Multicultural Assessment Perspectives for Professional Psychology

RICHARD H. DANA

Regional Research Institute
Portland State University

ALLYN AND BACON

Boston London Toronto Sydney Tokyo Singapore

Copyright © 1993 by Allyn and Bacon
A Division of Simon & Schuster, Inc.
160 Gould Street
Needham Heights, Massachusetts 02194

Library of Congress Cataloging-in-Publication Data

Dana, Richard H. (Richard Henry).
    Multicultural assessment perspectives for professional psychology
  / Richard H. Dana
        p.   cm.
    Includes bibliographical references and index.
    ISBN 0-205-14092-0
    1. Minorities—Psychological testing.   2. Psychological tests for
minorities.   3. Minorities—Psychology.   I. Title.
    [DNLM: 1. Cultural Characteristics. 2. Minority Groups—
psychology. 3. Psychological Tests—methods.   WM 145 D169m]
    RC473.P79D36   1993
155.2'8'08693—dc20
DNLM/DLC
for Library of Congress   92-17630
                                                                CIP

Printed in the United States of America

10 9 8 7 6   96

Contents

Preface

This book has been written primarily for middle-class Anglo-American psychologist service providers in order to provide necessary information for culturally competent assessment practice. Culturally competent assessment services stem from efforts to understand persons who differ in the realities that they have constructed to endow their lives with meaning and dignity and to offer respect for varied solutions to basic problems of living.

This book deals with the acquisition of a knowledge base concerning application of existing assessment instruments and current research on new assessment instruments relevant to several major cultural groups in American society. I am concerned with several training issues reflected in this book: (a) minimal interest in training for cultural competence among most graduate students; (b) programs that do not encourage students to contextualize persons in their life settings; (c) haphazard applications of research findings in practice; and (d) professional identity that is characterized by an increasing separation between researchers and practitioners.

During the past 20 years, I have found little enthusiasm among graduate students in either Boulder Model or professional psychology programs at the prospect of providing services to multicultural populations. This insensitivity is a result of unexamined biases, incorrect assumptions, and insufficient information about persons who differ in their cultural identities. Nonetheless, survey evidence suggests that practitioners, at least in California, do learn about the cultures of their clients and appear to be consistently sensitive to cultural differences (López & Hernandez, 1986). However, learning about other cultures is a lifelong task that is part and parcel of learning about oneself in a context with other persons who all differ in some degree. It is not sufficient to invite multicultural clients into a collaborative assessment relationship that provides education for the service provider. Although this argument may be based on good will, sincerity, and openness on the part of service providers, it minimizes the extent of world-view differences and the amount of training and experience required to provide culturally competent services.

Cultural competence is now one part of the fabric of general clinical competence. A major emphasis of training in the 1990s should be the development of positive attitudes toward assessment practice in a pluralistic society. Such an attitude will not only require new methods for assessment of multicultural populations but will demand a questioning of the adequacy of our Eurocentric model of science as expressed in psychometric technology.

A second concern in assembling these materials is to recognize the emergence of a new era in professional psychology. With the establishment of a clear professional identity as independent practitioners and a potentially viable research basis for practice, psychologists are now working with new populations, using new technologies, and discovering new arenas for practice. These new opportunities are present, but there are increased restrictions on practice and societal demands for accountability, coupled with a greater number and variety of competing practitioners and an increasing power of insurance providers to dictate the parameters of professional practice.

I share with Stan Schneider (1990) unanswered questions concerning the integrity and coherence of contemporary psychology. These questions may only be partially addressed by training. Schneider argued for a new training model in which the process is designed to focus on persons in environmental settings over time and to examine the mutual influences of persons, settings, and systems. As a result, the person can be contextualized not only within family, community, and society but in a personal and social history as well. We need to rediscover a context for our assessment technologies in the lives of clients. The 1990s thus afford an opportunity to develop into an even more respected profession, although a temptation to pursue the middle-class ethic of exploiting the marketplace remains present.

A third personal concern pertains to the persistent difficulty in applying academic and research knowledge to practice. As psychologists we have experienced a history of limitations inherent in the grand design for a unique profession that integrated research and training—the Boulder Model. I have followed Seymour Sarason (1988) in his lifelong pleas for imbuing our research endeavors with practicality and relevance. It is now more vital than ever before in our history to maintain the bifurcated or "bicultural" identity of scientist-practitioner, albeit with an enlarged science base. This base should be explicit with respect to the personal contribution of the scientist to the research process, especially taking into consideration whatever advocacy stance has been espoused, either unwittingly or explicitly. This science base should also emphasize that differing world views will generate alternative models of science, none of which are sacred, and all of which can directly promote responsible practice.

A fourth concern is with the professional identity of clinical psychologists. At a time when our professional organization, the American Psychological Association, has split into practice and academic/research components, the very identity we sought to achieve with the Boulder Model is jeopardized. I suspect that during my professional lifetime we have lost some of the first-generation skill in processing assessment data that was exemplified by Silvan Tomkins, Roy

Schafer, David Rapaport, and many others. We have gained a repertoire of psychometric technologies for assessment, but some of the personal immersion of the service provider in the complex human transaction with clients has been replaced by these technological accoutrements. Thus, when megatrends characterizing our time period were examined, the emphasis on technology outweighed the "high touch," or personal contribution of the provider to quality of service (Dana, 1984). Quality of service has a human dimension in addition to mere technical competence. Clients often experience this quality not only as understanding but as respect for the cultural dimension that defines their identity and may largely determine their perceptions of health/illness and provider competence.

I have tried to convey in this book my own awareness of being encapsulated in Eurocentric thinking in the face of many new populations who anticipate—often with trepidation—a gift of professional skill and high-quality care. I have suggested that our identity and integrity as a profession may now require an openness to ethnorelativistic thinking in order to continue to provide high-quality care. This book is a means for me to acknowledge my own discomfort with current service-delivery systems by examining in detail the dilemmas inherent in providing services to persons who are culturally different from an Anglo-American provider. The best hope for amelioration of the many large community, societal, and planetary problems lies in an appreciation and acceptance of all persons. Such an understanding implies that we need to learn more about our own culturally imposed construction of reality and the impact of this Eurocentric world view on research, training, assessment/intervention technology, and ethical considerations.

References

Dana. R. H. (1984). Megatrends in personality assessment: Toward a human science psychology. *Journal of Personality Assessment, 48,* 562–590.

López, S., & Hernandez, P. (1986). How culture is considered in evaluations of psychotherapy. *Journal of Nervous and Mental Disease, 176,* 598–606.

Sarason, S. (1988). *The making of an American psychologist: An autobiography.* San Francisco: Jossey-Bass.

Schneider, S. F. (1990). Psychology at a crossroads. *American Psychologist, 45,* 521–529.

Acknowledgments

This book owes its existence to a fortuitous early retirement in 1988 from the University of Arkansas and the good will of persons in the Psychology Department there, especially Dave Schroeder and Tom Jackson, who continued to provide me with an office and research support through the Howells' Fund. A second event in the form of my association with the Regional Research Institute at Portland State University was equally vital to the completion of this book. Participation in writing a center grant proposal with Barbara Friesen, Director of the Research and Training Center in the Regional Research Institute, led to two and one-half years as Principal Investigator of the Minority Initiative Project. During this time I had the opportunity to examine literature and be involved in research on cultural competence with the assistance of Terry Gonwa, Tina Landroche, Mary Elizabeth Rider, and Holly Winzurk. Holly Winzurk is responsible for gathering many of the general references used here. Her enthusiasm, good nature, and persistence have been appreciated more than she knows. During this period I have also benefited from the resources of the Northwest Indian Child Welfare Institute and the generosity of Terry Cross, the Institute Director. I was fortunate in being able to meet Steven López and become familiar with his major contributions in the areas of culturally competent assessment and training. Since April 1991, through the kindness of Bill Feyerherm, Director of the Regional Research Institute, I have been able to devote full time to this book and enjoy some facilitation from the Institute.

The area of concern in this book grows out of a lifelong professional preoccupation with assessment research and practice. Although I have been influenced by many persons, my first mentor, Silvan Tomkins, modeled for me a method of inquiry into personality that set the stage for my entire professional life.

The multicultural focus of this book may be attributed largely to the influence of Rodger Hornby, a community practitioner and Sinte Gleska University instructor. Rodger has provided me with an example of how a culturally competent psychologist can function in a multicultural society and be innovative, effective, and perdurable in encountering the special problems of professional identity and responsible practice. Rodger introduced me to Chicano society and later to Native American reservation society and encouraged me to attempt to use my assessment skills with his friends and clients. Over a period of many years, I learned that what I thought I knew as an assessment specialist on the basis of research and practice, primarily with Anglo-Americans, was largely inapplicable in reservation settings. Most of what I needed to know had little to do with assessment technology but with a style of service delivery that was provided in an atmosphere of ongoing relationships. Even an acceptable style meant little when the instruments had origins in personality theory and psychometric logic that was European and American in origin. The paradox for me was how to apply a technology that was inapplicable because of irreconcilable differences in world view. This book is a tentative step in dealing with this paradox.

There are many other persons whose assistance has been welcome and necessary. Continuing friendship and support from Ted May awakened me to vistas of social and professional change that otherwise would have been beyond my academic tunnel vision. Guiseppe Costantino and Bob Malgady were kind enough to go over some specific sections of Chapter 8. John Exner and Charlie Spielberger were generous with their time and resources. The helpful comments of two reviewers provided an opportunity for me to do a complete revision of the manuscript prior to publication. They were Professor Robert Martin of the University of Manitoba in Winnipeg and Professor Joseph F. Aponte of the University of Louisville, Kentucky.

Additionally, a lifetime of working with students who often became colleagues and friends has permitted me to remain open to new ideas. Specifically, I want to acknowledge Arne Dahlke, John Condry, Rod Cocking, Phil Comer, Shirley Leech, Phil Barling, Tom Hoffmann, John Monopoli, Rick Whatley, and Mike Conner. Rod Cocking, Tom Hoffmann, and John Monopoli all did master's theses on assessment of Native Americans. Finally, the interest, good will, and involvement of my wife, Joan Dayger Behn, has made the process continuously enjoyable and coextensive with our life together.

CHAPTER ONE

Psychological Services for Multicultural Populations

Introduction

The four major multicultural populations in the United States are African Americans, Asian Americans, Hispanic Americans, and Native Americans. These populations have a history of receiving mental health services that are often perceived as inadequate and/or inappropriate. This chapter provides an overview of cultural issues contributing to an underutilization of mental health services as a result of a system of services and providers that was designed originally to meet the needs of persons in the dominant Anglo-American society. A discussion of the general issues will provide an introduction to descriptions of each of these populations in Chapters 2–5. An assessment paradigm for multicultural populations in the United States is presented in Chapters 6–9. Chapter 10 outlines a format for assessment practice with these populations.

More specifically, underutilization of services will be considered as one outcome of provider ignorance of cultural expectations for services and cultural rules for appropriate delivery of these services. An understanding of these cultural rules and their applications with clients should be present in all parts of the service-delivery system. Such an understanding will be conveyed by the terms "cultural sensitivity" to connote awareness and "cultural competence" to suggest a translation of this awareness into credible provider behaviors. The training of professional psychology service providers, including assessors, for cultural competence will be presented as both necessary and feasible.

Cultural differences among groups are described in this chapter under the rubric "world view." World view includes group identity, individual identity, beliefs, values, and language. These components contribute to a construction of reality that determines perceptions of legitimate services, service providers, and service-delivery etiquette or style. Following this general introduction to world view, some effects of the dominant society's Anglo-American world view on professional psychology practice, particularly assessment, will be suggested. Descriptive materials will be provided on the four major ethnic minority cultures, including their world views. These world views represent the cultures and influence acceptable definitions of health or illness and perceptions of legitimate services.

Finally, the chapter provides an introduction to several sources of potential confusion in assessment practice that are largely unrecognized and/or unverbalized by service providers. These potentially disruptive concerns include etic-emic perspectives, assimilation versus pluralism, group personality versus individual differences, and racism.

Service Utilization and Cultural Competence

Mental health services in the United States were originally designed by middle-class Anglo-Americans for clients who were similar to themselves. Populations from other cultures were provided services on the basis of the belief that these clients were either highly similar to Anglo-Americans or would inevitably become more similar over time as they assimilated into the melting pot of American society. As a result these services were underutilized because they were often perceived by potential consumers as inappropriate and/or ineffective.

Multicultural persons have been less likely to seek services, and the services they received differed in kind and/or quality from services delivered to Anglo-Americans. For example, S. Sue (1977) examined patterns of services to 14,000 clients in 17 community mental health centers over a 3-year period. Multicultural persons saw fewer psychologists and psychiatrists and more teachers, vocational rehabilitation counselors, or nonprofessionals than did Anglo-Americans. African-American clients, in particular, received less group or marital therapy and more inpatient treatment. Fewer than one half of these minority patients returned after the first session, and those who did return received significantly fewer sessions than the Anglo-American patients. Premature termination of treatment for multicultural clients occurred as a result of "a series of frustrations, misunderstandings, distortions, and defensive reactions" that included "language problems, role ambiguities, misinterpretations of behavior, differences in priorities of treatment" (S. Sue & N. Zane, 1987, p. 44).

Service utilization has changed somewhat over time for some groups because of a larger minority presence in a community (Cuellar & Schnee, 1987), or for all groups in some geographic locales (O'Sullivan, Peterson, Cox, & Kirkeby, 1989). However, Mollica (1990) stated that the "slow death by asphyxiation" of the community mental health system and continued stratification by class and race has been responsible for maintaining the status quo in availability and utilization of services by most Americans of minority cultural origins. In more recent examples, Solomon (1988) found that African Americans not only received more diagnoses of schizophrenia but continued to receive fewer services than Anglo-Americans, and Mexican Americans still underutilized outpatient services (Hough, Landsverk, & Karno, 1987).

Nonetheless, culture-compatible services can result in increased utilization. Flaskerud (1986) demonstrated the potential effectiveness of culture-compatible services for Asian-American, African-American, Mexican-American, and mixed ethnic/racial populations in four full-service, public, metropolitan mental health agencies. A culture-compatible approach included therapists who shared the clients' culture, language, or language style; use of family members in brief therapy; referrals to clergy and/or traditional healers; agency location in the client community; flexible hours/appointments, and involvement of consumers directly in determining, evaluating, and publicizing services. Culture-compatibility scores were derived for each agency and related to dropout rates. These agencies were relatively homogeneous on culture-compatibility scores and all were moderately successful in retention of clients. Furthermore, therapist-client language and ethnic/racial match, in addition to agency location, were suggestive of therapy continuation.

The Flaskerud study suggested that cultural competence is dependent on a style of service-delivery that is perceived by clients as *credible and giving* (S. Sue & N. Zane, 1987). Credibility invokes client perception that the therapist is effective and trustworthy. Giving implies client recognition that something of value has been received in the clinical situation.

Culturally knowledgeable Anglo-American service providers are believed to be able to provide appropriate services to multicultural populations (Abel, Metraux, & Roll, 1987). An increasing utilization of available services can occur as a result of training Anglo-American students and practitioners for cultural competence. A knowledge of client culture is required in order to engage in the quality of ethnorelativistic thought and behavior required for culturally competent service delivery. Moreover, culturally competent descriptions of personality are dependent on knowledge of group cultural identity and the ingredients of personal identity. In addition, however, cultural competence also must be developed at the levels of agency administration, policy, and the consumer community so that an agency can be perceived by minority clients as providing culturally relevant services (Cross, Bazron, Dennis, & Issacs, 1989). At the consumer level, cultural competence not only suggests the necessity for advocacy in promoting recognition of culture-specific community needs but also the importance of accurate perceptions of the Anglo-American culture by each minority community.

At the agency administrative level, a context is available for development of cultural competence. Recruitment of minority staff should be required. In addition, an agency self-assessment of cultural sensitivity should be followed by relevant inservice training to develop cultural knowledge and skill requirements for all staff or consultants who provide contracted services. Physical facilities can be developed to include culturally appropriate decor, settings that are less threatening because of shared occupancy with non-mental health services, and locations within minority communities. The agency can provide sponsorship for new programs or adjustments in existing programs and services to fit the problems perceived as important by specific client populations. Linkage to outreach and community systems is essential in this process. Data regarding services to minority communities can be shared with consumers in annual reports.

Cultural competency at the agency level has been explored in a variety of agencies using a Cultural Competence Checklist (Dana, Behn, & Gonwa, 1992). This checklist was constructed from a systematic examination of the research literature. The checklist includes culturally competent practices as reflected in agency policy, staff selection, and staff attitudes; available services; relationships to ethnic communities; training; and research.

Opportunities for development of policymaking competence are present in community/local, state, and national contexts. Community competence in policymaking occurs as a result of involvement in policy-shaping settings that include boards, advisory committees, commissions, and task forces. Linkages with existing networks in minority communities are necessary to provide culture-sensitive standards for services, requirements for training agendas, and use of research findings in local agencies. Community input at the legislative level can result in new laws, modifications of existing laws, and pressure for appropriate use of available funds and other resources. Finally, cultural competence at the consumer level means the ability of ethnic minority groups to articulate the importance of their own cultures and to provide advocacy for necessary services and/or system changes in order to obtain these services.

Cultural competence thus implies more than cultural knowledge per se or culture-specific intervention techniques that have been recognized as distal to psychotherapy outcome (S. Sue & N. Zane, 1987). In this formulation, cultural knowledge is more remote from the goals of intervention than is an emphasis on therapeutic techniques and process. Mental health services for cultural minorities have been prone to rely on specific techniques rather than a service-delivery context that begins with consumer involvement in policy and requires administrators and service providers to have in-depth knowledge and experience with diverse cultural beliefs and practices. It is necessary to have bilingual/bicultural service providers and culture-specific parallel services for large ethnic communities, but it will be of even greater importance to embed new service delivery systems in legal, social service, and language programs (S. Sue, 1977).

Training for Service Providers

When minority population growth in this country was compared with proportions of minority members of the American Psychological Association (APA), minority doctoral recipients, and minority doctoral students, large and increasing discrepancies were shown (Bernal, 1986). Between 1980 and 1990, only 1 psychology faculty member in 20 represented a minority group, and these academics were less likely to be of tenured rank (Jones, 1990; Pion, Bramblett, Wicherski, & Stapp, 1985). From 1973 to 1981 the number of minority doctorates in all areas of psychology increased from 4 percent to 11 percent, and remained static for 1984–1985. Only 10 percent of these new minority doctoral recipients accepted academic positions (Russo, Olmedo, Stapp, & Fulcher, 1981). Health service providers graduating from doctoral programs in 1984 included 4.8 percent African Americans, 3 percent Hispanic Americans, 1.2 percent Asian Americans, and 0.2 percent Native Americans (Howard et al., 1986). These cultural groups now have approximately a 15 percent representation in psychology graduate programs and an 8 percent representation in APA membership. They could not address the service needs for the populations they represent even if they restricted their practices to persons sharing their own cultures.

Training for services to multicultural groups should be provided for all professional psychology graduate students. However, ethnic minority curriculum and training simply has not existed in most accredited clinical, counseling, and school psychology graduate programs (Bernal & Padilla, 1982; Wyatt & Parham, 1982). For example, an APA survey (American Psychological Association [APA], 1982) of 398 psychology departments found only 4.3 percent requiring courses or practica in psychological assessment of ethnic minorities and 9.5 percent with an elective course or practicum.

In a second example, Dunston (1983) reported a survey response rate of 41 percent from APA-accredited graduate and internship programs. Although 60 percent of these program directors indicated that ethnic minority content was included in their training programs, integration of content was provided primarily by elective courses in graduate departments and by required training in some internships. At that time, few respondent programs included appreciable numbers of culturally diverse students and most programs made no provision for faculty development to teach relevant content.

Psychologist practitioners will inevitably provide their services to clients similar to themselves and different in culture of origin. Anglo-American service providers can expect to encounter many persons with multicultural origins, as well as foreign students and other sojourners in the United States. Without specific training for these professional encounters, assessment data may be distorted, subsequent interpretations will be incomplete, and intervention services may not materialize or may be substantially reduced in quality.

The statistical documentation of inadequacies of training and training outcomes during the 1980s has had a dramatic impact on the APA. Accreditation policy and procedures now put pressure on programs to provide training for multicultural services and service delivery. In addition, there are APA offices, boards, committees, task forces, and divisions to provide for a continuing sensitivity and advocacy for ethnic minority issues. The Minority Fellowship Program provides support for multicultural graduate students. Moreover, in 1991, the APA Council of Representatives approved the Guidelines for Providers of Psychological Services to Ethnic and Culturally Diverse Populations (Myers, Wohlford, Guzman, & Echemendia, 1991, Appendix D).

As a result of these guidelines, APA official policy recognizes not only cultural diversity, but also the impact of socioeconomic and political factors on the psychological development and sociocultural identifications of ethnic minority members is emphasized. An understanding of the interaction effects of culture, gender, and sexual orientation on behavior is called for, as well as help for clients with problems of sociocultural identification.

In response to APA policy, graduate training programs have examined models that require adding courses, substituting courses, and integrating relevant material into an entire program. However, most programs have opted to use new courses (an additive model), although at least three programs now have formal areas of concentration (California School of Professional Psychology, Los Angeles; University of California, San Francisco; and New York University) (Myers, Echemendia, & Trimble, 1991). Radical changes in philosophy or cultural perspective have not been forthcoming.

Culturally Relevant Training Approaches

Many other disciplines that provide professional training have also been concerned with training for services to multicultural populations. For example, Copeland (1982) suggested four approaches to make culturally relevant training available: (a) a separate course in ethnic studies that focuses on a single group, using an historical perspective, with provision for development of positive attitudes and intensive experience in a cross-cultural setting; (b) an area of concentration that includes a core of courses, and prepracticum skills-building exercises, with specialized practicum/internship sites; (c) an interdisciplinary approach to provide depth of knowledge and cooperation in both research and practice; and (d) an integration approach to provide instruction for all students in all courses and cooperation from all faculty, using sites that provide multicultural services. The details of each approach as applied to counselor training programs are contained in Table 1-1.

Training for Ethnorelativistic Thinking

The approaches to training identified above are structural devices for acquainting students with multicultural service issues and thereby enhancing intercultural sensitivity. However, the ultimate purpose of training for cultural

TABLE 1-1 • *Summary of Approaches to Training*

Approach	Advantage	Disadvantage
Course	Coverage; uses adjunct faculty; no program evaluation required.	No total faculty commitment; ancillary; not part of program.
Area of concentration	In-depth study; offers practice opportunity; experience with diverse groups; study of similarities/differences.	Does not necessarily reach all students working with minorities.
Interdisciplinary	Varies courses; broad experiences; minimizes course redundancy.	Not necessarily used by all.
Integration	Total program evaluation; involves faculty, students, and practitioners.	Requires faculty commitment and time.

Source: Adapted from Copeland, 1982, p. 192.

competence is to develop ethnorelative thinking. M. J. Bennett (1986) has described a six-stage process that moves from ethnocentric thinking characterized by denial (Stage 1), defense (Stage 2), and minimization (Stage 3) to progressively greater ethnorelativistic thinking evidenced by acceptance (Stage 4), adaptation (Stage 5), and integration (Stage 6).

Although few students in graduate programs are likely to be extremely prejudiced as defined by denial (i.e., belief in genocide) or defense (i.e., reaction to threat by denigration of differences), many students unwittingly opt for minimization (trivialization of differences) in the interest of preserving their own world view. Minimization (Stage 3) acknowledges differences that are not negatively evaluated but are tolerated by means of a physical or transcendent universalism. Cultural differences then become permutations of underlying rules and all persons are believed to be products of a single principle or law.

Acceptance (Stage 4) implies that it is all right for other people to exhibit different behaviors, including language, communication style, and nonverbal patterns. Moreover, the underlying cultural value differences and organizations of reality that are responsible for these overt differences are also not only comprehensible but acceptable as well. Most middle-class Anglo-American graduate students in human service programs require training or a history of relatively atypical life experiences to be at Stage 4 or beyond.

Stage 5 (adaptation) means that both behavior and thinking can be temporarily modified in the presence of culturally different behaviors. Processing of reality changes, shown by empathy, includes a shift in world view and permits culturally appropriate actions to occur automatically. Bicultural or multicultural persons have habitualized this empathic shift. Finally, integration (Stage 6) involves application of ethnorelativism to one's own identity by using contextual relativism—the ability to evaluate phenomena relative to cultural context.

Stage 4 Training   Training for Stage 4, acceptance, has been outlined in four domains (Copeland, 1983): consciousness raising; cognitive understanding; experiential or affective understanding; and skills training. Consciousness raising implies familiarity with the particular culture, including the history and present environment. J. M. Bennett (1986) described a variety of educational methods under the general heading of cultural awareness; these included Contrast America (CA). Intercultural Workshop (ICW), and Cultural Self-Awareness Training (CSA). CA uses role-play and case study to examine conflict with generalized American values. ICW uses small-group experiences with trained facilitators and members of two different cultures and is often packaged as an upper-division college course. CSA uses videotapes of critical incidents to aid trainees in recognizing their own values.

Cognitive understanding may be gained from ethnographic data that should include socioeconomic status, family structure, socialization, employment, literacy, and education. Henderson (1979) has suggested that cognitive understanding may be gained from these sources, from a study of the history of the particular culture, and from an examination of sources of bias in oneself and in the prejudicial attitudes of the majority society. Cognitive understanding has been measured by the Cultural Attitudes Repertory Technique (Neimeyer & Fukuyama, 1984), which identifies constructs of both service provider and client as a basis for sharing subjective culture. The Ethnic Validity Model (Tyler, Sussewell, & Williams-McCoy, 1985) provides a framework for understanding the service delivery process by examining convergence, divergence, and conflict between different world views. The manner in which these world-view dimensions become salient in client/service provider interactions becomes the arena for increasing understanding.

Experiential understanding has been approached by t-group and role-playing for self-awareness. Simulation area training (Harrison & Hopkins, 1967), as used by the Peace Corps, reproduces situations and conditions representative of a particular culture. Although such intensive residential training would probably not be cost-effective for professional psychology training, it may be as effective as a living experience or sojourn in another culture.

Skills training has been accomplished by reinforcing culturally appropriate behaviors (David, 1972) and preferably by teaching attributions commonly made by members of another culture, in order to interpret events as would persons from that culture (Albert & Triandis, 1985; Brislin, 1986). Attribution training, using a format of short episodes with alternative attributions for programmed learning, is of demonstrated effectiveness (Albert, 1983). Pedersen (1981) described an-

other format in which simulated interviews are mediated by a second counselor—an anticounselor or procounselor—who represents the client culture by
translating implicit cultural messages. Immediate videotaped feedback serves to
reduce defensiveness and anxiety.

World View

The first part of this chapter has described the dilemma of underutilization of
mental health services by persons who are culturally different; the relatively
small numbers of professional service providers from minority populations; and
recent APA policy aimed at increasing the availability and quality of culturally-
relevant training. Reasons for the poor fit between services, service providers,
and multicultural consumers will now be considered in terms of world-view
differences between service providers and clients.

World view provides some of the unexamined underpinnings for perceptions and the nature of reality as experienced by individuals who share a common
culture. The world view of a culture functions to make sense of life experiences
that might otherwise be construed as chaotic, random, and meaningless. World
view is imposed by collective wisdom as a basis for sanctioned actions that
enable survival and adaptation. The study of world view, or culturally specific
cognitions, includes nonverbal behaviors, language, and assumptions concerning
causality, time, and human nature that remain largely unverbalized (Kearney,
1975).

The world views of service providers and consumers have been described
as philosophies that affect transactions (Ibrahim, 1985). A philosophy consists of
presuppositions and assumptions regarding the composition of the world, the
place of human beings in the world, and the causes of their behavior. World
views of service providers and consumers may clash or coincide. To the extent
that these views diverge, the services tendered may be unacceptable. As a result
these services may be neither understood nor utilized. Some dimensions of world
view that are germane to professional practice have been organized into a format
and used a basis for perceptions that affect utilization of services, service providers, and service delivery (Figure 1-1).

The world-view components included in this format are group identity,
individual identity or self-concept, values, beliefs, and language. A group identity, or collective consciousness, is based on a unique history of development of
a cultural heritage. This identity includes not only retention of native language
and group-sanctioned behaviors but the perceptions of health/illness, credible
services, service-delivery styles, and the values and beliefs that define parameters of meaning. An individual or personal identity is predicated on the cultural
elaboration of a self-concept. A system of values permits meaning in terms of a

FIGURE 1-1 • *World-View Components and Perceptions*

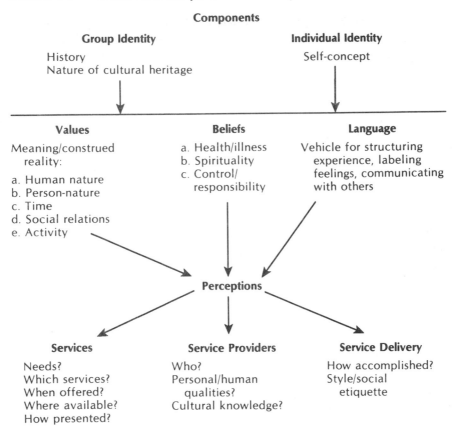

consensual construed reality as a basis for problem-solving and group survival. Beliefs include the causes and nature of health and illness, spirituality, and the extent of perceived control and responsibility over one's own life. Values, beliefs, and language provide a basis for perception of the need for particular services, relevant kinds of service, desired qualities in service providers, and a culturally acceptable style of service delivery. Language is a potential avenue for examination of the structure of thinking, for describing feelings, and for understanding the nature of culturally specific communication.

These world-view components will be used in Chapters 2–5 to describe the world views of each group as they influence perceptions of service providers, services, and service-delivery style. In Figure 1-1, these dimensions have been artifically decontextualized in order to emphasize the extent and quality of differences among groups.

World-View Components

Group Identity Most human beings develop both a group identity and an individual or personal identity. The group identity is a group cultural conscious- ness that includes the history of the group and those behaviors that are sanctioned by the group (Dana, 1988). Group identity probably exists only in the form of predominant or modal personality, which has also been referred to as traditional personality (DeVos, 1968). Some individuals do not share this traditional identity because they reject the their original cultural group and identify with the domi- nant culture (nontraditional), some identify with both cultures (bicultural), and still others may reject both the original and the dominant culture (marginality).

Individual Identity Individual or personal identity may be labeled as the self-concept. The descriptions of self, self-concept, or personal identity in this country have usually referred to a self of western European origin (Baumeister, 1986). Our knowledge of self-concept stems almost entirely from research on Anglo-Americans, individuals of the dominant culture in American society. The self for this population has firm boundaries that enclose what has been described as self-contained individualism, or egocentrism, characterized by personal con- trol and a self-concept that excludes other persons (Sampson, 1985, 1988). Until recently it was assumed by most social scientists that the self-concept of persons from other cultures could be defined similarly. One obvious result of this as- sumption was that persons from other cultures have typically appeared as defi- cient in self-esteem as indicated by personality measures.

In describing the identity of persons with non-European origins, it is necessary to consider an ensembled, extended, or sociocentric self (Sampson, 1985, 1988). This augmented self is responsible and obligated to a variety of other persons who are affected by the individual's actions and have to be consid- ered in all decision-making and problem-solving situations.

Beliefs Both group and individual aspects of identity are derived from shared beliefs, a structure of values, common language, and similar life experi- ences. These shared beliefs include the nature of health and illness, consensual spirituality, and the extent of responsibility and control over personal well-being.

Physical illness is not necessarily related exclusively to the germ theory of disease causation in groups of non-European origins but may also be related to a variety of folk and natural influences including magic, dreams, spirit events, forces in nature, and malevolent others. In Anglo-American society, physical health is ordinarily an absence of disease, but other cultures may conceive of health in holistic terms as a balance or harmony maintained by the practice of certain rituals. As a result, mental health may not be separable from physical health. Since health and spirituality are often intertwined, both are encompassed under the same rubric of beliefs in some cultures.

Values Value dimensions were originally developed by anthropologist Florence Kluckhohn (1960), based on the assumption that a limited number of problems exist for which human beings must find solutions. Each society may have a preferred mode of problem-solving, but the entire range of solutions usually exists within a particular culture.

Five prototypical problems and their potential solutions are:

1. An innate human nature, which may be understood as good, evil, or a mixture of both.
2. The relation of the person to nature, described as subjugation to nature, harmony with nature, or mastery over nature.
3. A temporal focus on the present, past, or future.
4. Relationships with other persons, conceived as either individualistic with primacy of individual goals, collateral with primacy of laterally extended groups, or lineal, in which age, generation, or cultural tradition are definitive of relationships.
5. Human activity that involves either Doing (in the sense of accomplishing something), Being-in-Becoming (emphasizing personal development), or Being (constituting a spontaneous expression of the personality).

More detailed descriptions of value orientations may be found in Kluckhohn (1954) and Kluckhohn and Strodtbeck (1961). These value orientations were

TABLE 1-2 • *Value Dimensions for Five Major Groups*

| Group | Dimension* | | | | |
	Human Nature	Person-Nature Relationship	Time Focus	Relationships	Activity
Anglo-American	Evil	Mastery of nature	Future	Individual	Doing
African American	Good/evil	Harmony with nature	Future	Individual	Doing
Asian American	Good	Subjugation to nature	Past	Lineal	Being-in-Becoming
Hispanic American	Good/evil	Subjugation to nature	Present	Lineal	Being
Native American	Good/evil	Harmony with nature	Present	Collateral	Being/Doing

*These dimensions are subject to extreme within-group variations due to age, generation, and cultural orientation. They are used here as illustrative guidelines.

originally used to compare Zuni, Navajo, Mormon, Hispanic-American, and Texan (Anglo-American) samples.

These prototypical problems and their most frequent solutions in Anglo-American and minority groups are presented in Table 1-2. This table is intended only to provide a set of expectations that can be modified in accord with additional client information. Values and value changes have been associated with number of generations in this country, urban-rural residence, desire to assimilate, extent of individual acculturation, and degree to which traditional culture has been retained.

Language   Language provides a means for communicating shared characteristics over time and exposes idiosyncratic patterns of thought that exemplify the salient characteristics of a particular world view. The extent to which language influences thought and hence affects the understanding of constructs in other cultures is not known (Hunt & Banaji, 1988). Nonetheless, language is one vehicle for imposing perception upon reality, or as Whorf (1956, p. 214) has stated, "All observations are not led by the same physical evidence to the same picture of the universe, unless their linguistic backgrounds are similar."

In "standard average European" (SAE) thinking, for example, the world is analysed in terms of things with unique spatial functions. Structure, by categorization, then may be provided by attributes of form and continuity. By contrast, in the Hopi language, the world is analyzed in terms of events whose parts interact whenever they occur simultaneously. Thus, in Hopi a rosebush is a process of budding, flowering, and decaying. In SAE thinking, a rosebush is a mental image representative of a rosebush, a distinct entity with a specific location.

World View in Anglo-American Culture

Katz (1985) has delineated the components of Anglo-American culture that make up world view. Some of the values, beliefs, and behaviors that are unequivocally accepted by most middle-class Anglo-Americans as the basis for their thinking about other persons are juxtaposed in Table 1-3 with parallel structures implicit in professional services.

These components include independence and autonomy to describe a stance in which each person potentially controls the natural and constructed environments. Competition is lauded and invokes a preoccupation with winning by using a pragmatic, action orientation. Decision-making occurs on the basis of the majority opinion of Anglo-Americans within a hierarchical format. Communication comes out of a written tradition in standard English, with verbal communication requiring direct eye contact, limited physical contact, and controlled emotion. Power and status are measured by money, possessions, titles, and

TABLE 1-3 • *Anglo-American Society and Professional Services: Parallel Values and Beliefs*

Culture	Services
Individualism/competition	Autonomy focus: intrapsychic, historical method.
Action orientation	Personal mastery/control by direct action.
Hierarchical power	Provider of service technology is credentialed, professionalized, highly paid. Perceived as uniquely effective.
Controlled communication	Verbal with reflective listening, eye contact, self-disclosure demand. Rigid time requirement.
Protestant ethic	Service is hard work for work provider/client.
Scientific method	Provider is objective, neutral, rational, linear, causal, quantitative, evaluative by using mind/body dualism.
Progress/history	Task-specin. , sequential, goal-oriented.
Family structure	Nuclear family with explicit sex roles desirable.
Religion/history/aesthetics	Provider understanding of client reality: WASP (white, Anglo-Saxon, Protestant)/YAVIS (young, attractive, verbal, intelligent, successful).

positions that are bolstered by belief in the inherent necessity and desirability of the American political and economic system. A Protestant work ethic includes rigid time schedules, planning, delayed gratification, and valuing of progress. The nuclear family structure with stereotyped sex roles comes from a European background. Physical preferences also have a basis in European cultures. Religion is defined by association with Christianity. Scientific method dictates structure of thinking that is quantitative, dualistic, objective, rational, and linear, with cause-and-effect relationships.

The core construct of this world view is an individualism that permeates American culture and includes a sense of personal identity, self-actualization, locus of control, and post-conventional principled moral reasoning (Waterman, 1981). This individualism, espoused especially by middle-class Americans, is both utilitarian and expressive. By means of the utilitarian component, human life becomes an effort to maximize self-interest in the form of power. The expressive component provides a unique core of feeling and intuition that may unfold and potentially be displayed as individuality (Bellah, Madsen, Sullivan, Swidler, & Tipton, 1985). Such an ideology cannot easily come to grips with culturally different persons because there is no idiom for bestowing on culturally different groups a common moral order in an egalitarian society. As a consequence, lip-service attention to the culturally different is combined with hope that these persons will abandon their cultural distinctiveness upon assumption of middle-class status and acceptance of values that include individual achievement, rational control over things/events, and an orientation toward the future. Although ethnic differences are usually diluted by the third generation, these cultural differences can also become exaggerated over time for groups who have been assimilated coercively, to whom middle-class status is largely denied, or whose differences in values and traditions have historically been more distinct.

An orientation toward private and personal interests, or individualism, may be contrasted with collectivism, which is an orientation toward the interests of other persons (Parsons, 1951). In the dominant society, collectivism has often been equated with codependence and is perceived by service providers as undesirable for competent social functioning. However, as Hornby and Dana (1992) have indicated, in a Native American education context, collectivism may not only be necessary for group survival but may contain something of value for interpersonal relations in the dominant society as well.

Hui and Triandis (1986) used a questionnaire with a world-wide sample of 46 psychologists and anthropologists in order to describe dimensions of a collectivist orientation. These dimensions include openness, concern, sharing, belief, and feeling. An openness to the opinions and values of others leads to greater conformity. There is concern with regard to self-presentation and the effects of actions/decisions on a wide spectrum of other persons. Material benefits and nonmaterial resources are shared. There is belief in interdependence and sharing of outcomes for the common good. Finally, there are feelings of involvement with others and integumentation within the lives of many other persons.

Anglo-American World View and Practice

To invite more careful consideration of ordinarily unexamined bases for practice, several strands of the Anglo-American world view shared by many professional psychologists will be contrasted with alternatives found in the world views of other cultures. It is recognized that many Anglo-American psychologist service providers are culturally marginalized (Henry, Simes, & Spray, 1971) and either will not necessarily share all of the modal Anglo-American world-view characteristics or will have considerable awareness of the implications of their own cultural identity.

Three areas of Anglo-American world-view effects on assessment practice will be considered: individualism, model of science, and control and responsibility. Cultural options in each of these areas are relevant to the perception and utilization of assessment services by ethnic minority clients.

Self-Contained and Ensembled Individualism

Professional psychology emerged in mid-twentieth-century service society with an immensely successful entrepreneurship in which mainstream, middle-class American traditions of individualism and self-sufficiency were emphasized. Psychologist service providers have shared with other psychologists a world view that is basically one of self-contained individualism (Wallach & Wallach, 1983). This world view is characterized by an unquestioning belief in the use of personal control resulting from money, power, and recognition, to achieve an orderly world and satisfactory self-definition (Sampson, 1985). Moreover, these service providers often practice their skills on the basis of an isolated professional stance that fosters a sense of personal control over their professional and personal destinies.

The world view of psychologists extends to their clients, who are presumed to be similar to themselves and hence are expected to aspire toward internal control and an exercise of personal responsibility in their own lives. Self-contained individualism leads to the assumption that services constitute a contractual and negotiated exchange grounded in participants' exclusive responsibility for themselves. This professional stance may implicitly signal to clients an ultimate self-responsibility, an expectation that one's resource repertoire will be maximized in order to live life in a more autonomous manner. Clients are then encouraged to behave in ways that confirm their separate and essentially solitary identities.

In contrast to the self-contained individualism of many middle-class Anglo-American clinical psychologists, the majority of persons on this planet have alternative realities and beliefs about what is required to be a cohesive and integrated person. Ensembled individualism implies a blurred distinction or permeable boundary between oneself and other persons as a result of crosscutting ties and many-sided relationships (Sampson, 1985, 1988). The relentless focus on the self provided by most existing services may also be alien and disquieting to persons with cultural values that define the self only in concert with others and perceive autonomy and individualism as undesirable or even unnecessary.

For persons who rely on more fluid boundaries between the self and other persons, and traditional family, group, and community forms for contextualization and derived meaning, experience with this professional service-delivery stance can be dehumanizing. For example, an Anglo-American world view that emphasizes the ideal of individual happiness has become a major export (see statements by Amos Oz in To See Ourselves . . . , 1986), especially to developing countries. Modernization has contributed to the acceptance of this individual happiness ideal as a substitute for an historic concern with happiness as a collective ideal embodied in the well-being of the group.

Model of Science

A second facet of this world view that affects practice is the prevailing model of science that has formed the core of training for most professional psychologists. Psychologists have found their need for cognitive certainty, as embodied in a self-contained individualism, documented by the positivist, empiricist scientific attitude (Koch, 1981).

To describe this attitude, Kimble (1984) developed an Epistemic Differential Scale that presents a listing of the premises of the prevailing scientific attitude: scientific values, determinism, objectivism, data, laboratory investigation, the historical, heredity, nomothesis, concrete mechanisms, elementarism, cognition, and reactivity. The opposite terms of each of these provide perspective for a human science that is more relevant to cross-cultural research and practice: human values, indeterminism, intuitionism, theory, field study, the ahistorical, environment, idiogaphy, abstract concepts, holism, affect, and creativity.

There are major areas of disagreement between conventional logical positivism and an emerging human science as defined by the Epistemic Differential Scale. Wittig (1985) suggested that these differences include underlying values of either science or humanism, knowledge sources that contrast objectivism and intuition, and methodologies that favor nomothesis or idiography. It is not surprising that scientific values, objectivism, and nomothesis have condoned an exercise of power in professional relationships with students and clients, one that has coexisted with a lack of interest in legitimizing cross-cultural issues (Dana, 1987b).

The psychologist practitioner is considered to be an expert as defined by training, professional socialization, and a community of peers to provide credentials and legitimization for clinical practice. This expertise stems from a value-neutral science that is impersonal, descriptive, and manipulative. Even if the clinician does not pattern his or her professional behavior on medical-model service delivery and expect the complementary role of a "good" patient, there is still some invocation of power derived from special knowledge and special skills. How professional psychologists use their power/skills in providing a context for understanding the roles of assessment and/or intervention in collaborative problem-solving may determine the usefulness of these services for particular clients (Heller, 1985; Pinderhughes, 1989). For example, the acceptability to the client of giving or receiving personality-relevant information may be defined in cross-cultural settings either on the basis of the quality of the personal relationship as experienced by the client cross-culturally or by the status/expertise of the service provider.

The historic and prevailing model of psychological science has definite limits even within Western society. This model is now undergoing rapid and fundamental changes that have been reviewed elsewhere (Dana, 1982, 1984;

Manicas & Secord, 1983; Rychlak, 1977). A positivist, empiricist science is being gradually exchanged for a constructionist view in which attempts are made to explain behavior over an extended range of phenomena, using an augmented methodology.

Social constructionism provides meaning as a product of consensus from linguistic and conceptual categories (Gergen, 1985). Attitudes that inform social constructionists provide an interpretation of reality as a cultural/historical product that leads to questioning of the status quo. For example, several new dimensions of the constructionist view (Wittig, 1985) will affect assessment practice.

First, the new human science emphasizes that explanations of human behavior require knowledge of persons in social contexts; that knowledge includes motives, expectancies, intentions, and capacities for change. The assessment paradigm is thus expanded from the role of individual tests, or test batteries, to encompass other informants, other sources of data, observations of behavior in several settings, and the goodness-of-fit between persons and a variety of environmental demands (Dana, 1986).

Second, there are many specific and interacting causes for behavior, as well as multiple and simultaneous system effects on behavior. As a result, a systems approach can help to prioritize these multiple causes by identifying the impingement of biological, personal, interpersonal, family, small group, organizational, community, and societal effects (Taplin, 1980). This equation is never static because of the complex and changing interplay of behavior and our professional knowledge of it. Causes that stem from family, community, and societal effects have greater salience in some cultures and represent resources that are typically underutilized by Anglo-American service providers.

Third, the methods, including tests and other assessment devices, are incomplete in themselves and require modification to be useful in providing competent services to clients from diverse cultural origins. Historically, interpretation of assessment data has been regarded as a primary province of the assessor. However, interpretation has to include the importance of subjective meaning as determined by world view and cultural experience. The client must play an increasing role in interpretation to clarify the multiple causal effects and the cultural meanings of behavior and experience. Augmentation of methods may be addressed by training clinicians to expand their awareness of clients' subjective experience to include cultural considerations. Careful sharing of assessment process and honest feedback of findings to clients by using a culture-specific service-delivery style becomes an important part of this process (Dana, 1985).

Personal Control and Responsibility

A final facet of Anglo-American world view pertains to potential provider-client cultural differences in personal control and responsibility that influence the service-delivery process and the utilization of assessment findings. These provider-client differences can affect assessment practice by leading to false assumptions and expectations for client compliance. Personal control and responsibility will be examined using locus of control (LC) and locus of responsibility (LR) formulation and by examples of culturally determined expectations for responsibility with regard to problems and/or solutions.

Locus of Control/Locus of Responsibility   LC and LR world-view components have been described as independent beliefs that interact to form four quadrants when plotted graphically (D. W. Sue, 1978a, 1978b). These quadrants are internal control-internal responsibility (IC-IR), external control-internal responsibility (EC-IR), external control-external responsibility (EC-ER), and internal control-external responsibility (IC-ER). Many Anglo-Americans epitomize an IC-IR that embodies belief in personal power for active problem-solving. However, many minority persons passively accept second-class status, an ER-IC world view. Some minority persons hold an ER-EC view in which society is blamed for life circumstances and the person feels powerless to initiate ameliorative changes. Other minority persons, however, hold an IC-ER world view and believe themselves able to endure and prevail in spite of strong environmental pressures for failure.

There is one research demonstration of an LC/LR world view (Macaranas-Sittler, 1986). The internal-external Locus of Control Scale (I-E) (Rotter, 1966) was used with a specially constructed locus of responsibility scale to contrast African-American, Asian-American, Mexican-American, and Native-American college students with Anglo-American college students. All of the other cultural groups differed significantly from the Anglo-Americans in viewing the world from EC-IR dimensions rather than from IC-IR dimensions.

I-E scale scores and components or subscales have been used in many cross-cultural research studies. However, as Munroe (1979) indicated, the scale does not systematically vary situations, agents of action, outcomes, and consequences. Reynolds (1976) noted that only individual differences in expectancy (rather than motivation) are measured by items that are politically loaded and high in social desirability. Trimble and Richardson (1982) demonstrated that the same meanings for LC component scores do not necessarily occur in different cultural groups. Native Americans, for example, display both external personal control and internal group or societal control (Trimble & Richardson, 1983). The standard I-E scales (Rotter, 1966) are not often used for assessment of individuals in clinical populations, because the differences among groups, although significant, are generally too small for individual predictions.

Nonetheless, information on culture-specific LC and LR styles may be relevant as moderator variables in context with other assessment data. However, any hypothesis regarding the client's LC/LR needs to be verified in the context of service delivery, regardless of the client's social class or cultural identity. The reasons for such verification lie in the client's predisposition to find relevant the services that accord with belief in the efficacy and desirability of personal control and personal responsibility.

Professional psychologists now have the option of using instruments to provide direct evidence in this area. For example, in health assessment (Wallston, Wallston, & DeVellis, 1978) a Multidimensional Health Locus of Control (MHLC) instrument separates internal control from control by powerful others and chance. Nonetheless, the use of this instrument with multicultural populations has been infrequent (Stein, Smith, & Wallston, 1984; Tait, DeGood, & Carron, 1982), and these MHLC components should be examined and validated for use with each ethnic minority group.

Responsibility for Problems and Solutions   Models of helping/coping predicated on world view focus on service-delivery distinctions between responsibility for problems and responsibility for solutions (Brickman et al., 1982). These investigators examined moral, medical, compensatory, and enlightenment models. In the moral model, people have responsibility for both creating and solving their own problems. In the medical model, people are responsible for neither problems nor solutions. In the compensatory model, people are not responsible for problems but are responsible for solutions. In the enlightenment model, people are responsible for problems but not for solutions. In all models, value judgments are inherent to perception of self, actions expected of the self, others besides the self who must act, and the actions expected of others. There is an implicit accompanying view of human nature and a description of potential pathology for each model. In making use of these models, it is important to be aware of the fit between the model and the specific cultural world view of illness/mental illness as well as legitimate or acceptable interventions.

Real-world settings were cited in which the moral model was represented by Erhard seminar graduates, the medical model by students in a college infirmary waiting room, the compensatory model by members of a national evangelical group, and the enlightenment model by participants in a job training program. Acceptability of a service-delivery model is thus facilitated by who one is, including cultural identity, and the setting in which services are provided.

Sources of Confusion in Practice

S. Sue (1983, 1991) has identified several unverbalized sources of potential confusion in professional practice with multicultural groups. These issues must always be recognized and explored as they can affect the acceptability and usefulness of assessment services to ethnic minority clients. These issues include; etic versus emic perspectives; assimilation versus pluralism; group personality versus individual differences; and presence or absence of racism.

Etic and/or emic perspectives influence both the selection and interpretation of assessment devices. Assimilation-pluralism refers to the cultural orientation of the client. An assessor must have information concerning the cultural orientation of a client prior to any assessment process. Group personality-individual differences is a major concern because within-group differences will be as great (or greater) than between-group differences. The assumption of ethnic group homogeneity must be examined carefully and skeptically for each client. Finally, clients who have experienced prejudice and discrimination often have special problems with Anglo-American service providers and acceptance of services, as a result of their personal histories. A discussion of some potential effects of these issues on assessment practice at this point will serve as an introduction to detailed considerations later in this book.

Etic and Emic

Psychologists have traditionally preferred an etic perspective that emphasizes universals among human beings by using examination and comparison of many cultures from a position outside those cultures. Unfortunately, an imposed etic has frequently been applied, one using the middle-class Anglo-American as the standard for comparison with other groups. For example, the original norms of the Minnesota Multiphasic Personality Inventory (MMPI-1) described a 35-year-old, white, rural, married, semi-skilled person with an eighth-grade education (Dahlstrom, Welsh, & Dahlstrom, 1972) although this person was described differently for the MMPI-2, the standard continues to be predominantly middle-class. By this standard, cultural differences can be treated as statistical differences that describe a departure from normality. By contrast, an emic perspective is culture-specific and examines behavior from within a culture, using criteria relative to the internal characteristics of that culture. An emic approach acknowledges that persons from non-Anglo-American cultural groups must be understood on their own terms.

However, etic-emic differences can only provide avenues toward useful methodologies. These terms were extrapolated from a distinction in linguistics between phonetics, or generalization from different languages to all languages (etic), and phonemics, or sounds used in one language (emic) (Pike, 1966). The formulation of precise meaning for etics, or universals, is difficult (Van de Vijver & Poortinga, 1982). The emic, while elusive, may be found by painstaking immersion in a particular culture (Trimble, Lonner, & Boucher, 1983). Such immersion may involve becoming a long-term resident in a Native American reservation community, for example, to appreciate the ways in which an alternative world view can affect individual lives.

Jahoda (1977) noted that these etic-emic distinctions have practical utility either in a linguistic context or as a caution to psychologists not to ignore social-structural features in favor of pseudo-universals. For example, López et al. (1989) have described a seminar model of developmental stages of cultural sensitivity in which etic and emic perspectives are applied by students to illustrative vignettes. These stages included unawareness of cultural issues, heightened awareness, consideration of issues, and movement toward integration of culture in clinical work.

In American society, many clients remain rooted in their original culture while simultaneously enmeshed in the social and economic realities of the middle-class, predominantly Anglo-American culture. For professional psychologists who may be encapsulated by training and personal identity in this mainstream culture, the nature of this dilemma is crystallized by the etic-emic distinction. One resolution of this dilemma may be found in a multicultural stance that involves a Stage 4 openness, appreciation, and acceptance of culturally dissimilar lives (M. J. Bennett, 1986).

Assimilation Versus Pluralism

A second source of confusion lies in the contrast of assimilation and pluralism as desirable goals for multicultural persons in American society. At one time in this country, the melting pot ideal presumed that homogenization of different ethnic groups would produce a prototypical American. However, much of the strength contained in American character is to be found in what Bellah and colleagues (1985) have described as a "commitment of memory," in which people remember their historical sufferings and virtues in concert with their future aspirations, as a context for meaning in their individual lives. Such cultural identity has become a source of strength for members of minority groups who attempt to persevere with dignity in the face of overt discrimination and limitations on opportunity.

A cultural pluralism accepts individual differences as personal assets and aspires to maintain separate institutions for distinct social groups within a single political unit (Padilla & Keefe, 1984). The problem for culturally different populations is how to maintain essential ingredients of their unique and historic identities and still participate fully as citizens in mainstream American life. Nonetheless, there has been criticism of what is termed the "cult of ethnicity," or too intense cultural identity as a potential source of increased societal distress in the immediate future (Schlesinger, 1991).

Service providers must be aware that this dilemma of assimilation versus pluralism may be evident in individuals by the extent to which acculturation has occurred. Acculturation is a moderator variable in assessment (see Chapter 7). The application of moderator variables may provide the only defensible rationale for continuing to use imposed etic measures for populations that are culturally different from standardization populations. However, this approach is clearly compensatory and time-limited in usefulness. Nevertheless, in a psychometric climate that minimizes group differences, the additional data provided by these measures can alert assessors to inadequacies in their norms and thereby modify or qualify interpretation.

Group Personality Versus Individual Differences

A third source of confusion relates to group personality versus individual differences. Psychologist service providers often act on the basis of research evidence that emphasizes group differences rather than within-group variation, although it has been acknowledged that within-group differences are greater than differences between groups (Argyle, 1969).

Group personality research includes studies of national character (Inkeles & Levinson, 1969); modal personality research has used pooled individual Rorschach scores in a group psychogram, or synthetic pattern (Kaplan, 1961). Rorschach examples for Native American tribes have been reported (Wallace, 1952). Such examples require a large sample and measures of central tendency and standard deviation, as well as knowledge of the form of the distribution. Nonetheless, adding Rorschach scores across persons ignores interactions among scores and the fact that different numbers of responses will occur in each record (Cronbach, 1949). While MMPI-1 and MMPI-2 solve some of these problems, the assumption of within-group homogeneity permits so-called measurement errors to be confused with variance due to subject variability. Stereotyped images of culturally different persons may result and can bias subsequent test interpretations (Dana, 1988).

Racism

A final dilemma lies in the continued virulence of racism in American society. Both subtle and overt racism still permeate mainstream American society. Although each culturally different group has its unique history of discrimination, prejudice, and racism (see Chapters 2–5), most ethnic minority groups have been historically depicted as culturally deficient on both socially desirable and devalued attributes (Howard & Scott, 1981). Baratz and Baratz (1970) cite ignorance of cultural influences on socialization as responsible for acceptance of surface similarities between cultural groups. In the absence of ethnohistoric perspectives, these differences in behavior, intelligence, or cognition have been used as evidence for genetic deficit or for poverty and discrimination effects. These pejorative social science attitudes have affected the health and mental health services available to multicultural groups.

Historically, in graduate psychology training programs, racism was reflected by restricted admissions and subsequent "cooling out" of minority students, exclusion of cross-cultural content in training, and absence or only token representation of culturally different faculty members. Racism was also found in some early psychological tests and techniques, using for example, inappropriate test content or culturally unrepresentative items, bias in standardization procedures and sampling, skewing for socioeconomic status, examiner/language bias, measurement of different constructs and differential predictive validity, and distorted interpretation as a result of stereotyping with inequitable social consequences (Reynolds & Brown, 1984).

In the larger society, racism still exists overtly in some right-wing religious groups, the Ku Klux Klan, and the American Nazi party and affiliates. Recently, there has been a dramatic increase in unprovoked assaults and murders of persons who are identifiably different from the majority of Anglo-Americans. In spite of federal laws, racism continues to exist covertly in both the public and private sectors. For example, overt discrimination, especially in housing, has continued almost unabated; per capita income levels of African Americans were 57 percent of Anglo-Americans' income in 1971 and 1984; and prejudice continues, as the societal goal of assimilation has been gradually relinquished (Jaynes & Williams, 1989). Racism continues to be responsible for differential opportunity and contributes to poverty, hunger, and homelessness for a substantial number of Americans.

Resolution of Conflicts

An understanding of these sources of potential confusion is relevant not only to professional psychology practice with multicultural clients but to the future development and greater functional integration of our society. In order to be consistent with historic traditions that combine freedom and justice with individualism, it is necessary now to acknowledge explicitly the fact of cultural diversity as one focus for maintaining the strength of our society, based upon acceptance of differences as well as similarities among persons. For assessors, this can be accomplished by actively questioning the Eurocentric assumptions and values that undergird the development and use of specific assessment technologies for multicultural professional practice. Ultimately, competent services for multicultural populations will be dependent on formulation of new social policies rather than on technology per se. Unfortunately, the use of assessment technology in this society has not been preceded by any development of relevant social policy (Dana, 1987a).

References

Abel, T. M., Metraux, R., & Roll, S. (1987). *Psychotherapy and culture*. Albuquerque, NM: University of New Mexico Press.

Albert, R. D. (1983). The intercultural sensitizer or culture assimilator: A cognitive approach. In D. Landis & R. Brislin (Eds.), *Handbook of intercultural training: Vol 2. Issues in training methodology* (pp. 186–217). Elmsford, NY: Pergamon.

Albert, R. D., & Triandis, H. C. (1985). Intercultural education for multicultural societies. *International Journal of Intercultural Relations, 9,* 319–337.

American Psychological Association. (1982). *Survey of graduate departments of psychology.* Washington, DC: Author.

Argyle, M. (1969). *Social interaction.* New York: Atherton.

Baratz, S. S., & Baratz, J. C. (1970). Early childhood intervention: The social science base of institutional racism. *Harvard Educational Review, 40*(1), 29–50.

Baumeister, R. F. (1986). *Identity: Cultural change and the struggle for self.* New York: Oxford University Press.

Bellah, R. N., Madsen, R., Sullivan, W. M., Swidler, A., & Tipton, S. T. (1985). *Habits of the heart: Individualism and commitment in American life.* New York: Harper & Row.

Bennett, J. M. (1986). Modes of cross-cultural training. *International Journal of Intercultural Relations, 10,* 117–134.

Bennett, M. J. (1986). A developmental approach to training for intercultural sensitivity. *International Journal of Intercultural Relations, 10,* 179–196.

Bernal, M. E. (1986). *Issues and concerns regarding the preparation of psychologists for service and research with ethnic minority populations.* Washington, DC: American Psychological Association.

Bernal, M. E., & Padilla, A. M. (1982). Survey of minority curricula and training in clinical psychology. *American Psychologist, 37,* 780–787.

Brickman, P., Rabinowitz, V. C., Karuza, J., Jr., Coates, D., Cohen, E., & Kidder, L. (1982). Models of helping and coping. *American Psychologist, 37,* 368–384.

Brislin, R. W. (1986). A culture general assimilator. *International Journal of Intercultural Relations, 10,* 215–232.

Copeland, E. J. (1982). Minority populations and traditional counseling programs: Some alternatives. *Counselor Education and Supervision, 21,* 187–193.

Copeland, E. J. (1983). Cross-cultural counseling and psychotherapy: A historical perspective, implications for research and training. *Personnel and Guidance Journal, 62*(1), 10–15.

Cronbach, L. J. (1949). Statistical methods applied to Rorschach scores. *Psychological Bulletin, 46,* 393–429.

Cross, T. L., Bazron, B. J., Dennis, K. W., & Issacs, M. R. (1989). *Toward a culturally competent system of care.* Washington, DC: CAASP Technical Assistance Center, Georgetown University Child Development Center.

Cuellar, I., & Schnee, S. B. (1987). An examination of utilization characteristics of clients of Mexican origin served by the Texas Department of Mental Health and Mental Retardation. In R. Rodriguez & M. T. Coleman (Eds.), *Mental health issues of the Mexican origin population in Texas* (pp. 100–115). Austin, TX: Hogg Foundation for Mental Health, University of Texas.

Dahistrom, W. G., Welsh, G. S., & Dahistrom, L. E. (Eds.). (1972). *An MMPI handbook, Volume I: Clinical interpretation.* Minneapolis: University of Minnesota Press.

Dana, R. H. (1982). *A human science model for personality assessment with projective techniques.* Springfield, IL: Thomas.

Dana, R. H. (1984). Megatrends in personality assessment: Toward a human science psychology. *Journal of Personality Assessment, 48,* 562–590.

Dana, R. H. (1985). A service delivery paradigm for personality assessment. *Journal of Personality Assessment, 49,* 598–604.

Dana, R. H. (1986). Clinical assessment. In G. S. Tryon (Ed.), *The professional practice of psychology* (pp. 69–87). Norwood, NJ: Ablex.

Dana, R. H. (1987a). Health psychology technology and/or values? *Contemporary Psychology, 32,* 695–696.

Dana, R. H. (1987b). Training for professional psychology: Science, practice, and identity. *Professional Psychology: Nesearch and Practice, 18,* 9–16.

Dana, R. H. (1988). Culturally diverse groups and MMPI interpretation. *Professional Psychology: Research and Practice, 19,* 490–495.

Dana, R. H., Behn, J. D., & Gonwa, T. (1992). A checklist for examination of cultural competence in social service agencies. *Research on Social Work Practice, 2*(2), 220–233.

David, K. H. (1972). *Intercultural adjustment and application of reinforcement theory to problems of culture shock.* Hilo, HI: Center for Cross-Cultural Training.

DeVos, G. (1968). National character. In D. L. Sills (Ed.), *International Encyclopedia of the Social Sciences* (Vol. 11, pp. 14–19). New York: Macmillan and Free Press.

Dunston, P. J. (1983). Culturally sensitive and effective psychologists: A challenge for the 1980s. *Journal of Community Psychology, 11,* 376–382.

Flaskerud, J. H. (1986). The effects of culture-compatible intervention on the utilization of mental health services by minority clients. *Community Mental Health Journal, 22,* 127–141.

Gergen, K. J. (1985). The social constructionist movement in modern psychology. *American Psychologist, 40,* 266–275.

Harrison, R., & Hopkins, R. (1967). The design of cross-cultural training: An alternative to the university model. *Journal of Applied Behavioral Science, 3*(4), 431–460.

Heller, D. (1985). *Power in psychotherapeutic practice.* New York: Human Sciences Press.

Henderson, G. (1979). *Understanding and counseling ethnic minorities.* Springfield, IL: Thomas.

Henry, W. E., Simes, J. H., & Spray, S. L. (1971). *The fifth profession: Becoming a psychotherapist.* San Francisco, CA: Jossey-Bass.

Hornby, R., & Dana, R. H. (1992). Human services training in tribal colleges. *Tribal College: Journal of American Indian Higher Education, 3*(3), 24–27.

Hough, R. L., Landsverk, J. A., & Karno, M. (1987). Utilization of health and mental health services by Los Angeles Mexican-American and non-Hispanic whites. *Archives of General Psychiatry, 44,* 702–709.

Howard, A., Pion, G. M., Gottfredson, G. D., Flattau, P. E., Oscamp, S., Pfafflin, S. M., Bray, D. W., & Burstein, A. G. (1986). The changing face of American psychology: A report from the committee on employment and human resources. *American Psychologist, 12,* 1311–1327.

Howard, A., & Scott, R. A. (1981). The study of minority groups in complex societies. In R. H. Munroe & B. B. Whiting (Eds.), *Handbook of cross-cultural development* (pp. 113–152). New York: Garland Stem.

Hui, C. H., & Triandis, H. C. (1986). Individualism-collectivism: A study of cross-cultural researchers. *Journal of Cross-Cultural Psychology, 17,* 225–248.

Hunt, E. B., & Banaji, M. R. (1988). The Whorfian hypothesis revisited; A cognitive science view of linguistic and cultural effects on thought. In J. W. Berry, S. H. Irvine, & E. B. Hunt (Eds.), *Indigenous cognition: Functioning in cultural context* (pp. 57–84). Boston: Martinus Nijhoff.

Ibrahim, F. A. (1985). Effective cross-cultural counseling and psychotherapy. *The Counseling Psychologist, 13,* 625–638.

Inkeles, A., & Levinson, D. J. (1969). National character: The study of modal personality and sociocultural systems. In G. Lindzey & E. Aronson (Eds.), *The handbook of social psychology* (2nd ed.) (Vol. 4, pp. 418–506). Reading, MA: Addison-Wesley.

Jahoda, G. (1977). In pursuit of the emic-etic distinction: Can we ever capture it? In Y. H. Poortinga (Ed.), *Basic problems in cross-cultural psychology* (pp. 55–63). Amsterdam: Swets and Zeitlinger.

Jaynes, G. D., & Williams, R. M., Jr (Eds.). (1989). *A common destiny: Blacks and American society.* New York: National Research Council.

Jones, J. M. (1990, June). A call to advance psychology's role in minority issues. *APA Monitor, 21*(6), 23.

Kaplan, B. (1961). Cross-cultural use of projective techniques. In F. L. K. Hsu (Ed.), *Psychological anthropology* (pp. 235–254). Homewood, IL: Dorsey.

Katz, J. H. (1985). The sociopolitical nature of counseling. *The Counseling Psychologist, 13,* 615–624.

Kearney, M. (1975). World view theory and study. In B. J. Siegel (Ed.), *Annual Review of Anthropology* (Vol. 4, pp. 247–270). Palo Alto, CA: Annual Reviews.

Kimble, G. A. (1984). Psychology's two cultures. *American Psychologist, 39,* 833–839.

Kluckhohn, F. R. (1954). Dominant and variant value orientations. in C. Kluckhohn & H. A. Murray (Eds.), *Personality in nature, society, and culture* (pp. 342–358). New York: Knopf.

Kluckhohn, F. R. (1960). A method for eliciting value orientations. *Anthropological Linguistics, 2*(2), 1–23.

Kluckhohn, F. R., & Strodtbeck, F. L. (1961). *Variations in value orientations.* Homewood, IL: Dorsey.

Koch, S. (1981). The nature and limits of psychological knowledge. *American Psychologist, 36,* 257–269.

López, S. R., Grover, K. P., Holland, D., Johnson, M. J., Kain, C. D., Kanel, K., Mellins, S. A., & Rhyne, M. C. (1989). Development of culturally sensitive psychotherapists. *Professional Psychology: Research and Practice, 20,* 369–376.

Macaranas-Sittler, N. (1986, April). *Psychological frames of reference: Cross-cultural dimensions.* Poster presented at the Southwestern Psychological Association meeting, Ft. Worth, TX.

Manicas, P. T., & Secord, P. F. (1983). Implications for psychology of the new philosophy of science. *American Psychologist, 38,* 399–413.

Mollica, R. (1990, March). *A look to the future.* Paper presented at the conference on Mental Health of immigrants and Refugees, World Federation for Mental Health and Hogg Foundation for Mental Health, Houston, TX.

Munroe, D. (1979). Locus of control attribution among blacks and whites in Africa. *Journal of Cross-Cultural Research, 10,* 157–172.

Myers, H. F., Echemendia, R. J., & Trimble, J. E. (1991). The need for training ethnic minority psychologists. In H. F. Myers, P. Wohlford, L. P. Guzman, & R. J. Echemendia (Eds.), *Ethnic minority perspectives on clinical training and services in psychology* (pp. 3–11). Washington, DC: American Psychological Association.

Myers, H. F., Wohlford, P., Guzman, L. P., & Echemendia, R. J. (Eds.). (1991). *Ethnic minority perspectives on clinical training and services in Psychology.* Washington, DC: American Psychological Association.

Neimeyer, G. J., & Fukuyama, M. (1984). Exploring the content and structure of cross-cultural attitudes. *Counselor Education and Supervision, 23,* 214–225.

O'Sullivan, M. J., Peterson, P., Cox, G. B., & Kirkeby, J. (1989). Ethnic populations: Community health services ten years later. *American Journal of Community Psychology, 17,* 17–30.

Padilla, A. M., & Keefe, S. E. (1984). The search for help: Mental health resources for Mexican Americans and Anglo Americans in a plural society. in S. Sue & T. Moore (Eds.), *The Pluralistic society: A community mental health perspective* (pp. 77–115). New York: Human Sciences.

Parsons, T. (1951). *The social system.* New York: Free Press.

Pedersen, P. (1981). Triad counseling. In R. J. Corsini (Ed.), *Handbook of innovative psychotherapies* (pp. 840–854). New York: Wiley.

Pike, K. L. (1966). *Language in relation to a unified theory of the structure of human behavior.* The Hague: Mouton.

Pinderhughes, E. (1989). *Understanding race, ethnicity, and power: The key to efficacy in clinical practice.* New York: Free Press.

Pion, G., Bramblett, P., Wicherski, M., & Stapp, J. (1985). *Summary report of the 1984–85 survey of graduate departments of Psychology.* Washington, DC: American Psychological Association.

Reynolds, C. R. (1976). Correlational findings, educational implications, and locus of control research: A review. *Journal of Black Studies, 6*(3), 221–256.

Reynolds, C. R., & Brown, R. T. (1984). Bias in mental testing: An introduction to the issues. In C. R. Reynolds & R. T. Brown (Eds.), *Perspectives on bias in mental testing* (pp. 1–39). New York: Plenum.

Rotter, J. B. (1966). Generalized expectations for internal vs. external control of reinforcement. *Psychological Monographs, 80*(1, whole No. 609).

Russo, N. F., Olmedo, E. L., Stapp, J., & Fulcher, R. (1981). Women and minorities in psychology. *American Psychologist, 36,* 1315–1363.

Rychlak, J. F. (1977). *The Psychology of rigorous humanism.* New York: Wiley.

Sampson, E. E. (1985). The decentralization of identity: Toward a revised concept of personal and social order. *American Psychologist, 40,* 1203–1211.

Sampson, E. E. (1988). The debate on individualism; Indigenous psychologies of the individual and their role in personal and societal functioning. *American Psychologist, 43,* 15–22.

Schlesinger, A. M., Jr. (1991). *The disuniting of America.* Knoxville, TN: Whittle Direct Books.

Solomon, P. (1988). Racial factors in mental health service utilization. *Psychosocial Rehabilitation Journal, 11,* 3–12.

Stein, M. J., Smith, M., & Wallston, K. A. (1984). Cross-cultural issues in health locus of control beliefs. *Psychological Studies, 29*(1), 112–116.

Sue, D. W. (1978a). Eliminating cultural oppression in counseling. *Journal of Counseling Psychology, 25,* 419–428.

Sue, D. W. (1978b). World views and counseling. *Personnel and Guidance Journal, 56,* 458–462.

Sue, S. (1977). Community mental health services to minority groups—some optimism, some pessimism. *American Psychologist, 32,* 616–624.

Sue, S. (1983). Ethnic minority issues in psychology; A reexamination. *American Psychologist, 38,* 583–592.

Sue, S. (1991). Ethnicity and culture in psychological research and practice. In J. D. Goodchilds (Ed.), *Psychological perspectives on human diversity in America* (pp. 51–85). Washington, DC: American Psychological Association.

Sue, S., & Zane, N. (1987). The role of culture and cultural techniques in psychotherapy. *American Psychologist, 42,* 37–45.

Tait, R., DeGood, D., & Carron, H. (1982). A comparison of health locus of control beliefs in low-back patients from the U. S. and New Zealand. *Pain, 14,* 53–61.

Taplin, J. R. (1980). Implication of general systems theory for assessment and intervention. *Professional Psychology, 11*, 722–727.

To See Ourselves as Others See Us. (1986, June 16). [Opinions about what Americans do best, from notables on five continents]. *Time,* pp. 52–53.

Trimble, J. E., Lonner, W. J., & Boucher, J. D. (1983). Stalking the wily emic: Alternatives to cross-cultural assessment. In S. H. Irvine & J. W. Berry (Eds.), *Human assessment and cultural factors* (pp. 259–271). New York: Plenum.

Trimble, J. E., & Richardson, S. S. (1982). Locus of control measures among American Indians: Cluster structure analytic characteristics. *Journal of Cross-Cultural Psychology, 13*, 228–238.

Trimble, J. E., & Richardson, S. S. (1983). Perceived personal and societal forms of locus of control measures among American Indians. *White Cloud Journal, 3*(1), 3–14.

Tyler, F. B., Sussewell, D. R., & Williams-McCoy, J. (1985). Ethnic validity in psychotherapy. *Psychotherapy, 22*, 311–320.

Van de Vijver, F. R. J., & Poortinga, Y. H. (1982). Cross-cultural generalization and universality. *Journal of Cross-Cultural Psychology, 13*, 387–408.

Wallace, A. F. (1952). The modal personality structure of the Tuscarora Indians as revealed by the Rorschach test. *Bureau of American Ethnology, 150*, 1–120.

Wallach, M. A., & Wallach, L. (1983). *Psychology's sanction for selfishness: The error of egoism in theory and therapy.* San Francisco: Freeman.

Wallston, K. A., Wallston, B. S., & DeVellis, R. (1978). Development of the Multidimensional Locus of Control (MHLC) Scales. *Health Psychology Monographs, 6*(2), 160–170.

Waterman, A. S. (1981). Individualism and interdependence. *American Psychologist, 36*, 96–112.

Whorf, B. L. (1956). *Language, thought and reality.* Cambridge, MA: MIT Press.

Wittig, M. A. (1985). Metatheoretical dilemmas in the psychology of gender. *American Psychologist, 40*, 800–811.

Wyatt, G., & Parham, W. (1982). *Summary of findings on inclusion of culturally sensitive materials in graduate schools and training programs.* Washington, DC: Board of Ethnic Minority Affairs, American Psychological Association.

CHAPTER TWO

African Americans

Introduction

The 1990 census reported that approximately 25 percent of the population of the United States were persons of non-Anglo-American origins, from four major ethnic/racial groups. These groups included approximately 30 million African Americans, or 12.1 percent of the population. It has been estimated that the African-American population will increase by 22 percent, or 6.6 million persons, by the year 2000. By the middle of the next century, the combined populations of African Americans, Asian Americans, Hispanic Americans, and Native Americans will probably constitute a majority of the United States population (Henry, 1990).

This chapter and the next three will describe the cultures of these four groups, including their histories and experiences with discrimination and racism. This material will be presented in a format that follows Figure 1-1, beginning with group and personal identity, proceeding to values and beliefs, including spirituality and health/illness, and finally examining perceptions of services, service providers, and service-delivery style.

Cultural Differences

Identity

Group Identity The term "African American" will be used throughout this book. This term is potentially less stigmatizing than other terms such as "Black" or "Negro," which have been associated historically with negative racial attitudes and represent changes from one European language to another (Fairchild, 1985). Fairchild also suggests that "African American," hyphenated or unhyphenated, is preferable to "Black" or "Negro" because it formalizes the African connection, avoids the ambiguity inherent in the capitalization/non-capitalization issue, adds a consciousness-raising dimension of self-respect and dignity, and may even attenuate hostile Anglo-American attitudes. In research with Anglo-American college students, Fairchild found consistent stereotyping of "Blacks" and "Negroes" with more negative traits than were ascribed to "African Americans." However, "African American" is not used here synonymously with an Afrocentric cultural orientation, as that orientation is only one of four distinct orientations shared by a heterogeneous population.

African Americans have a turbulent and poignant history in this country, which has been accompanied by racism in the form of terrorism, lynchings, and property destruction. Their upward mobility has been restricted by poverty and discrimination in a society they did not choose but of which they now consider themselves an integral part, for better or worse. This history began with forcible removal from Africa, their continent of origin, and chattel slavery in the United States, followed by Emancipation, Reconstruction, and Black Codes or Jim Crow laws from 1877 to 1914. From 1940 to 1970 there was a migration away from the South to the North and West, with a gradual shift from rural residence in the South to predominantly urban residence. A cultural renaissance from 1915 to 1930 was followed by a social movement that included civil rights and militancy from 1954 to 1975.

Baker (1987) has described the low profile and passive role of most African Americans at the beginning of this century, an attitude that preceded later group self-assertiveness and accompanying social changes. As a result of these changes, expectations were fueled for an improved quality of life that has not materialized. A profound disappointment of these hopes during the 1980s has been accompanied by economic retrenchment. In the 1990s, a majority of African Americans still have lifestyles that are significantly affected by racism. The most blatant indicators of the cumulative results of discrimination and racism are found in health, income, education, and occupation statistics that all show significant and increasing discrepancies between African Americans and Anglo-Americans. Some comparative statistics, for example, include ratios for infant mortality for African Americans and Anglo-Americans of 2.1 to 1, adult mortality of 1.5 to 1, homicide for men of 10 to 1, and poverty of 3 to 1 (for details, see Tienda, 1990).

All of these factors have contributed to a unique ethnicity, or group identity, that may be described in terms of a common historical style, shared behaviors, values and perceptions, as well as distinctive patterns of cultural communication (Kochman, 1987). This group identity of African Americans is complex, as a result of large within-group differences and an admixture of cultural orientations. Four cultural orientations will be described on a group identity spectrum. All four of these orientations probably retain some qualities that can be called a racial identity as a result of a shared history in which some group behaviors and group consciousness have fostered survival. It is recognized that there is an element of arbitrariness in the construct of cultural orientations for African Americans for this reason. Nonetheless, the ability to recognize cultural identity options and orientations for African Americans provides an explicit recognition of their heterogeneity. In addition, the premise that assessor knowledge of cultural orientation should antedate any assessment procedure is necessary for provision of competent services.

The group identity spectrum includes persons who desire to belong to a unique cultural group of African heritage and are actively engaged in identity formation/consolidation (traditional or Afrocentric). While the percentages of persons in each group are unknown, 23 percent of a male urban college population were found to be involved in an identity transformation process leading to Afrocentrism, as indicated by stage scores on racial identity measures (Whatley & Dana, 1989).

Many other African Americans may prefer to identify with the dominant Anglo-American culture (nontraditional), although such identification has limits as long as distinctive skin color is present. Others may attempt to be part of both groups (bicultural). This option is also difficult because identifiable African Americans are still subjected to discrimination and racism, although denial and/or preoccupation often leads to overachievement and aspirations for middle-class status (Pinderhughes, 1982).

Finally, persons who are marginal and have neither a clear Afrocentric nor a Eurocentric cultural tradition are characterized by marginality. Marginality describes those who have been trapped in what Pinderhughes (1982) has called a "victim system" that affects identity formation and mental and/or physical health and places limits on community improvement because it constitutes a circular feedback process. This system was created by poverty, racism, and discrimination and limits opportunity, education, and development of skills, resulting in underemployment or unemployment. There is increased stress in relationships and fulfillment of family roles. As a consequence, poor health, psychosomatic illness, depression, child/adult abuse, and homicide are endemic.

Marginality has created a subculture with distinct values. These include cooperation as a bastion against powerlessness, strict obedience to authority within local subcultural groups, toughness, an unremitting focus on life in the present, suppression of feelings and displacement to music, and belief in luck, magic, and spirituality (Pinderhughes, 1982). Cultural marginality probably describes a significant percentage of the African-American population in this country, as 60 percent of African-American children have been exposed to early poverty, neighborhoods with high crime rates, poor schools, and substandard housing.

Many Anglo-American researchers have assumed that within-group differences among racially identified persons are negligible or may be equated with social class differences in the dominant society. However, social classes among African Americans are different in income, occupation, and educational representation from the class structure of the dominant society (Bass, 1982; Stricker,

1980). The African-American upper class contains 10 percent, the middle class includes 40 percent, and the lower class has 50 percent of the African-American population, with three subgroups in the middle and lower classes, including approximately 13 percent of nonworking poor persons. By contrast, for Anglo-Americans there is a six-class structure, with 15 percent in capitalist and upper-middle classes, 60 percent in approximately equal-sized middle and working classes, and 25 percent in the working poor and underclasses (Gilbert & Kahl, 1987). These differences are underscored by the fact that 34 percent of African Americans were below the poverty line in the 1990 census. When the qualifiers "at" and "close to" the poverty line are added, there were over 42 percent in this category in 1984, when the average net worth of Anglo-American families was 13 times greater than for African-American families (Bonacich, 1990). Furthermore, neighborhood of residence does not suggest homogeneity of residents for African Americans, as there is a mixture of the three lower-middle classes in segregated urban neighborhoods (H. F. Myers, 1982).

The personalities of African Americans have been assumed by many Anglo-American researchers to be the result of oppression (Baldwin, 1984) and/or socioeconomic characteristics as contained in a "culture of poverty" (O. Lewis, 1966). Although it is a fact that a history of oppression has contributed to personality problems and to development of survival-oriented coping strategies, the components of group identity formation are contained in what has been called Afrocentrism, "a viability of people, customs, beliefs, and behavior emanating from African lands" (Jackson, 1986, p. 132). The relationship between African-American cultural adaptation, or racial identity, and socioeconomic status has been equivocal in empirical studies. However, when the Racial Identity Attitude Scale (RIAS) was used to measure cultural adaptation, socioeconomic status could not be predicted (Carter & Helms, 1988). This finding suggested that socioeconomic status and racial identity are separate constructs.

Racial identity as described by Afrocentricism, or the development of Nigrescence measured by RIAS stages, is thus distinct from the history of social oppression in the United States. Afrocentricism is a recognition and/or relearning of ancestral roots together with an emphasis and pride in the remnants of an earlier world view that was clearly present in the components of group identity. This movement began in the 1960s and included college Black Studies programs, advocacy by leaders like Malcolm X, Eldridge Cleaver, Marcus Garvey, and Martin Luther King, and cognitive developmental psychological models of Nigrescence, or becoming African American.

Nigrescence has been described in cognitive developmental models by Cross (1971) and Thomas (1971) in different but conceptually analogous terms. Table 2-1 summarizes and compares these models by stage. Stage I constitutes a disturbed identity as a result of partial identification with the dominant society. Stage II provides the beginnings of a painful and confused awareness. Stage III involves an emotional responsiveness to the impact of an augmenting cultural identity. Stage IV provides evidence for consolidation of this new identity. Stage V indicates perspective, context, and stability.

Information on class, gender, and regional differences was omitted from these stage conceptions, as were descriptions of the family and social conditions that lead to Stage V (Ramseur, 1989). Nonetheless, these models of Nigrescence have stimulated the development of independent psychological measures of African-American identity (see Chapter 3) that are applicable to the results of standard imposed etic tests such as MMPI-1 and MMPI-2. However, Parham (1989) has argued convincingly that a focus on college populations not only limits the usefulness of these developmental models, but also implies that identity development occurs exclusively in late adolescence and is resolved by a personal cycle through the stages.

This conceptualization of Nigrescence should not be equated with Afrocentrism, although it does provide a context for describing the development of Afrocentrism in individuals. If one chooses to emphasize process, attention will be given to an elaboration of individual psychological functioning as hypothesized by the stages of Nigrescence that are relevant to the assessment of both psychological health and psychopathology of African Americans. However,

TABLE 2-1 • *Thomas and Cross Developmental Cognitive Models of Nigrescence*

	Model	
Stage	*Thomas*	*Cross*
I	*Negromachy:* mental illness resulting from dependence on white society; subservience, repressed rage, alienation.	*Pre-encounter:* Eurocentric worldview; denigration of Blackness; political naivete; exploitation of others. Psychological disturbance.
II	*Withdrawal/Testifying:* pain, anxiety, confusion, self-denial.	*Encounter/Reinterpretation:* motivated (frantic) search for identity.
III	*Information Processing:* developing awareness of cultural identity.	*Immersion-Emersion:* Whiteness denigrated; Black rage/guilt/pride; intense feelings at first, then leveling off.
IV	*Activity:* action for personal linkage to own culture/experience.	*Internalization:* Incorporation of III, fixation or nihilism for new security.
V	*Transcendence:* unity with mankind.	*Internalization-Commitment:* confidence and control expressed in long-term focus on social change.

Sources: Thomas, 1971; Cross, 1971, 1978.

if an Afrocentric identity is emphasized, then the focus of attention is on a culturally distinctive world view that not only provides a rationale for culturally relevant assessment, but also opens an avenue to understanding and respecting the integrity of an alternative construction of human reality. Afrocentrism is a state of consciousness that requires substantial attention to Stages IV and V of the Nigrescence model.

An attempt will be made here to delineate some of the major consensual components of Afrocentrism as a religion/philosophy/world view. Since these terms are interchangeable, "world view" will be used consistently here. Central to this world view is a collective unconscious that Nobles (1980) described as "a kind of faith in a transcendental force and a sense of vital solidarity" (p. 24). Although man has always been considered to be the center of the universe, spirits, human beings, plants, animals, and natural phenomena were all interconnected and ordered in a field of force or power. In this holistic conception, the life cycle is unending and the harmony with nature is perdurable. This collective unconscious expressed a community unity and a continuous reaffirmation of existence. In addition, this collective unconscious is manifest at a conscious level and acted upon in everyday life by means of an oral tradition.

African-American scholars have made a strong case for a distinctiveness in their natural consciousness that would be described as an altered state from a Eurocentric world view (McGee & Clark, 1974). Reality is perceived differently with respect to a variety of basic attributes of existence including spirituality, apprehension of time units, reconciliation of paradox, and expression of emotion. A spiritual reality is invoked by synchronicity and extrasensory perception. This spirituality is a pervasive essence that unites the individual self with the community, past and present. A culture-specific sequencing of time units constitutes a conspicuous cross-cultural dimension of human reality that has been largely overlooked in the literature (Hall, 1984). A diunital logic, or union of opposites, is characteristically employed in thinking (L. J. Myers, 1987). Diunital existence means that positive and negative qualities coexist. As a result, people may be viewed as good and evil simultaneously (Rodgers-Rose, 1982/83). There is an immediacy and primacy to affect, an openness to feelings and their expression that makes for an emotional vitality. This vitality is expressed through an oral tradition that makes possible a resilience to tragedy (White, 1984).

A vocabulary with origins in a Eurocentric world view has difficulty in capturing the essence of an Afrocentric world view, as a result of different historical assumptions concerning the nature of man. Molefi Kete Asante (1987) and other scholars have provided the new set of terms used here, as well as much of the content contained in this description of African-American world view.

The collective unconsciousness communicates with the consciousness by means of an oral tradition, Ebonics. Within this oral tradition, "the generative and productive power of the spoken word" (Asante, 1987, p. 17), or "nommo," occurs within a structured linguistic code, using a physical style and rhythm to create rapport and relationship with an audience. In the African-American community, both credibility and power have been associated with the use of common or street language. Power was attained by means of public orature in which the leader fascinated the audience using creative energy and a logic that yielded concrete images invoking inner needs and providing for relationships. The purpose of orature in Africa and in this country has been to produce community stability and unity.

A residue of this communication system is to be found in the Southern, rural, "sacred" style of speaking that includes a rhythmic pattern in which sound is emphasized. In this improvised and spontaneous interaction with an audience, there is a "call and response" and signifying, or speech that is intended to be provocative in a context of imagery and ideas that focus on the present (Smitherman, 1973). Such learned orature originally provided communication between a king or priest and the people, in order to influence communal behavior in a context of spirituality. The speaking style has retained some of the original spiritual significance by association with ministers, gospel singing, the church, and group survival in this country.

This description of Afrocentrism may seem alien to many readers, but there is strong empirical evidence in African-American children of an historic West African origin for some of their cultural behaviors (Dodson, 1983). Data were collected by a variety of methods and evaluated on a continuum of expressive behaviors, including West African historical origin, overt changes associated with experience in this country, and behaviors that could not be associated with either historic or contemporary cultural origins. In this study, there were extreme differences between children of working-class parents and those with parents in "caretaker" positions (i.e., supervisory, civil service, professional, or business occupations). In areas of musical preference and religion, the caretaker children had strong African-origin behaviors, and in food preferences both groups had strong African content.

Personal Identity　African identity would render the individual simultaneously one with an infinite consciousness and with a separate personal self (L. J. Myers, 1987). One Afrocentric residue of this original holomony lies in the retention by many African Americans of a distinctive sociocentric self that is shown in kinship, neighboring, and friendship groups. However, not all African Americans can be characterized as sociocentric, because of dilution of values, especially at Stage 1 of Nigrescence. Nonetheless, for many African Americans the concept of self has remained strongly sociocentric, as a result of African roots and the need to survive in this country by means of mutual support and collective sharing.

Kinship in the form of an extended family once provided the means by which each person was related not only to tribal ancestors, including spirits and the unborn, but to all other living persons as well. Historically, the naming of children linked them to the spirit world, the supernatural, and the environment. In African societies, the first name represented the "okra," or supernatural cultural community or spiritual identity, and the surname or last name referred to the "ntoro" and "sunsum" of the father or the ancestral communication community. In African-American culture, nicknames are considered by Asante (1987) to "serve as markers of the African presence in the 'sound sense' of black America" (p. 73).

Anglo-American professional persons once believed that African-American families were brutalized and pathologized images of dominant culture families. However, African-American families have demonstrated a stability and cohesive functioning that is often culture-specific (H. F. Myers, 1982). J. M. Lewis and J. G. Looney (1983) found that competence among intact inner-city African-American families included shared power, strong parental coalitions, closeness without sacrificing individual ego boundaries, and negotiation in problem-solving. The competence of these intact inner-city families was related to a significantly higher income than neighboring families. Nonetheless, many of these competent families are at risk, due to economic conditions and the uncertain employment status of family members.

As a result of economic conditions, families are often of three-generation composition. They do not necessarily include only blood relations but may have uncles/aunts, cousins, "play sisters," and "home boys/girls." These co-residential extended families make possible an elastic kinship-based exchange network that may last a lifetime (Stack, 1975). These families exhibit role flexibility and interchangeability in which male-female relationships are often egalitarian, due to the presence of working wives, mothers, and grandmothers. There may also be "child-keeping" by members of the extended family, using an informal adoption network (Hines & Boyd-Franklin, 1982).

African-American men have identity as the nominal heads of household, tied in to their ability to provide for the family. However, it is girls who are socialized by their mothers for strength, economic independence, family responsibility, and daily accountability (Wilson, 1986). Women are identified as possessing fortitude, perseverance and strength during adversity. Women are also identified as "mother," and 47 percent of households have a female head (Staples, 1988).

Women are also generally more religious than men and function to tie the family into a complete church-centered support system of persons in particular roles, activities, and social life. This is especially notable in Baptist churches. Other major religious groups with some similar functions include the African Methodist, Jehovah's Witnesses, Church of God in Christ, Seventh Day Adventist, Pentecostal, and Nation of Islam sects (Hines & Boyd-Franklin, 1982).

This culture-specific description of the African-American family is not intended to suggest that all families are extended and non-consanguineous in composition. In fact, there has been a recent trend toward single life, and marriages have an increasing fragility in the African-American community (Staples, 1988). In addition, many African Americans have opted for identification with the dominant Anglo-American culture and will be more egocentric in lifestyle and less communal in orientation. As a result, African Americans may show greater within-group differences in egocentrism-sociocentrism than, for example, Native Americans. To the extent, however, that they become explicitly Afrocentric, middle-class persons especially will deal with their individual life experience in a collective manner, with a strong emphasis on flexibility, sharing, and consideration for the welfare of other persons within their sphere of responsibility and influence.

Values

The values of African Americans have been examined within the Kluckhohn dimensions of human nature, man-nature relationship, time, human relationships, and activity (Table 1-2). During the 1970s, the general pattern includes viewing other persons as both good and evil, subjugation to nature, a present-time focus, and a Being orientation (Kendrick, MacMillan, & Pinderhughes, 1983). However, more recently Carter and Helms (1987) have reported harmony in man-nature relationships, a future-time focus, an individualized relational stance, and a Doing activity orientation. This value pattern is identical to that reported for the dominant-culture configuration with regard to time, relational stance, and activity (Sue, 1981). These discrepancies indicate that many African Americans not only resemble dominant-culture persons in value orientations but reiterate the expectation for extreme within-group differences.

A focus on present or future time in the Kluckhohn dimensions does not adequately express the African origins of time perception. The perception of time was fluid and dealt with the direct experience of the present as it is composed of past events. Mbiti (1970) has described a period of immediate concern for people, or nearness and nowness ("sasa" in Swahili), that is expressed in personal recollections. Sasa is of indeterminate length and varies with the particular tribe and the age of the individual. A larger context or field for time is expressed by "zamani," which includes sasa but is not separable from it. Zamani binds persons and their environment together to express the consciousness of the entire tribe. Whenever time is structured in Anglo-American terms and schedules take precedence over spontaneity, especially in prioritizing human interactions, African Americans may be unable to fully engage their feelings (Jackson, 1986).

Beliefs

Spirituality   African spirituality, at least in a Ghana tribe, the Akan, has meant that the individual was linked to a spirit community by a constant flow of energy, or "okra," as manifested by intuitive knowledge, creative insight, or bizarre behavior. Another spiritual substance, "sunsum," was believed to be responsible for temper and character as transmitted from the father by "ntoro." Ntoro stood for reason and control of feeling. Thus, the sunsum combined objectivity with subjectivity. Finally, "mogya," or blood, is both literal and symbolic as a means of understanding ancestral community traditions. This view of human society is embedded in a more detailed and elaborate context and has been labeled by Asante (1987) as personalism.

Spirituality need not be associated with church membership for African Americans but often includes the abiding belief that it is possible to reach out to a superior power for strength and solutions to problems. Spirituality and the belief that God will solve problems may be expressed in several ways—by viewing the problem as punishment from God, by seeing the church as one's personal salvation, and by the occasional practice of witchcraft and voodoo (Knox, 1985).

Religion plays a role in help-seeking behavior; particular church affiliation may be critical in directing persons toward informal or formal service providers (Gary, 1987b). For example, preferences for institutional support, private practitioners, and informal supports differed. The majority of Holiness Church members preferred informal supports; Baptists and Lutherans expressed only a slight preference for informal supports; Catholics preferred private practitioners. Gary indicated that religious networks within the African-American community still include faith healers, prophets and advisors, missionary societies, Bible study groups, prayer meetings, and preachers.

Health/Illness Africans connected medicine with everything else in a holism that included religion, agriculture, nature, and the village. The African idea of sudicism represented a spiritual commitment to harmony. The healthy person was harmonized with self, others, nature, the spirit world, and the universe by connections, interactions, and meetings, using an oral tradition. The life task of each African was to become human in concert with others, using libations and rituals to release energy and stimulate transcendence. The nommo quality of "possession" constituted harmony, to be achieved by personal volition in a group setting accompanied by music and incantation. Bizarre behavior, speech that could not be understood, and performances contrary to harmony with the group were believed to be produced by bad okra.

Traditional African belief systems are similar to those found among Native Americans and Hispanic Americans. These systems all recognize illness as having natural, occult, or spiritual origins (Murdock, 1980). Natural illness has physical causes, and herbs, barks, teas, and other natural substances are used by folk doctors for treatment. Occult illness results from supernatural forces, including evil spirits and their agents. Spiritual illness results from deliberate violations of sacred beliefs, or sin. Folk practitioners use their own powers for prevention and healing of these illnesses. Survivals of African folk medicine include voodoo or hoodoo, shango, santería, and curanderísmo (Watson, 1984). Santería and curanderísmo are associated with Hispanic-American populations and will be described in Chapter 4. Voodoo continues to be practiced in Haiti, Louisiana, the Sea Islands of the Carolinas, and some southeastern United States subregions. Shango still exists in Trinidad-Tobago, Jamaica, Brazil, and elsewhere in South America. Beliefs in folk medicine have persisted in this country, especially among older African Americans in rural, isolated settings who share a common culture in kinship-based villages. Within these settings many residents still have faith in folk medicine and access to its practitioners (Blake, 1984).

Perceptions

Services Gary (1987a) reviewed attitudes of African Americans toward community mental health centers and discovered a recent shift toward more positive attitudes. An earlier review had found widespread shame accompanying use of mental health services, as well as beliefs that these services were without value and were used only by crazy people (Parker & McDavis, 1983). Gary used a random sample of community households and discovered that not only were people more knowledgeable about services but that the services were increasingly available. Married individuals with an augmented racial consciousness and higher educational level held more favorable attitudes. Nonetheless, nearly half of this sample had neutral attitudes, often as a reaction to negative experiences with mental health personnel who were not culturally competent. However, when there is relative social isolation from the larger society, little money to pay for services, and limited access to insurance, it is not surprising that many African-American women, at least, believe that professional services are not vital to their well-being (Amaro, Beckman, & Mays, 1987).

Other recent studies also suggest perceptions of services. Patients interviewed in an urban family planning clinic (Pugh & Mudd, 1971), agreed that problems had to be severe before services would be sought. Survey data from the Boston area has been used to profile six ethnic groups (Cleary & Demone, 1988). These groups included Protestants, Jews, and Italian, Irish, and Spanish Catholics as well as African Americans. Although the African Americans were younger and clearly had less income, higher rates of separation/divorce, and greater unemployment and responsibilities, their problem areas were not distinctively different from persons in the other groups. However, African Americans were less likely to seek counseling.

Post-hospital agency contact among African Americans has been slightly more frequent than for matched Anglo-Americans (Solomon, 1987), but these clients actually received less service and different kinds of service and remained in treatment for shorter periods than their Anglo-American counterparts. The study suggests that difficulties in obtaining services continue to be associated with expectations for services.

Service Providers   In the Pugh and Mudd study (1971) discussed earlier, men were less willing to be interviewed. They were cautious, concerned with the qualifications/competence of providers, less open or trusting, and tried to maintain an appearance of strength. Women ranked mothers, female friends, the family physician, and their minister as priority sources of help, before husband or father and professional persons. Men selected their mothers and their minister as primary help sources and ranked wife, father, and professionals lower. The major problems reported were money and marriage, and women were more positive regarding outcomes of help than were men. Neither men nor women felt that the race of the provider was of primary importance, but the fee, profession, and availability of the helper were emphasized. Women anticipated reassurance, being told what to do, understanding of self and others, and goal-setting. Men anticipated more concrete outcomes including answers, goal-setting and implementation, in addition to understanding.

A developing consciousness of racial identity has been found to be related to the perceptions of provider cultural competence (Pomales, Claiborn, & LaFromboise, 1986). African-American college students with racial identity concerns measured by the Racial Identity Attitude Scale stages of Encounter and Internalization perceived Anglo-American counselors who were culturally sensitive as also being culturally competent.

Service-Delivery Style   African Americans generally need to accept the humanity and cultural understanding of a service provider prior to making any commitment or becoming engaged with the proffered services. This process of sizing up and checking out has been described by microstages that include both agency/client concerns and the provider's behavior as it is evaluated in treatment relationships (Gibbs, 1985) and mental health consultations (Gibbs, 1980).

Stage I is an appraisal in which the client may be guarded, reserved, aloof, or superficial while waiting for provider signs of genuineness and approachability or personal authenticity. Stage II is investigative, with challenges to personal qualifications, values, or beliefs, to determine the provider's culturally relevant experience. The underlying or implicit question being asked is whether or not any differences in ethnicity or background can be equalized. Stage III only occurs when the client is satisfied by earlier investigation and develops a partial identification with the provider. This identification will often include overtures designed to establish a more personal relationship. Stage IV occurs as a result of flexible and sensitive efforts by the provider in Stage III. Loyalty and personal regard for the provider in Stage IV permit the client to be less defensive and oriented to testing the provider's intentions. In Stage V, engagement, the treatment can begin with full involvement of the client. Problems will then be revealed and attention given to treatment goals. Although this process may take several sessions, the client has come to acknowledge the provider's interpersonal competence and to experience trust in instrumental competence.

This description has a counterpart in the African-American community in response to the presence of an Anglo-American (Berg, 1977). Gaining trust within the African-American community is difficult for an Anglo-American. However, it can be done by surviving tests of availability and presence in the community and by maintaining confidentiality, which may be more difficult to deal with in an agency setting.

References

Amaro, H., Beckman, L. J., & Mays, V. M. (1987). A comparison of Black and White women entering alcoholism treatment. *Journal of Studies on Alcohol, 48*, 220–228.

Asante, M. K. (1987). *The Afrocentric idea*. Philadelphia, PA: Temple University Press.

Baker, F. M. (1987). The Afro-American life cycle: Success, failure, and mental health. *Journal of the National Medical Association, 79*(6), 625–633.

Baldwin, J. A. (1984). African self-consciousness and the mental health of African-Americans. *Journal of Black Studies, 15*, 177–194.

Bass, B. A. (1982). The validity of socioeconomic factors in the assessment and treatment of Afro-Americans. In B. A. Bass, G. E. Wyatt, & G. J. Powell (Eds.), *The Afro-American family: Assessment, treatment, and research issues* (pp. 69–83). New York: Grune & Stratton.

Berg, K. R. (19771. Trust as a factor in working with residents of a Black community. *Hospital and Community Psychiatry, 28*, 619–620.

Blake, J. H. (1984). "Doctor can't do me no good": Social concomitants of health care attitudes and practices among elderly Blacks in isolated rural populations. In W. H. Watson (Ed.), *Black folk medicine: The therapeutic significance of faith and trust* (pp. 33–40). New Brunswick, NJ: Transaction Books.

Bonacich, E. (1990). Inequality in America: The failure of the American system for people of color. In G. E. Thomas (Ed.), *U. S. race relations in the 1980s and 1990s: Challenges and alternatives* (pp. 187–215). New York: Hemisphere.

Carter, R. T., & Helms, J. E. (1987). The relationship between Black value-orientations and racial identity attitudes. *Measurement and Evaluation in Counseling and Development, 19*(4), 185–195.

Carter, R. T., & Helms, J. E. (1988). The relationship between racial identity attitudes and social class. *Journal of Negro Education, 57*(1), 22–30.

Cleary, P. D., & Demone, H., Jr. (1988). Health and social service needs in a Northeastern metropolitan area: Ethnic group differences. *Journal of Sociology and Social Welfare, 15*(4), 63–76.

Cross, W. E., Jr. (1971, July). The Negro-to-black conversion experience. *Black World*, 13–27.

Cross, W. E., Jr. (1978). The Thomas and Cross models of psychological Nigrescence: A review. *Journal of Black Psychology, 5*(1), 13–31.

Dodson, J. E. (1983). Black families: The clue to cultural appropriateness as an evaluative concept for health and human services. In A. E. Johnson (Ed.), *The Black experience: Considerations for health and human services* (pp. 43–52). Davis, CA: International Dialogue Press.

Fairchild, H. H. (1985). Black, Negro, or Afro-American? The differences are crucial! *Journal of Black Studies, 16*(1), 47–55.

Gary, L. E. (1987a). Attitudes of Black adults toward community mental health centers. *Hospital and Community Psychiatry, 38,* 1100–1105.

Gary, L. E. (1987b). Religion and mental health in an urban Black community. *Urban Research Review, 7*(2), 5–7, 14.

Gibbs, J. T. (1980). The interpersonal orientation in mental health consultation: Toward a model of ethnic variations in counseling. *Journal of Community Psychology, 8,* 195–207.

Gibbs, J. T. (1985). Treatment relationships with black clients: Interpersonal vs. instrumental strategies. *Advances in Clinical Social Work.* Silver Spring, MD: National Association of Social Workers.

Gilbert, D., & Kahl, J. A. (1987). *The American class structure: A new synthesis.* Chicago: Dorsey.

Hall, E. T. (1984). *The dance of life: The other dimension of time.* New York: Anchor.

Henry, W. A., III. (1990, April 9). Beyond the melting pot. *Time, 135*(15), 28–31.

Hines, P. M., & Boyd-Franklin, N. (1982). Black families. In M. McGoldrick, J. K. Pearce, & J. Giordano (Eds.), *Ethnicity and family therapy* (pp. 84–107). New York: Guilford.

Jackson, G. G. (1986). Conceptualizing Afrocentric and Eurocentric mental health training. In H. P. Lefley & P. B. Pedersen (Eds.), *Cross-cultural training for mental health professionals* (pp. 131–149). Springfield, IL: Thomas.

Kendrick, E. A., MacMillan, M. F., & Pinderhughes, C. A. (1983). A racial minority: Black Americans and mental health care. *American Journal of Social Psychiatry, 3*(2), 11–18.

Knox, D. H. (1985). Spirituality: A tool in the assessment and treatment of Black alcoholics and their families. *Alcoholism Treatment Quarterly, 2*(3–4), 31–44.

Kochman, T. (1987). The ethnic component of Black language and culture. In J. S. Phinney & M. J. Rotheram (Eds.), *Children's ethnic socialization: Plualism and development* (pp. 219–238). Beverly Hills, CA: Sage.

Lewis, J. M., & Looney, J. G. (1983). *The long struggle: Well-functioning working class Black families.* New York: Brunner/Mazel.

Lewis, O. (1966). *La vida.* New York: Random House. Mbiti, J. S. (1970). *African religions and philosophies.* Garden City, NY: Anchor.

McGee, D. P., & Clark, C. X. (1974). Critical elements of Black mental health. *Journal of Black Health Perspectives,* 52–58.

Murdock, G. P. (1980). *Theories of illness: A world survey.* Pittsburgh, PA: University of Pittsburgh Press.

Myers, H. F. (1982). Research on the Afro-American family: A critical review. In B. A. Bass, G. E. Wyatt, & G. J. Powell (Eds.), *The Afro-American family: Assessment, treatment, and research issues* (pp. 35–68). New York: Grune & Stratton.

Myers, L. J. (1987). The deep structure of culture: Relevance of traditional African culture to contemporary life. *Journal of Black Studies, 18*(1), 72–85.

Nobles, W. W. (1980). African foundations for Black psychology. In R. E. Jones (Ed.), *Black Psychology* (2nd ed., pp. 23–36). New York: Harper & Row.

Parham, T. A. (1989). Nigrescence: The transformation of Black consciousness across the life cycle. In R. L. Jones (Ed.), *Black adult development and aging* (pp. 151–166). Berkeley, CA: Cobb & Henry.

Parker, W. M., & McDavis, R. J. (1983). Attitudes toward mental health agencies and counselors. *Journal of Non-White Concerns, 11,* 89–98.

Pinderhughes, E. (1982). Afro-American families and the victim system. In M. McGoldrick, J. K. Pearce, & J. Giordano (Eds.), *Ethnicity and family therapy* (pp. 108–122). New York: Guilford.

Pomales, J., Claiborn, C. D., & LaFromboise, T. D. (1986). Effects of Black students' racial identity on perceptions of white counselors varying in cultural sensitivity. *Journal of Counseling Psychology, 33,* 57–61.

Pugh, T. J., & Mudd, E. H. (1971). Attitudes of Black women and men toward using community services. *Journal of Religion and Health, 10,* 256–277.

Ramseur, H. P. (1989). Psychologically healthy Black adults: A review of theory and research. In R. L. Jones (Ed.), *Black adult development and aging* (pp. 215–241). Berkeley, CA: Cobb & Henry.

Rodgers-Rose, L. F. (1982/83). Theoretical and methodological issues in the study of Black culture and personality. *Humboldt Journal of Social Relations, 10,* 320–338.

Smitherman, G. (1973). White English in blackface, or who do I be? *The Black Scholar, 4*(8–9), 32–39.

Solomon, P. (1987). Racial factors in mental health service utilization. *Psychosocial Rehabilitation Journal, 11*(2), 3–12.

Stack, C. (1975). *All our kin: Strategies for survival in a Black community.* New York: Harper & Row.

Staples, R. (1988). The Black American family. In C. H. Mindel, R. W. Habenstein, & R. Wright, Jr. (Eds.), *Ethnic families in America: Patterns and variations* (pp. 303–324). New York: Elsevier.

Stricker, L. J. (1980). "SES" indexes: What do they measure? *Basic and Applied Social Psychology, 1,* 91–101.

Sue, D. W. (1981). *Counseling the culturally different; Theory and practice.* New York: Wiley.

Thomas, C. S. (1971). *Boys no more.* Beverly Hills, CA: Glencoe.

Tienda, M. (1990). Race, ethnicity, and the portrait of inequality: Approaching the 1990s. In G. E. Thomas (Ed.), *U. S. race relations in the 1980S and 1990s: Challenges and alternatives* (pp. 137–159). New York: Hemisphere.

Watson, W. H. (1984). *Black folk medicine: The therapeutic significance of faith and trust.* New Brunswick, NJ: Transaction Books.

Whatley, P. R., & Dana, R. H. (1989). *Racial identity and MMPI group differences.* Unpublished paper, Department of Psychology, University of Arkansas, Fayetteville, AR.

White, J. L. (1984). *The psychology of Blacks: An Afro-American perspective.* Englewood Cliffs, NJ: Prentice-Hall.

Wilson, P. M. (1986). Black culture and sexuality. *Journal of Social Work and Human Sexuality, 4*(3), 29–46.

A core pan-Asian world view will be emphasized that may be extrapolated with caution to some other Asian groups. However, neither pan-Asian similarities nor differences among groups should be accepted without question, because of unique cultural histories and extensive differences among language families represented in the 32 groups. Readers are encouraged to develop their own bibliographies of research studies for groups not described in detail in this book.

Cultural Differences

Identity

Group Identity: General Asian Americans of different national origins have different histories of immigration and acculturation. (For a comprehensive review, see Kitano & Daniels, 1988.) A frequently violent racism accompanied the entry and early history of each group in this country and is still evident in the experiences of recent refugees on the basis of their visibility (Starr & Roberts, 1982).

The recent research literature on Asians in this country deals primarily with mental health/personality description of Chinese and Japanese immigrants (e.g., 11 reviews are cited by Nakanishi, 1988). Earlier literature was largely devoted to stereotyped mental health beliefs in these same populations (Morishima, Sue, Teng, Zane, & Cram, 1979).

Japanese Americans were the single largest Asian-American group in the 1970 census. However, Japanese immigration has almost ceased, due to a strong economy in Japan. By the year 2000, it has been estimated that Asian Indians will have increased from approximately 373,000 to 1,683,000, Filipinos from 782,000 to over 2 million, Koreans from 346,000 to 1,321,000, and Vietnamese from 245,000 to 1,574,000 (Gardner, Robey, & Smith, 1985). As a result, Filipinos soon will be the largest single group, or 21 percent; Koreans will account for over 13 percent and the Japanese will only rank sixth numerically in the estimated Asian-American population.

Mental health agencies have had to provide services for trauma victims by using interpreters and translations of assessment instruments because many Southeast Asian refugee immigrants are not English-speaking. Since the influx of Asians from Korea, India, and the Philippines has been very recent, there are few available services for them and a dearth of published research on these populations. Instead, new services have been focused on the multinational and multilingual Southeast Asian refugees because their mental health and health problems on entry to the United States were so acute and severe. It will be necessary to develop culturally competent services for all of these Asian-American groups as soon as possible.

Asian Americans from India, the Philippines, and Korea will soon be major recipients of services, as will Chinese Americans and Southeast Asian refugees. Although most other Asian-American groups have a lower birth rate in this country than do Anglo-Americans. Southeast Asians have a birth rate comparable to Hispanic Americans, and their current entry rate into the United States is over 4,000 per month (P. Leung & R. Sakata, 1988).

Group Identity: Chinese Americans   From 1840 until the advent of the 1882 Chinese Exclusion Act, approximately 125,000 Chinese from Kwangtung, a small area in South China, entered the United States. These Chinese were almost exclusively men, who entered this country primarily to work on the railroads. The federal discrimination associated with the exclusion act followed lynchings, murders, and race riots and resulted in a rapid decline in the Chinese American population to about 77,000 by 1940.

By 1917 there was a "barred zone," where Asian immigrants were not allowed to enter, except for Filipinos, Samoans, and Japanese, who were added to the list in 1924. Although the original exclusion act was replaced by a token quota system in 1941, the McCarren-Walter Act removed racial and ethnic restrictions in 1952 but continued with a national-origins model. Between 1952 and 1964, over 100,000 non-quota immigrants of Chinese and Japanese origin entered this country. During this period, most of the Chinese were women and family members. Finally, the 1965 Immigration Act abolished the national-origins system in favor of hemisphere quotas.

As a result of the earlier immigration policies and racism, a segregated bachelor society was created, with its own social institutions and mores, that was highly resistant to acculturation. Single clans or family associations organized emigration, typically as temporary sojourners. These clans also provided protection and mutual aid in Chinese ghettos (pejoratively called "Chinatowns") and facilitated political linkage to the surrounding population.

In addition to these clans, there were anti-establishment secret societies, the tongs, which provided opportunities for gambling, opium use, and prostitution in the Chinese-American community. Although political power in China was vested in a scholarly, non-emigrating bureaucracy, in the United States this power was largely in the hands of immigrant merchants, some of whom also participated in clan and tong leadership. Many small cities originally had their Chinatowns, but by 1940 there had been a population shift to a few major urban centers, especially San Francisco, often for reasons of increased physical safety. By 1960, 60 percent of Chinese Americans were in the four Pacific states, and over 90 percent were in only 13 states and the District of Columbia.

In spite of this history of racism and restrictions on immigration, Asian Americans were never deprived of their familial, political, and social institutions and then coercively assimilated as were African Americans (Lyman, 1968).

As a result of this history in the United States, the Chinese-American population was dichotomized (de Rios & Cheung, 1982). The majority of old residents and recent immigrants form an impoverished, traditional, Chinese language and culture community, in contrast to a relatively smaller, educated, marginally affluent, bicultural community (Lyman, 1968). Nonetheless, there has been an increasing desire among college-educated Chinese Americans to assimilate and become part of American social, political, and economic institutions (Kuo, 1982). Evidence for assimilation may be found in the relatively small differences in self-images of Chinese-American adolescents and adolescents representative of the general U.S. population (Chen & Yang, 1986), although Chinese in Taiwan remain remarkably different from both of these groups in the United States. Chinese Americans continue to struggle with identity issues involved in maintaining a traditional culture, adopting Western values, or rejecting both old and new cultures to develop Asian-American values (S. Sue & D. W. Sue, 1973) and a new Asian consciousness (Chen & Yang, 1986).

In the 1930s, the image of Chinese Americans as a despised, feared, and persecuted minority began to change with the popular novels of Pearl S. Buck, including *The Good Earth* and *Dragon Seed*. A positive backlash from the anti-Japanese hysteria during the 1940s reinforced this favorable image, at least until the cold war of the 1950s. During the late 1970s and 1980s, some major events included the establishment of economic ties between the United States and China, and in China there was a welcoming of foreign tourists and a modest encouragement of private enterprise. The June 1989 Tiananmen Square massacre of students resulted in a period of mild political estrangement between the United States and China.

Modernization came to China in the form of the 1949 Communist revolution and its aftermath, the Cultural Revolution of 1966. In this tumultuous process, a vigorous attempt was made to replace the traditional collectivity, defined by unquestioning allegiance to the ancestry, family, and kinship network, with a new collective emphasizing the state, Chairman Mao, and the party leadership (Chu, 1985). This transformation experience included psychologically sophisticated thought-reform in which milieu control, guilt/shame/confession, group analysis, and emotional appeals were used in six-month college courses between 1948 and 1952 (Lifton, 1961).

These revolutions in China eroded the sociocultural underpinnings of the family by dispersing the traditional kinship network and creating working parents with latchkey children who discovered a precocious and precarious freedom. Women now preferred to marry an only son of their own choosing, one who had deceased parents, good appearance, and sufficient financial advantages, including adequate housing and income (Chu, 1985). As a result, earlier values and virtues of filial piety and absolute submission to the family's wishes were increasingly questioned in an atmosphere of utilitarian and material bases for human relations.

Group Identity: Japanese American   At the close of the last century, rural Japanese men began to immigrate to Hawaii and then to California, to provide agricultural and road-maintenance labor. Japan had a strong national government and was an emerging nation in the international context during this period. As a result, Japan could provide these immigrants with a degree of protection that Chinese immigrants did not share (Kagiwada, 1982/83). For example, a gentlemen's agreement between the United States and Japan in 1907–1908 permitted family members of Japanese immigrants to enter this country, and the Japanese government also sponsored self-help organizations to encourage acculturative behaviors in the United States.

Japanese-American experience is usually described by generation in this country. The first generation, or issei, were born in Japan and emigrated between 1890 and 1942; they were not permitted to become naturalized citizens. In this country they were isolated and segregated in a static culture that probably changed less than did Japan during this period. The second generation, or nisei, were born in the United States and had citizenship as a result, but were exposed to the adolescent trauma of internment during World War II and abrupt entry into American society thereafter. The nisei were predominantly a middle-class, low-profile group who devoted their energies to economic recovery from the effects of the war years. The sansei, or third generation, had their beginnings in the 1970s and, with the fourth generation yonsei, are usually assimilated and ordinarily have not experienced the intense discrimination suffered by earlier generations. These generations are now described by a broader term, nikkei, that refers to all Japanese Americans.

The watershed historical event for Japanese Americans was a four-year period of internment during World War II. Immediately after the Pearl Harbor attack, approximately 120,000 Japanese Americans—issei adults, nisei adolescents, and sansei children—had their assets frozen and lost their property. These persons were relocated to internment camps. Persons of Japanese ancestry in Hawaii and those who were able to move from the designated West Coast areas lived in an uneasy stasis during the war years. Although men were initially excluded from military service, later they were forced to serve or be imprisoned.

Since the end of the war in 1945 and statehood for Hawaii in 1959, there has been an increased acceptance of Japanese Americans and a token societal reparation. Nonetheless, it has taken many years for the Japanese-American community to come to terms with the racism of the internment experience. Perhaps the least conspicuous residue of internment has been a pervasive cynicism concerning the American credo. Nonetheless, by 1980, Japanese Americans were primarily college-educated, urban residents, with 71 percent living in California or Hawaii. Some intermarriage has increased their assimilation and reduced the identifiability of their children as non-Anglo-Americans. However, outside of California and Hawaii, residues of racism persist.

Group Identity: Southeast Asian Americans Five major groups of Southeast Asians have entered the United States since the fall of Saigon in 1975; they include Vietnamese, Laotians, Cambodians, Hmong (from Laos), and ethnic Chinese (Kitano & Daniels, 1988). The term "refugee" encompasses those who flee a country under economic or political duress as well as those who voluntarily emigrate for a variety of personal reasons, especially the hope for a better life. No explicit refugee policy existed for America prior to 1980. In that year, the Refugee Assistance Act was passed, allowing an annual admission of at least 50,000 persons; it recognized the principle of asylum and provided federal aid and reimbursement for refugee-related expenses.

Skinner (1980) described two separate waves of Southeast Asian refugee immigration: pre-1975 and post-1975. The first wave fled for political reasons and contained heterogeneous urban, educated, often affluent groups of middle- and upper-class multilingual persons, equally divided between Catholics and Buddhists. The second wave included more Buddhists, ethnic Chinese, and many rural persons who were younger, less well-educated, and more naive concerning American culture. These persons fled for economic reasons and as a result of fear of relocation to re-education centers or work camps in Vietnam.

By 1985, this refugee population of over 1 million persons in the United States was 63 percent Vietnamese, 22 percent Cambodian, and 16 percent Laotian. Although 11 other Southeast Asian refugee groups have been identified in California (California Department of Mental Health Refugee Project, 1986), only these three groups will be discussed here, as they represent a majority of the refugee population. Most of them have settled in California, Washington, and the Sunbelt states, especially Texas.

Before 1975, Vietnam had been in turmoil for over 50 years, with rebellions against French rule, conquest by the Japanese in 1940, a postwar French reoccupation, a civil war from 1945 to 1975, and an increasing American military presence after 1961. An estimated 2 to 3 million Vietnamese were killed during the Vietnam War, and there were at least 3 million refugees from 1965 to 1968. Buddhism was the primary religion for 90 percent of the Vietnamese population, but the minority Catholic population included a Francophile, educated, middle-class political elite (Boman & Edwards, 1984).

The Hmong emigrated from China to Laos early in the nineteenth century. Although they had a 3,000-year history in China, they have had a written language only during the last 50 years. Their spoken language and culture were markedly different from their Chinese neighbors. As Laos experienced a recent history of colonization and conquest similar to that of Vietnam, the Hmong shared these upheavals on the basis of their geographic location. Although Laotian independence was recognized in 1954, the country was already divided between the Royal Lao government and the Pathet Lao. The Vietnam War spread to Laos, and the Hmong suffered approximately 15,000 combat deaths; bombing created a refugee population estimated at 600,000. In the United States, the Hmong have settled primarily in the San Joaquin Valley around Fresno and in the Sunbelt states. Typically, Hmong arrived in this country without financial resources and with a world view markedly unlike that of the dominant-culture population.

The Cambodians (Kampucheans) are about 85 percent Khmer, with the remainder of the population being Chinese and Vietnamese. Cambodia was once home to a major civilization, between the ninth and fourteenth centuries A.D., and later was absorbed by invaders from Vietnam and Siam. In 1863, France began to provide an indirect colonial rule that endured until changes in Cambodian political leadership in 1955. By 1966, Cambodia had become another casualty of the Vietnam War, in spite of an attempted neutrality, and by 1975 there were over 3 million refugees when the Khmer Rouge, led by Pol Pot, took over the government. At least a million persons were murdered in the succeeding years, and perhaps another million new refugees were created as a result of Khmer Rouge terror, a subsequent invasion by the Vietnamese, and famine (Kitano & Daniels, 1988).

These refugees from Vietnam, Laos, and especially Cambodia constituted a large population of severely traumatized persons with histories of work camp, prison, or first-asylum refugee camps in which physical abuse, torture, illness, and malnutrition and/or starvation were commonplace. These experiences were often augmented by equally harrowing trauma during the process of escape and relocation. The refugees have settled in other Southeast Asian countries, China, Australia, Canada, and the United States.

There are ethnic and cultural differences between the Asian-American groups described here, differences that include language, religion, and unique cultural histories of customs and traditions. Nonetheless, some commonalities will be considered under the heading of group identity; some of the differences in temperament, expressive style, and rigidity of social structure among these groups will be examined in the section on personal identity.

Group Identity: Pan-Asian American   Chinese culture was historically a major influence on the core cultures of Japan, Vietnam, and Korea. The group identity of Asian Americans has sources in the cultural impact of Confucianism, Buddhism, and Taoism, which have become somewhat blended over time (Abbott, 1970; Boman & Edwards, 1984). Confucianism is a humanistic code of behavior involving a life of virtue structured by filial piety in the contemporary and historic family to sustain a hierarchical society. Confucianism was concerned with maintaining a proper balance or regulation of forces with as little direct action as possible. As a philosophy it is eclectic, systematizing, and compromising.

The Buddhist ideal advocates avoiding ordinary human activity in favor of meditation and prayer as approaches to the true reality of oneness in nirvana. The Buddhist cultural impact is reflected in the noble truths that see life as suffering;

suffering stems from desire and may be reduced by absence of desire as a result of following the eightfold path. This path consists of right conduct, effort, meditation, speech, purpose, thinking, and understanding. Behavioral results include impassivity and stoicism as reactions to pain or adversity.

Taoism, the philosophy of Lao-Tzu, emphasized harmony between human beings and with nature. Confrontation was to be avoided, and the natural and orderly course of life was directed toward perfection. Identification with the reality of the natural, a natural paradise, led to avoidance of falsity, fabrication, selfishness, and worldiness. Being Chinese therefore was "natural," as was the absorption of new people and new ideas. The water symbol in Taoism speaks to the concern with being unaggressive, absorbing attack, and seeking one's own level with self-replenishment and self-purification.

These philosophical approaches all share a common focus on quietude or inactivity that potentially can eliminate overt aggression, competition, and conflict. Courage, energy, conviction, and self-examination are required in order to live in concert with other persons and nature.

In lieu of the Western premise of cause and effect, the Chinese believe that the world, or universe, is in constant harmonious movement, oscillating between indistinct poles, and cyclic, returning to its point of origin. All humans, supernatural forces, and ghosts are relative and connected and part of this process that cycles through time and other worlds. "Ho," or harmony, is the vital heart of existence, because human beings are enmeshed and without control in this unending process. Harmony in the universe is the key ingredient in relationships among persons, between persons and social institutions, between persons and nature, and between persons and gods or spirits. Substance and activity only exist within the matrix of rules and order that permits righteousness, self (jen), and harmony to emerge. This system is not based on constant reexamination of the empirical world and even puts restrictions on any such investigation. As a result, the focus is internal and only can direct the individual toward manipulation of well-known categories in the interest of good functioning (Abbott, 1970).

To summarize these group characteristics, Viqui Claravall (Irigon, Claravall, & Christian, 1990) identified pan-Asian characteristics of world view that include a holistic perception in which mind and body are not separable and a pluralistic world in which many approaches are integrated. Illness is perceived as physical and caused by bad spirits or a curse, or as punishment, curable or reversible by exorcism or strengthening the nervous system by herbs or tonics. The desired goal of intervention is a restoration of balance or harmony. Such restoration occurs within the family system and as a direct consequence of family harmony, and also secondarily in the life of the individual.

Personal Identity   Hsu (1985) distinguished between "greater" and "smaller" selves of traditional Chinese, and Dien (1983) identified "big me" and "little me." The greater self referred to a concern for society and even humanity, and the smaller self included the individual and immediate family. Hsu (1971, 1985) identified seven irregular, concentric layers of self from the unconscious to the outer world, including both the greater and smaller selves. These layers constituted a psychosocial homeostasis theory applicable to both Chinese and Japanese. The traditional self included several distinct layers of role and intimacy relationships. Roles that resulted in proper relationships had been originally described by Confucius as existing between prince and minister, father and son, husband and wife, elder brother and younger brother, or friend and friend (Tseng, 1973). All of these role relationships were contexts for verbalized communication, emotional support, and mutual receptivity; intimacy relationships were considered to be life-sustaining because they provided meaning and a sense of individual identity.

Hsu (1985, 1971) used the Confucian virtue of jen, which he considered to be synonymous with man or his greater self. Jen has been rendered literally as benevolence, humaneness, humanity, or love (Tseng, 1973). Jen was collective or sociocentric, predominantly external to the person, and described by the variety of role relationships that existed across several layers of personality as well as by consciousness contained in the smaller self.

Jen is in a state of dynamic equilibrium, being responsive primarily to the obligations of kinship, as expressed by filial piety. Filial piety was seen as the glue that permitted love to be expressed in a manner that maintained harmony in the family and in the social order. Filial piety included unquestioning obedience as shown by concern, understanding, and scrupulous attention to the wishes and needs of family members within the prescribed role relationships. Whenever accepted, filial piety also involved reciprocity, or appropriate benevolent responsiveness. Filial piety thus became a primary condition in the individual for the development of self-respect and self-worth. Filial piety was generalized to all authority as expressed in the etiquette of role relations outside of the family by respect, deference, and submission to law and government. This traditional sociocentric or ensembled self was committed primarily to family, including ancestors, but not to gods and spirits, which were deemed to be malevolent and dangerous by traditional Chinese.

D. W. Sue (1983) described the family life of Chinese and Japanese. The family is patriarchal, with authority and communication exercised from top to bottom, interdependent roles, strict adherence to traditional norms, and minimization of conflict by suppression of overt emotion. Guilt and shame are used to control family members; obligations to the family take precedence over individual prerogatives. Under the aegis of the family, there is sufficient discipline and self-control to provide an impetus for outstanding achievement to honor the family. Negative behaviors such as delinquency, school failure, unemployment, or mental illness are considered as family failures that disrupt the desired harmony of family life. Moreover, there is belief in external control, a fatalism that allows an equanimity and acceptance without question of life as it unfolds (Ho, 1976).

In China and in the United States, absolute control by the family as a major ingredient in the formation of a traditional self-concept has not only diminished but is being openly questioned. In spite of this questioning of traditional filial identity, there is strong evidence, at least among Hong Kong Chinese students, for the continued presence of an extended self, or collective orientation.

This collectivity has been defined, using an Individualism-Collectivism Scale (INDCOL) developed in Hong Kong, as "a set of feelings, beliefs, behavioral intentions, and behaviors related to solidarity and concern for others" (Hui, 1988, p. 17). There are role-specific subscales for parent, spouse, kin, neighbor, friend, and co-worker; these subscales have documented extreme differences between Chinese and Americans as functions of culture.

Similarly, in Japan there has been an increasing emphasis on the importance of collectivity, particularly in the form of corporate family effectiveness instead of intra-family lineal authority or filial piety. However, this collectivity may be also expressed in humanistic or socialistic terms (Caudill & Scarr, 1962).

In the United States, the problems faced by first- and second-generation Chinese may differ as a result of inability to express filial piety properly (S. Sue & D. W. Sue, 1973). Although first-generation men in particular are required to achieve and/or to be good providers for the family, sufficient achievement to fulfill family expectations has not always been possible for them. Second-generation individuals also may fail to be unquestioningly faithful to the traditional values of their parents. Their self-worth is increasingly defined either by dominant-culture values or by pan-Asian values in which a common response to racism and personal pride may take precedence over filial piety. As a result, individuals in both generations may experience considerable guilt and anxiety. It may be argued that the locus of loyalty within the Chinese community is in the process of shifting from the family, including ancestors, to other collectivities, including the pan-Asian community in the United States.

Values

The Confucian value that human nature is basically good is generally accepted. In spite of this premise, however, it was necessary for human beings to erect a panoply for protection of the self, family, and social institutions from potentially disruptive or harmful feelings. Historically, subjugation to nature, as shown by fatalism, was characteristic. The temporal focus was on the past, with ancestor worship and respect for tradition. Relationships were predominantly lineal. Age and generation determined the behavioral prerogatives of the various roles. In human activity, Being-in-Becoming was the prevailing position in which personal development occurred within the constraints of filial piety (see Table 1-2).

Caudill and Scarr (1962) examined Kluckhohn value orientations in Tokyo area high schools, to document the process of cultural change as it affected family and individual behavior in occupational, political, and religious life. Depending on the area of focus, man-nature relationships involved mastery in work situations and harmony otherwise. Relationships with other persons were often collateral initially and ultimately became individualistic. Time orientations also differed by context, with a future perspective in technology and a present focus in social relations. The largest generational changes in these values occurred in political considerations, and the smallest changes were in religious life.

E. Lee (1982) provided a convenient summary of Chinese values that restates the Kluckhohn categories in more popular terms. A predominantly agricultural civilization with Confucianist, Buddhist, and Taoist religions has predisposed persons to a logic of the heart and a quest for harmony. These values are implemented culturally by rigidity of roles and status, suppression of individuality and emotion in favor of conformity, and mutual dependence (including financial dependence) that includes collective responsibility, fatalism, and conservatism.

Beliefs

Health/Illness In China, mental illness was believed to be caused by wrath of the gods and/or the ancestors and was directed toward the family, or a particular family member, in retribution for misconduct at any time in their history. Mental illness was believed to be multifaceted. Moral, religious, physiological, psychological, social, and genetic explanations for mental illness have all been widespread (T. Y. Lin & M. C. Lin, 1981).

A physiological explanation for health/illness was found in the 5,000-year-old yin-yang theory of the balance of forces in nature (R. N. F. Lee, 1986). Yin and yang account for differences and changes within a system of categorization (Abbott, 1970). Yang, a male principle, was a positive, active, strong, constructive energy or power, producing light, warmth, and fullness. Yin, a female principle, constituted a negative, passive, weak, destructive power, producing darkness, cold, and emptiness.

This yin-yang identification has had effects on masculine and feminine roles and psychosocial development and functioning. Little girls are forced to be passive and weak; little boys are required to be strong and active. A girl who is active or a boy who is passive is considered to be out of harmony with the universe, not merely failing to meet role expectations (Abbott, 1970).

Any imbalance of yin-yang forces is believed to exert power on humans in the form of emanations or illness. Numbness, wildness, insanity, speech disturbances, and anger were recognized dysfunctions. It is also believed that any physiological excess also could result in dysfunction (i.e., breathing, eating, bowel function, sexual activity, physical exhaustion).

This physiological format for expression of distress came about because the Chinese lacked experience in labeling, describing, and communicating affect, and as a consequence emotion was not easily expressed directly. Confucian teachings required repression of emotion in order to maintain correct social behavior. Any emotional excess was stigmatized; public and private expressions of affect were very different. Moreover, emotion was potentially dangerous and needed to be controlled because it could disrupt the harmony in familial and social relations. Since the Chinese had been culturally trained to "listen" within their bodies, subjective discomfort was transformed into descriptions of internal bodily functions and thereby somatized and endowed with physical symptomatology (Saner-Yiu & Saner-Yiu, 1985).

The prevalence of somatization has also been explained as the result of a situation-oriented approach to life (Hsu, 1963). Being situation-specific in behaviors is a practical, concrete way of dealing with the complexities of the role system in effecting psychosocial homeostasis (T. Y. Lin, 1983). In addition, somatization provides a defense against guilt and shame; it is produced by the symptomatology and effectively removes the individual from his or her usual obligations.

There are distinctive Chinese psychopathologies, including neurotic disorders in the form of culture-bound syndromes and depression (T. Y. Lin, 1982). These conditions occur with high frequency among the 20 million overseas Chinese and among mainland Chinese (E. S. Tan, 1981). These culture-bound syndromes include neurasthenia, koro, frigophobia, and spirit possession. Neurasthenia literally refers to weak nerves and weak kidneys; it has always affected young adult males and currently accounts for two-thirds of the neurotic patients in China (Wang & Tuan, 1957). This condition is experienced as a loss of semen leading to emaciation or death and is usually accompanied by extreme anxiety and multiple hypochondriacal somatic complaints. Sexual excess is believed to result in premature ejaculation and impotence as well. A belief underlying this condition is that of one drop of semen is derived from 10 drops of blood and 100 grains of rice (E. S. Tan, 1981). As a result, semen loss is perceived as being potentially life-threatening.

Koro, a second culture-bound syndrome, is fear of death due to belief that there has been a shrinking of the penis, or of the nipples, breasts, and labia in women. Koro is considered to be caused by loss of yang. Frigophobia, a third culture-bound syndrome, is fear of cold, regardless of temperature or protective clothing. Frigophobia is attributed to fear of excess yin in males. A fourth disorder, spirit possession, is a diagnosis invoked whenever the symptoms are bizarre and cannot be understood by yin-yang polarity (E. S. Tan, 1981).

Depression in Chinese patients is prevalent, but is also expressed primarily by somatic symptoms, including fatigue, low energy, loss of appetite, constipation, and sleep disturbances, with little expression of dysphoric affect (T. Y. Lin, 1982). In Japan, however, depression has been identified with "shinkeishitsu," or nervousness; it is internalized and has primarily subjective components that include an exaggerated anxiety concerning minor changes in physical or mental functions, introversion, and self-consciousness, self-deprecation, and suicidal ideation (Rin, Schooler, & Caudill, 1973).

These neurotic, or neurasthenic, disorders have been attributed to stress resulting from social change or migration, because they occur least frequently in urban persons who are secure in a traditional Chinese identity but have also become adapted to modernization (T. Y. Lin, 1982). During the 1950s in China, neurasthenia may have been the vehicle for expressing the political, social, and physical stresses that accompanied life. Moreover, these stress disorders had also been identified in Japan at an earlier date, using the concept of shinkeishitsu (T. Y. Lin, 1990).

These neurotic conditions with their somatic emphases have persisted in the Chinese-American community in the United States. However, there is evidence that Western affective cognitive norms are being internalized at different rates by urban and rural mainland Chinese, Hong Kong Chinese, and the five generations of Chinese in the United States (Fong, 1965). Hong Kong Chinese and fifth-generation Chinese Americans have the most complete internalization of these norms.

Perceptions

Services T. Y. Lin (1982) described family perceptions of services that were required for major and minor disturbances. Persons with major emotional disturbances, such as schizophrenia, were usually isolated and cared for at home over long periods of time in an atmosphere of denial, intense shame, and pervasive guilt. Trusted outsiders, including the family physician, eventually would be enlisted to facilitate hospitalization of the afflicted family member. Individuals with minor disturbances such as depression or neurosis were usually willing and able to talk about their symptoms and to seek help outside of the family, from Western-trained doctors and/or traditional Chinese practitioners. Whether hospitalization or individually initiated help-seeking was the outcome, the family usually ultimately rejected the disturbed family member, thereby completing the pattern that T. Y. Lin and M. C. Lin (1981) have described as "love, denial, and rejection."

These observations are in accord with perceptions in China that result in delayed hospitalization and a diagnosis of schizophrenia in 83.7 percent of these patients (S. M. R. Leung, M. H. Miller, & S. W. Leung, 1978). In addition to treatments used in Western hospital settings, hospital treatment in China included herbal medication, acupuncture, and discussion of Mao Tse-Tung's writings. These discussions may represent a therapeutic adjunct to the earlier thought-reform conducted using principles of psychological intervention (Lifton, 1961).

Chinese-American families also keep their disturbed members at home for prolonged periods of isolation, restricted interpersonal contacts, and care, prior to seeking help in the community. Persistent and intensive involvement by key family members continues to be characteristic (K. M. Lin, T. S. Inui, A. M. Kleinman, & W. M. Womack, 1982). The presenting concerns of all Asian-American patients, excluding Filipino Americans, continue to be non-psychological in content. These complaints are typically of an educational/vocational nature rather than personal/emotional (Tracey, Leong, & Glidden, 1986).

Service Providers Asian-American university students generally preferred service providers who were also Asian American, but Japanese-American Buddhist students expressed no clear racial preference, possibly because they were more assimilated (Atkinson, Maruyama, & Matsui, 1978). Asian students also preferred counselors with training in medicine or education who did not use tests (H. Tan, 1967).

Some of these preferences may be related to culturally determined misunderstandings focused around problems in communicating a diagnosis and treatment plan whenever clients do not speak fluent English and service providers do not speak Chinese. For example, in one New York City study of children with developmental disabilities, their parents lacked Western concepts of etiology and instead attempted to understand in terms of physical agents, supernatural agents, and/or metaphysical elements (Ryan & Smith, 1989). Moreover, these parents had expectations for culture-specific cures that their social workers neither believed in nor were able to provide.

Although the clients described above were Chinese, rural Vietnamese and Laotians still believe in folk explanations of mental illness that include animistic and astrological explanations (Westermeyer & Wintrob, 1979). For illustration, during the 1970s in South Vietnam there were only 2,000 psychiatric beds in three hospitals providing custodial care to the chronic mentally ill. Folk healers were the primary caregivers, using exorcism by ritual summoning and offerings of food or golden votive papers (Boman & Edwards, 1984). If these techniques did not suffice, attempts might be made to frighten the spirit away by having the patient spit gasoline and igniting the spray, for example. Buddhist monks also served as counselors by listening, explaining, and prescribing pharmaceutical nostrums.

Service-Delivery Style Services are more likely to be accepted and ultimately effective when clients have faith in service providers and their interventions. Asian Americans use communication patterns that are directed by conformity to role relationships in which age, gender, and expertise are primary considerations (S. Sue & N. Zane, 1987). The credibility of these role relationships is related to both the ascribed status and the achieved status of the service provider. Status is ascribed, for example, on the basis of being male and older than the client. Expertise, or power, may be demonstrated by a display of confidence and communication of educational background, work experience, personal credentials, and willingness to assume multiple roles (E. Lee, 1982). Status is achieved on the basis of skills that are perceived as culturally competent and hence that stimulate hope and confidence.

Asian-American clients often believe that Western interventions will be inappropriate remedies for their problems. For example, talking about problems and feelings, especially with a professional service provider, is not considered to be a sine qua non for either decision-making or action. As a result, these clients need to experience some direct and immediate benefit in the form of a "gift" from the service provider so that the relationship can be strong enough for subsequent services to be accepted (S. Sue & N. Zane, 1987). This occurs because gift-giving has been ritualized in Asian relationships. These gifts may include an immediate reduction in anxiety or relief from depression; "normalization," which is a recognition that feelings or experiences are common to many persons; and cognitive clarity, in which there is understanding of a crisis situation.

S. Sue and N. Zane (1987) have suggested that this gift symbolizes the connection between work during the intervention and problem alleviation. This suggestion is based on the premise that credibility and giving per se are legitimate intervention goals, in addition to the cultural knowledge required to initiate the relationship. Credibility and the ability to be gift-giving need to be followed by a counseling style that is logical and structured (Atkinson et al., 1978). Asian-American students also responded favorably to direction by the counselor, including persuasion, influence, and moralism (H. Tan, 1967).

References

Abbott, K. A. (1970). *Cultural change, psychosocial functioning, and the family: A case study in the Chinese-American community of San Francisco.* Unpublished doctoral dissertation, University of California, Berkeley, CA.

Atkinson, D. R., Maruyama, M., & Matsui, S. (1978). Effects of counselor race and counseling approach on Asian Americans' perception of counselor credibility and utility. *Journal of Counseling Psychology, 25,* 78–83.

Boman, B., & Edwards, M. (1984). The Indochinese refugee: An overview. *Australian and New Zealand Journal of Psychiatry, 18,* 40–52.

Butterfield, F. (1991, February 24). Asian-American population explodes all around U. S. *The Sunday Oregonian,* p. A28.

California Department of Mental Health Refugee Project. (1986). Oakland, CA: Asian Community Mental Health Services.

Caudill, W., & Scarr, H. A. (1962). Japanese value orientations and culture change. *Ethnology, 1*, 53–91.

Chen, C. L., & Yang, D. C. Y. (1986). The self image of Chinese-American adolescents: A cross-cultural comparison. *International Journal of Social Psychiatry, 32*, 19–27.

Chu, G. C. (1985). The changing concept of self in contemporary China. In A. J. Marsella, G. DeVos, & F. L. K. Hsu (Eds.), *Culture and self: Asian and western perspectives* (pp. 252–277). New York: Tavistock.

de Rios, M. D., & Cheung, F. (1982). Recent trends in the study of the mental health of Chinese immigrants to the United States. In C. B. Marrett & C. Leggon (Eds.), *Research in race and ethnic relations: A research annual* (Vol. 3, Part 2, pp. 145–163). Greenwich, CT: JAI Press.

Dien, S. D. (1983). Big me and little me: A Chinese perspective on self. *Psychiatry, 46*, 281–286.

Fong, S. L. M. (1965). Cultural influences in the perception of people: The case of Chinese in America. *British Journal of Social and Clinical Psychology, 4*, 110–113.

Gardner, R. W., Robey, B., & Smith, P. C. (Eds.). (1985). Asian Americans: Growth, change and diversity. *Population Bulletin, 40*(4); 3–143.

Ho, M. K. (1976). Social work with Asian Americans. *Social Casework, 57*, 195–201.

Hsu, F. L. K. (1963). *Clan, caste, and club*. Princeton, NJ: D. Van Nostrand.

Hsu, F. L. K. (1971). Psychosocial homeostasis and Jen: Conceptual tools for advancing psychological anthropology. *American Anthropologist, 73*, 23–44.

Hsu, F. L. K. (1985). The self in cross-cultural perspective. In A. J. Marsella, G. DeVos, & F. L. K. Hsu (Eds.), *Culture and self: Asian and western perspectives* (pp. 24–55). New York; Tavistock.

Hui, C. H. (1988). Measurement of individualism-collectivism. *Journal of Research in Personality, 22*, 17–36.

Irigon, F., Claravall, V., & Christian, A. (1990, June). *Cultural issues related to effective mental health treatment for Asian/Pacific Islander population*. Workshop conducted at the Washington Second Annual State Wide Mental Health Conference, Yakima, WA.

Kagiwada, G. (1982/83). Beyond internal colonialism: Reflections from the Japanese American experience. *Humboldt Journal of Social Relations, 10*(1), 177–203.

Kitano, H. H. L., & Daniels, R. (1988). *Asian Americans: Emerging minorities*. Englewood Cliffs, NJ: Prentice-Hall.

Kuo, C. L. (1982). Perceptions of assimilation among the Chinese in the United States. In C. B. Marrett & C. Leggon (Eds.), *Research in race and ethnic relations: A research annual* (Vol. 3, Part 2, pp. 127–143). Greenwich, CT: JAI Press.

Lee, E. (1982). A social systems approach to assessment and treatment for Chinese American families. In M. McGoldrick, J. K. Pearce, & J. Giordano (Eds.), *Ethnicity and family therapy* (pp. 527–551). New York: Guilford.

Lee, R. N. F. (1986). The Chinese perception of mental illness in the Canadian mosaic. *Canada's Mental Health, 34*(4), 2–4.

Leung, P., & Sakata, R. (1988). Asian Americans and rehabilitation: Some important variables. *Journal of Applied Rehabilitation Counseling, 9*(4), 16–20.

Leung, S. M. R., Miller, M. H., & Leung, S. W. (1978). Chinese approach to mental health service. *Canadian Psychiatric Association Journal, 23*, 354–360.

Lifton, R. J. (1961). *Thought reform and the language of totalitarianism*. New York: Norton.

Lin, K. M., Inui, T. S., Kleinman, A. M., & Womack, W. M. (1982). Sociocultural determinants of the help-seeking behavior of patients with mental illness. *Journal of Nervous and Mental Disease, 170*, 78–85.

Lin, T. Y. (1982). Culture and psychiatry: A Chinese perspective. *Australian and New Zealand Journal of Psychiatry, 16,* 235–245.

Lin, T. Y. (1983). Psychiatry and Chinese culture. *Western Journal of Medicine, 139,* 862–867.

Lin, T. Y. (1990). Neurasthenia revisited: Its place in modern psychiatry. *Culture, medicine and psychiatry, 14,* 105–129.

Lin, T. Y., & Lin, M. C. (1981). Love, denial and rejection: Responses of Chinese families to mental illness. In A. Kleinman & T. Y. Lin (Eds.), *Normal and abnormal behavior in Chinese culture* (pp. 387–401). Dordrecht, Holland: D. Reidel.

Lyman, S. M. (1968). Contrasts in the community organization of Chinese and Japanese in North America. *Canadian Review of Sociology and Anthropology, 5*(2), 51–67.

Morishima, J., Sue, S., Teng, L. N., Zane, N., & Cram, J. (1979). *Handbook of Asian American/Pacific Islander mental health research.* Rockville, MD: National Institute of Mental Health.

Nakanishi, D. T. (1988). Seeking convergence in race relations research: Japanese-Americans and the resurrection of the internment. In P. A. Katz & D. A. Taylor (Eds.), *Eliminating racism; Profiles in controversy* (pp. 159–180). New York: Plenum.

Ponterotto, J. G., & Casas, J. M. (1991). *Handbook of racial/ethnic minority counseling research.* Springfield, IL: Thomas.

Rin, H., Schooler, C., & Caudill, W. A. (1973). Symptomatology and hospitalization: Culture, social structure, and psychopathology in Taiwan and Japan. *Journal of Nervous and Mental Disease, 157,* 296–312.

Ryan, A. S., & Smith, M. J. (1989). Parental reactions to developmental disabilities in Chinese American families. *Child and Adolescent Social Work, 6,* 283–299.

Saner-Yiu, L., & Saner-Yiu, R. (1985). Value dimensions in American counseling: A Taiwanese-American comparison. *International Journal for the Advancement of Counseling, 8,* 137–146.

Skinner, K. A. (1980). Vietnamese in America: Diversity in adaptation. *California Sociologist, 3*(2), 103–124.

Starr, P. D., & Roberts, A. E. (1982). Attitudes toward new Americans; Perceptions of Indo-Chinese in nine cities. In C. B. Marrett & C. Leggon (Eds.), *Research in race and ethnic relations: A research annual* (Vol. 3, Part 2, pp. 165–186). Greenwich, CT: JAI Press.

Sue, D. W. (1983). Ethnic identity: The impact of two cultures on the psychological development of Asians in America. In D. R. Atkinson, G. Morten, & D. W. Sue (Eds.), *Counseling American minorities: A cross cultural perspective* (pp. 85–96). Dubuque, IA: William C. Brown.

Sue, S., & Sue, D. W. (1973). Chinese-American personality and mental health. In S. Sue, & N. N. Wagner (Eds.), *Asian-Americans: Psychological perspectives* (pp. 111–124). Palo Alto, CA: Science & Behavior Books.

Sue, S., & Zane, N. (1987). The role of culture and cultural techniques in psychotherapy: A critique and reformulation. *American Psychologist, 42,* 37–45.

Tan, E. S. (1981). Culture-bound syndromes among overseas Chinese. In A. Kleinman, & T. Y. Lin (Eds.), *Normal and abnormal behavior in Chinese culture* (pp. 371–386). Dordrecht, Holland: D. Reidel.

Tan, H. (1967). Intercultural study of counseling expectancies. *Journal of Counseling Psychology, 14,* 122–130.

Tracey, T. J., Leong, F. T. L., & Glidden, C. (1986). Help seeking and problem perception among Asian Americans. *Journal of Counseling Psychology, 33,* 331–336.

Tseng, W. S. (1973). The concept of personality in Confucian thought. *Psychiatry, 36,* 191–202.

Wang, C. Y., & Tuan, S. C. (1957). Clinical statistic analysis of the hospitalized patients of the psychiatric hospital of Peking Medical School in a four year period. *Chinese Journal of Neurology and Psychiatry, 3,* 162–170.

Westermeyer, J., & Wintrob, R. (1979). "Folk" explanations of mental illness in rural Laos. *American Journal of Psychiatry, 136,* 901–905.

CHAPTER FOUR

Hispanic Americans

Introduction

The 1990 census reported 22.4 million persons of "Spanish origin." By contrast, in the 1980 census there were 14.6 million, not including 6 to 10 million undocumented aliens and 3.1 million Puerto Ricans living in Puerto Rico (U.S. Department of Commerce, Bureau of the Census, 1986). This "Spanish origin" group will continue to increase from 9 percent of the population in 1990 to 15 percent, or 47 million persons, by 2020, to become the largest of the four major multicultural populations in the United States (Davis, Haub, & Willette, 1988).

Hispanics are a diverse and heterogeneous population. In 1980, 55.6 percent of them designated themselves as white, 2.7 percent as black, 1.1 percent as Asian/Pacific Islanders, 0.6 percent American Indian, Eskimo, or Aleut, and 40 percent as "other." As Trevino (1987) has suggested, this "other" category would also be identified as white without their necessarily believing or understanding that they are, in fact, white. Although the designation "Hispanic American" may be considered as racially neutral, Hispanic Americans are now designated as "people of color."

In 1988, 74 percent of this Hispanic population was concentrated in four states (California, Texas, New York, and Florida), while five other states (Illinois, Arizona, New Jersey, New Mexico, and Colorado) had 15 percent of this population. The percentages of Hispanics in these state populations ranged from 35 percent in New Mexico to 7 percent in Illinois. Texas had 24 percent, California 23 percent, and Arizona 18 percent. Florida and New York each had 12 percent, Colorado had 11 percent, and New Jersey had 8 percent (Valdivieso & Davis, 1988).

There are three major subgroups in this Hispanic population: Mexican Americans or Chicanos (62 percent); Puerto Ricans or Puertoriqueños (13 percent); and Cubans or Cubanos (5 percent). These three groups accounted for 80 percent of the Hispanic-American population in 1988 (Valdivieso & Davis, 1988). In addition, there are new arrivals from at least 16 other Spanish-speaking countries of Latin America (12 percent) and elsewhere (8 percent), including Spain.

The history and experiences with discrimination and racism of these three major Hispanic cultural subgroups will be presented here. This material will be presented in a format that follows Figure 1-1, beginning with group and personal identity, including values, health and illness beliefs, and finally examining their perceptions of services, service providers, and service-delivery style.

Caution should be used in extrapolating the material presented in this chapter to the 20 percent of the Hispanic population that comes from Central and South America and elsewhere. Hispanics from other countries of origin are often political refugees with special problems of trauma, who may be less willing to acculturate. However, the descriptions should provide a basis for further examination of research on Hispanic Americans from other countries of origin.

Cultural Differences

Identity

Group Identity

The term "Hispanic" is of New Mexican origin and has become an official and sanctioned designation, although it has political overtones of obliterating class and ethnic distinctions by promoting "Americanness" (Melville, 1988). "Latino" has been preferred by many Mexican Americans because of a Spanish word origin that does not signify the conqueror Spain and parallels "La Raza," or "the race" (Buriel, 1987). These usages notwithstanding, "Hispanic American" will be used here to refer to a diverse population.

The Hispanic-American group thus includes persons from a variety of ethnic, racial, national, and cultural backgrounds, who differ markedly in education, income, and social class, as well as immigrants and "Hispanos," or "Californios," who trace their ancestry to Spanish colonists and Southwest Indians. Each of these groups of Hispanics has a different immigration history, concentration in different parts of the country, and experiences of contact, discrimination, and acculturation preferences and history. Migration histories within the United States also differ. For example, many Mexican Americans who settled in urban areas of California, Texas, and Illinois are descendants of twentieth-century immigrants.

Nonetheless, there is a consistency in the cultures of these Hispanic populations that includes their identities, values, beliefs, perceptions, and language (Figure 1-1). All of them originally came from Spanish-speaking nations, and about 85 percent are nominally Roman Catholic. Acosta-Belén (1988) reported that approximately 90 percent of them continue to speak Spanish with some degree of fluency, in spite of a national opposition to bilingualism that has been crystallized in an English-only movement (Padilla et al., 1991). This book will document a need for translated tests, particularly in Spanish. Test administration, as well as other assessment service delivery, should be in the first language of the client. Cultural competence requires first-language assessment not only for fairness and adequacy of obtained data, but for ethical reasons as well (see Chapter 10).

Mexican Americans   In addition to these similarities, however, there are also differences that are determined by countries of origin and experiential histories in the United States. Approximately 14 million Mexican Americans have come to this country, legally and illegally, largely for economic reasons. They have been a source of cheap labor, either as migrant farm workers or as factory and service workers in urban areas. Their economic stability is often precarious because they have had to depend largely on fluctuations of the economy. Poverty continues to be widespread, and educational/occupational status has been low.

For example, in 1987, 26 percent of all Mexican-American families and 47 percent of all female-headed families were below the poverty line; 54 percent of Mexican Americans completed high school and 8 percent completed college, by contrast with 62 percent and 12 percent completion rates for all Hispanics (Valdivieso & Davis, 1988). Poor educational preparation, compounded by a limited knowledge of English upon entering school, has resulted in an over-representation of Mexican Americans in poorly paid jobs with little opportunity for advancement. This history of economic exploitation, poverty, and only partial acceptance into the dominant Anglo-American society has often been accompanied by racism.

Nonetheless, the Mexican-American generation born in the United States (the so-called Chicano generation) has a desire for bilingual education, Spanish language fluency, and community membership. For this generation, biculturality has been increasingly common and is built on a strong sense of ethnic identity (Arce, 1987). This sense of Hispanic ethnic identity has resulted in political coalitions of Hispanic legislators from all three Hispanic-American groups, although these liaisons have become increasingly fragile during the present period of greater socioeconomic differentiation between ethnic groups (Tienda, 1990).

Puerto Ricans   Over 3 million Puerto Ricans have had easy access to urban areas, especially in New York, New Jersey, and Illinois, and there are also over 3.5 million persons resident in Puerto Rico. Many Puerto Ricans were displaced economically as a result of rapid industrialization of a colonial plantation economy in Puerto Rico. Puerto Rican culture is an admixture of European, African, Taino Indian, and American characteristics.

with belief in strong/weak character structure. An interaction was believed to occur between the strength or weakness of character and problem severity and pervasiveness.

An emotional problem was described as either minor and temporary, and therefore to be endured and resolved by oneself, or as being serious enough to require help, initially from a relative or friend. For more serious emotional problems, help was required from a professional. A mental disorder, "enfermidad mental," required help, especially for a nervous crisis ("crisis nerviosa," "ataque de nervios"), but being insane ("loco"), with complete loss of control or withdrawal, was believed to be only partially curable by intervention or institutionalization.

Good health and mental health for Mexican-American individuals implies a balance with God and a congruence or harmony with the family, other persons, and the customs of the church (Weclew, 1975). To restore this balance and harmony, Mexican-American, Puerto Rican, and Cuban folk-healing practices represent avenues that are perceived as acceptable for intervention with mental and emotional problems, especially by traditional Hispanics. These problems/illnesses may be addressed by a variety of systems and persons, often according to their relative availability to individuals in the community.

Perceptions

Services   The variables responsible for utilization of services by Mexican Americans are complex, and underutilization has been reported historically (see Chapter 1). However, underutilization of services by Mexican Americans has been disputed by López (1981) in a review of 47 studies. Utilization is apparently related to an increasing sophistication in reporting, concentration of a Hispanic population in a community, and differences among Hispanic groups in need, as well as accessibility and cultural compatibility of services available (Cuellar & Schnee, 1987).

All patients who come to outpatient clinic facilities apparently do so for similar reasons, regardless of differences in marital status, income, or gender. However, ethnicity does make a difference. For example, Hispanic-American patients more readily perceive their problems as external to themselves and more readily delegate responsibility for problem-solving to someone else than do African Americans or Anglo-Americans (Evans, Acosta, Yamamoto, & Hurwicz, 1986). Moreover, referral and discharge patterns for Hispanic Americans in one comprehensive mental health center differed from those of other groups. Premature dropout and infrequent referral back to the community were typical for these Hispanic Americans (Andrulis, 1977).

One of the major reasons for advocating culture-specific services for Hispanic Americans pertains to use of the Spanish language in assessment and treatment. There is a large literature that indicates ethnic and linguistic bias in assessment of Hispanic Americans and serious problems that attend interventions conducted in a second language for either client or service provider (Malgady, Rogler, & Costantino, 1987). Culture-specific alternative services in Spanish are available and utilized, especially by those Hispanic Americans who have a non-Eurocentric world view. These services include "curanderísmo," spiritism, "santiguando," "santerísmo," and "santería."

Curanderísmo, as practiced by Mexican and Mexican-American curanderos (curers), has Spanish-Catholic and Indian origins and involves the use of herbal remedies, special prayers to God or saints, and specific magico-religious practices primarily for minor illnesses (e.g., "empacho" or food bolus, and "caida de mollera," or fallen fontanelle). Curanderísmo is used also for folk illnesses caused by external forces such as "brujas," or witches, and "embrujados," or hexes, and imposed punishments for sins (Martinez, 1977).

The major Mexican-American folk mental illnesses include "mal ojo," "susto," and "mal puesto" (Rubel, 1960). Mal ojo, or evil eye, is an outcome of dangers inherent in social relationships. Mal ojo is believed to result from an unnatural bond due to excessive admiration or attention, especially damaging to women and children, who are considered weaker in nature than mature males. This bonding is ennervating, and the recipient is believed to be deprived of the will to act as a result of the entry of influence from the other person into his or her body. Susto comes from a fright or a result of the hassles of everyday social life it causes a part of the self, the "espíritu" (spirit), to leave the body. This soul loss is manifested by restlessness during sleep and when awake by listlessness, with lack of interest, weight loss, and depression. Mal puesto is a hex, willfully imposed as a result of jealousy or vengeance, often through food or a photograph.

Since many Mexican Americans do not distinguish between diseases that have natural, supernatural, and superstitious origins, all available interventions may be used (Tamez, 1978). Although low frequencies of visits to curanderos have been reported (see review by Newton, 1978), these surveys were not conducted in a confianza relationship and generally did not use rural, lower-class samples or examine respondent differences in acculturation and generation (Vega, 1982).

Puerto Rican folk healing includes spiritism, santiguando, and santerísmo, which is of Cuban origin. Santiguando (from the word for crossing oneself) is practiced by a santiguador and uses herbal remedies for intestinal disorders, muscle aches, and broken bones. Spiritism is belief in an invisible world inhabited by good and evil spirits, surrounding the visible world. Spiritual protection prevents illness by warding off evil spirits and hexes and fostering good luck. When this protection is inadequate, bad luck, illness in the form of pain and lethargy, or nervousness may occur (Delgado, 1988). Delgado reports that a majority of Nuyoricans use spiritism in the form of services by mediums or "espritistas." Lower-class persons in Puerto Rico have been reported to rely on spiritualist beliefs and interventions by espritistas (Rogler & Hollingshead, 1961).

Santería is an Afro-Cuban religious complex—worship of the Yoruba gods or "orchias." Santería is practiced by a priest or priestess medium who interprets beliefs, rituals, and mythology. Chants, dances, animal sacrifice, plants, and herbs are used. Disease is referred to as "ano" and may be natural or supernatural in origin. Witchcraft, or "bilongo," is believed to produce ailments by entering the body. Imitative or contagious magic may be initiated by an enemy, who uses a picture or other personal object to cause disease. Disease may also be caused by soul loss, spirit intrusion, or anger of gods. Sandoval (1977) has provided case examples, a clear discussion of the gods of santería who rule over specific body parts, and a rationale for the successful transplanting of santería to Miami by Cubans striving for middle-class status.

For Mexican Americans, Puerto Ricans, and Cubans, there are certain common elements in the practices of folk healers, including diagnosis and curing, often by touch; invocation of spiritual helpers; rituals; and herbs. They are practitioners of an ancient oral tradition that inspires hope, confidence, and faith. These individuals occupy the hub of an extensive social network and may have complex social and emotional relationships with their clients. They usually do not charge a fixed fee for services and may have other, full-time jobs. The process involves mutuality and has a follow-up that may include the combined efforts of different healers or referral to dominant-culture health/mental health resources if necessary (Vega, 1982).

Service Providers The indigenous service providers of folk medicine respect and understand the cultures of the people to whom they provide services, because their clients come from their own cultural, socioeconomic, and religious backgrounds. They employ spiritualistic conceptualizations for psychological problems that might be misinterpreted or pathologized by Anglo-American professional therapists. These problems include highly emotional seizure-like or trance-like states and talking to God. Furthermore, these practitioners are readily available, especially during crises, will come for home visits, and are willing to provide services at nominal cost. They share a human relationship with their clients, based upon respeto, personalismo, and confianza en confianza. As a result, the clients are comfortable and feel that they are not being stigmatized as insane, or loco, and that their problems are accepted as having external causes (Rosado, 1980).

Service-Delivery Style A service-delivery style that is comfortable and acceptable to Hispanic Americans must contain many of the ingredients described above for folk healers. Proper social etiquette requires using the cultural script of simpatía, in which there is knowledge and faithful attention to the behavioral implications of respeto, personalismo, and platicando. Moreover, whenever the Hispanic-American client is traditional in observance of cultural value orientations, the tempo of the interaction between client and provider will be dramatically altered in order to enable the client to accept the person who is providing services before becoming immersed in the services themselves. This acceptance is generated by a perception on the part of the client that the provider understands and is responsive to the major cultural entities of familism and church, as well as the meaning of the client's relationship to these cultural entities. However, it is difficult for an Anglo-American service provider to create the atmosphere of confianza en confianza that exists within the Hispanic-American community and with folk healers.

Service-delivery style also includes mandatory use of the client's first language, regardless of whether or not the client has some command of English or has little or no English. Whenever the client's first language is not used, affect may not be communicated readily or appropriately (Marcos, 1976; Rozensky & Gomez, 1983), cultural themes (e.g., fatalism, familism, spiritism, authoritarianism) may predominate (Edgerton & Karno, 1971), and less self disclosure may lead to fragmentary information (Levine & Padilla, 1980). When a second language has been learned as an adult, there may be speech distortions that can be misinterpreted (Peck, 1974). These are potent considerations for not conducting assessment or intervention services with Hispanic-American clients in English if English is a second language for the client.

Acceptance of services is thus dependent on use of the expected cultural script, ability of the provider to communicate that his or her knowledge of the culture is adequate, and communication in the first language of the client. A behavioral knowledge of cultural script, a cognitive understanding of the culture-personality interface, and language skills, whenever relevant, are ingredients of cultural competence. A fourth ingredient for professional psychologists is, of course, the culture-specific assessment and intervention technologies that will be presented in later chapters.

References

Acosta-Belén, E. (1988). From settlers to newcomers: The Hispanic legacy in the United States. In E. Acosta-Belén & B. R. Sjostrom (Eds.), *The Hispanic experience in the United States: Contemporary issues and perspectives* (pp. 81–106). New York: Praeger.

Andrulis, D. P. (1977). Referral patterns of a comprehensive mental health center. *Journal of Community Psychology, 5,* 231–237.

Arce, C. H. (1987, Winter). Maintaining a group culture. *ISR Newsletter,* Institute for Social Research, University of Michigan, pp. 7–8.

Buriel, R. (1987). Ethnic labeling and identity among Mexican Americans. In J. S. Phinney & M. J. Rotheram (Eds.), *Children's ethnic socialization: Pluralism and development* (pp. 134–152). Beverly Hills, CA: Sage.

Castro, F. G., Furth, P., & Karlow, H. (1985). The health beliefs of Mexican, Mexican American and Anglo American women. *Hispanic Journal of Behavioral Sciences, 6*, 365–383.

Comas-Díaz, L. (1989). Culturally relevant issues and treatment implications for Hispanics. In D. R. Koslow & E. P. Salett (Eds.), *Crossing cultures in mental health* (pp. 31–48). Washington, DC: SIETAR International.

Cuellar, I., & Schnee, S. B. (1987). An examination of utilization characteristics of clients of Mexican origin served by the Texas Department of Mental Health and Mental Retardation. In R. Rodriguez & M. T. Coleman (Eds.), *Mental health issues of the Mexican origin population in Texas* (pp. 100–115). Austin, TX: Hogg Foundation for Mental Health, University of Texas.

Davis, C., Haub, C., & Willette, J. L. (1988). U. S. Hispanics: Changing the face of America. In E. Acosta-Belén & B. R. Sjostrom (Eds.), *The Hispanic experience in the United States: Contemporary issues and perspectives* (pp. 3–55). New York: Praeger.

Delgado, M. (1988). Groups in Puerto Rican spiritism: Implications for clinicians. In C. Jacobs & D. D. Bowles (Eds.), *Ethnicity and race: Critical concepts in social work* (pp. 34–47). Silver Spring, MD: National Association of Social Workers.

Edgerton, R. B., & Karno, M. (1971). Mexican-American bilingualism and the perception of mental illness. *Archives of General Psychiatry, 24*, 286–290.

Evans, L. A., Acosta, F. X., Yamamoto, J., & Hurwicz, H. L. (1986). Patient requests: Correlates and therapeutic implications for Hispanic, Black, and Caucasian patients. *Journal of Clinical Psychology, 42*, 213–221.

Gomez, E., & Cook, K (1978). Chicano culture and mental health: Trees in search of a forest. *Chicano Culture and Mental Health Monograph Series,* No. 1. San Antonio, TX: Our Lady of the Lake University.

Inclán, J. (1985). Variations in value orientations in mental health work with Puerto Ricans. *Psychotherapy, 22*, 324–334.

Jackson, R. G. (1973). A preliminary bicultural study of value orientations and leisure activities. *Journal of Leisure Research, 5*(Fall), 10–22.

Kluckhohn, F. R., & Strodtbeck, F. L. (1961). *Variations in value orientations.* Homewood, IL: Dorsey.

Levine, E. S., & Padilla, A. M. (1980). *Crossing cultures in psychotherapy: Counseling for the Hispanic.* Monterey, CA: Brooks/Cole.

López, S. (1981). Mexican-American usage of mental health facilities: Underutilization reconsidered. In A. Baron, Jr. (Ed.), *Explorations in Chicano psychology* (pp. 139–164). New York: Praeger.

Malgady, R. G., Rogler, L. H., & Costantino, G. (1987). Ethnocultural and linguistic bias in mental health evaluation of Hispanics. *American Psychologist, 42*, 228–234.

Marcos, L. R. (1976). Bilinguals in psychotherapy: Language as an emotional barrier. *American Journal of Psychotherapy, 30*, 552–560.

Martinez, C., Jr. (1977). Curanderos: Clinical aspects. *Journal of Operational Psychiatry, 8(2), 35–38.*

Melville, M. B. (1988). Hispanics: Race, class, or ethnicity? *Journal of Ethnic Studies, 16*(1), 67–83.

Nelson, C., & Tienda, M. (1988). The structuring of Hispanic ethnicity: Historical and contemporary perspectives. In R. D. Alba (Ed.), *Ethnicity and race in the U.S.A.: Toward the twenty-first century.* (pp. 49–74). New York: Routiedge.

Newton, F. (1978). The Mexican American emic system of mental illness: An exploratory study. In J. M. Casas & S. E. Keefe (Eds.), *Family and mental health in the*

Mexican American community (pp. 69–90). (Monograph No. 7). Los Angeles, CA: Spanish Speaking Mental Health Center, University of California.

Padilla, A. M., Lindholm, K. J., Chen, A., Duran, R., Hakuta, K., Lambert, W., & Tucker, G. R. (1991). The English-only movement: Myths, reality, and implications for psychology. *American Psychologist, 46,* 120–130.

Papajohn, J., & Spiegel, J. (1975). *Transactions in families.* San Francisco: Jossey-Bass.

Peck, E. (1974). The relationship of disease and other stress to language. *International Journal of Social Psychiatry, 20,* 128–133.

Rogler, L. H., & Hollingshead, A. B. (1961). The Puerto Rican spiritualist as a psychiatrist. *American Journal of Sociology, 67,* 17–21.

Rosado, J. W., Jr. (1980). Important psychocultural factors in the delivery of mental health services to lower-class Puerto Rican clients: A review of recent studies. *Journal of Community Psycholgy, 8,* 215–226.

Rozensky, R. H., & Gomez, M. Y. (1983). Language switching in psychotherapy with bilinguals: Two problems, two models, and case examples. *Psychotherapy: Theory, Research and Practice, 20,* 152–160.

Rubel, A. J. (1960). Concepts of disease in Mexican-American culture. *American Anthropologist, 62,* 795–814.

Sabogal, F., Marín, G., Otero-Sabogal, R., VanOss Marín, B., & Perez-Sable, E. J. (1987). Hispanic familism and acculturation: What changes and what doesn't? *Hispanic Journal of Behavioral Science, 9,* 397–402.

Sandoval, M. (1977). Santería: Afrocuban concepts of disease and its treatment in Miami. *Journal of Operational Psychiatry, 8,* 52–63.

Sena-Rivera, J. (1979). Extended kinship in the United States: Competing models and the case of la familia chicana. *Journal of Marriage and the Family, 41,* 121–129.

Sjostrom, B. R. (1988). Culture contact and value orientations: The Puerto Rican experience. In E. Acosta-Belén & B. R. Sjostrom (Eds.), *The Hispanic experience in the United States: Contemporary issues and perspectives* (pp. 163–186). New York: Praeger.

Szapocznik, J., Scopetta, M. A., Aranalde, M., & Kurtines, W. (1978). Cuban value structure: Treatment implications. *Journal of Consulting and Clinical Psychology, 46,* 961–970.

Tamez, E. G. (1978). Curanderismo: Folk Mexican-American health care system. *Journal of Psychiatric Nursing and Mental Health Services, 16,* 34–39.

Tienda, M. (1990). Race, ethnicity, and the portrait of inequality: Approaching the 1990s. In G. E. Thomas (Ed.), *U.S. race relations in the 1980s and 1990s: Challenges and alternatives* (pp. 137–159). New York: Hemisphere.

Trevino, F. M. (1987). Standardized terminology for Hispanic populations. *American Journal of Public Health, 77,* 69–72.

Triandis, H. C., Marín, G., Lisansky, J., & Betancourt, H. (1984). Simpatía as a cultural script of Hispanics. *Journal of Personality and Social Psychology, 47,* 1363–1375.

U. S. Department of Commerce, Bureau of the Census. (1986). *National data book and guide to sources. Statistical abstract of the United States.* Washington, DC: U. S. Government Printing Office.

Valdivieso, R., & Davis, C. (1988). *U. S. Hispanics: Challenging issues for the 1990s.* Washington, DC: Population Reference Bureau.

Vega, W. (1982). The Hispanic natural healer, a case study: implications for prevention. In R. Valle & W. Vega (Eds.), *Hispanic natural support systems: Mental health promotion perspectives* (pp. 65–74). Sacramento, CA: State of California, Department of Mental Health.

Vélez, C. G. (1982). Mexicano/Hispano support systems and confianza: Theoretical issues of cultural adaptation. In R. Valle & W. Vega (Eds.), *Hispanic natural support systems: Mental health promotion perspectives* (pp. 45–54). Sacramento, CA: State of California, Department of Mental Health.

Weclew, R. V. (1975). The nature, prevalence, and level of awareness of "Curanderismo" and some of its implications for community mental health. *Community Mental Health Journal, 11,* 145–154.

Zinn, M. B. (1982/83). Familism among Chicanos: A theoretical review. *Humboldt Journal of Social Relations, 10,* 224–238.

CHAPTER FIVE

Native Americans

Introduction

The 1990 census reported just under 2 million Native Americans/Alaska Natives. Although this population has apparently not increased in comparison to the other groups, the extent of underreporting may be as high as 50 percent (Linkages for Indian Child Welfare Programs, 1990). Part of this underreporting may be because of a limitation in definition to only those persons having origins in North America. As a result, many immigrants from Central and South America who have indigenous origins have been categorized as Hispanic in the census (Forbes, 1988).

This chapter will describe some characteristics of Native American culture and world view, including their experience of cultural contact, discrimination, and attempted genocide. This material will be presented in a format that follows Figure 1-1, beginning with group and personal identity. Value orientations will be described, and beliefs in spirituality and health/illness will be discussed. Perceptions of services, service providers, and service-delivery style will be examined.

Native Americans, of course, do not constitute a homogeneous group, and their various cultures are neither intact nor entirely functional at the present time. Nonetheless, there does appear to be a core of world-view characteristics that have persisted and are perdurable reminders of an array of historic identities. This sense of Native American identity not only has minimized assimilation into the Anglo-American culture, but has also enabled life to be sustained under conditions of poverty, relative lack of educational opportunity, isolation, and the constant pressure of discrimination. Trimble (1988) has noted that 30 percent of the discrimination citations in a major bibliography (Kelso & Attneave, 1981) were related to problems of cultural adaptation and acculturation.

Cultural Differences

Identity

Group Identity Although Native Americans are numerically a small group, there are 517 different native entities that have been recognized by the federal government; state governments have recognized 36 tribes with unique customs, social organization, and ecology (LaFromboise & Low, 1989). These tribes once used over 200 different non-Indo-European languages, of which 149 are still in use, as well as hundreds of dialects (Manson & Trimble, 1982). The history of these tribes extends over thousands of years on this continent, and the relationships between tribes are complex. Their modes of subsistence included hunting, gathering, and agriculture, which made for a variety of distinct life-styles, with some tribes changing their subsistence patterns over time. The immense heterogeneity of the original tribes has remained apparent in their contemporary diversity.

Since the late 1940s, the Native American population has been almost evenly divided between rural and urban residence, although only about 60 percent of urban residents live in central city areas (as contrasted with 84 percent of African Americans). Many of these urban Native Americans moved to cities in the 20 years after World War II because of government policies, economic conditions on the reservations, and off-reservation experiences such as military service. There is also a history of Precolumbian urban population centers that survived hundreds of years in North America (Thornton, Sandefur, & Grasmick, 1982).

The history of cultural contact between the tribes and European fur traders, soldiers, and immigrants provided a different experience for each tribe. However, these tribes were consistently treated as conquered nations who either submitted passively to assimilation or were killed, relocated, isolated, or otherwise mistreated (Trimble, 1988). Covington (1990) described this history as one of multiple losses that included displacement from their homeland, forcible removal of children from the family, obliteration of community and family roles for men, and loss of language. The outcome of losing their traditional culture has been unresolved grief, anger, pain, and loneliness. Although the magnitude of these depredations varied, all tribes have experienced poverty, ill health, poor education, unemployment, and conflicts with the law that have not improved appreciably over time, largely due to incompatibility of Native American and Eurocentric world views (Malan, 1963). Novel practices and ways of thinking from the dominant culture were superimposed on existing patterns. Since these forms had not emerged from interior habits and/or perdurable racial memories, core cultural beliefs were not displaced.

As defeated nations and peoples, the majority of Native Americans are now part of a politically disempowered underclass that is engaged in a continuous adaptation to the wishes of the dominant society and a constant struggle for economic and cultural survival. To understand the intensity of this conflict with Anglo-American society and the potential effects on personality and/or psychopathology that may be observed in individuals, it is necessary to be aware of the many attempts to obliterate Native Americans' cultural identity. This has been done directly by business, industry, and education (Weyler, 1984) or by federal government "improvement" programs and educational practices, including the residential boarding schools (Fuchs & Havighurst, 1973).

Personal Identity   Trimble (1987) examined the literature on the so-called negative self-images of Native Americans and found that a variety of conceptual and methodological problems contributed to the general finding of low self-esteem. Trimble used an enlarged and culturally relevant definition of self that included esteem, acceptance of self, acceptance of others, and stability of self. Topical categories of alienation, esteem, control, stability, development, utilization, acceptance, values, interpersonal, motivation, and human nature were contained in self-perception items presented in survey format. Using a quota sampling with controls for age and gender, there were 791 respondents from 114 tribes in all geographic areas. When this enlarged definition of self was used, respondents consistently perceived themselves in a moderately positive manner, not as alienated persons. There were also feelings of being externally controlled, with some hopelessness but without feelings of being powerless.

Trimble (1987) described an extended self-concept with fluid boundaries that included others and provided for a location of power/control in a field of forces that extended considerably beyond the person. Rotenberg and Cranwell (1989) documented an extended self-concept among Native-American children by self-descriptions that indicated an emphasis on family ties, traditional customs and beliefs, and moral worth.

The presence and impact of these strong family ties once made possible the social controls that existed throughout life and shaped concepts of the self. In some tribes, during earlier periods, there was absolute control by the family over social behavior and sexuality during all phases of life (Gladwin, 1957). However, the power of these family ties has been diluted over time, and family life for Native Americans has become more difficult to characterize. The family now has an uncertain composition, and "extended family" refers to a village-type Native American community network in which responsibility is shared (Medicine, 1981).

This shared responsibility includes food, shelter, automobiles, and all available services, including child care. There are expectations within the Native

American community for decisions by tribal consensus, institutional sharing as a source of social esteem, and a characteristic indirection in attempts to control the behavior of others (Lurie, 1971). As a result of an extended concept of self, the community is enabled to enforce values and serve as a source of standards by using a loose structure or flexible nexus of support. For an example of extended self-concept, "tiospaye" in Lakota Sioux is used to refer to family in the broadest sense that is conducive to survival (Mohatt & Blue, 1982).

Another example, provided by Mowat (1975, p. 101) for the Ihalmiut, an inland Canadian Eskimo tribe, concerned the bestowing of the "song-cousin" relationship on an outsider. A song-cousin represented "a counterpart of each man who had adopted me . . . his reflected image, yet cloaked in the full flesh of reality." It was a gift of extended self that rendered the outsider forever attached in a complex and all-encompassing manner to his Eskimo friends. Although this particular outsider could not reciprocate the unconditional nature of this friendship by sharing ammunition vital to the continued survival of the Eskimo group, due to his Eurocentric self-concept, there was never any suggestion of withdrawing the privileges of this relationship as a result.

Examples of an extended self-concept include obligations to other human beings and to the native community. An extended self-concept serves to provide a continued group identity. This group identity increases the likelihood of prolonged individual survival in an alien and hostile mainstream culture in which the natural and social environments are increasingly less responsive to native persons.

The composition of the self-concept of any individual Native American also may be affected by his or her level of assimilation into the larger culture. However, in spite of education, occupation in nontraditional jobs, and bicultural status, there has been a significant retention of cultural values by many Native Americans. As a result, there may be greater homogeneity of beliefs among Native Americans than is characteristic of other cultural groups in this country. Without some clear understanding of an individual's self-concept in any service setting, it may not be feasible to provide adequate services, or even to know which services would be most helpful.

Values

The study of Native American values was originally the province of anthropologists, beginning with the classic conceptualization and collection of small samples (N=25) of Values Orientation data from five groups, including Navajo and Zuni people, by Kluckhohn and Strodtbeck (1961). In general, Native Americans understand innate human nature as a mixture of good and evil, experience a harmony with nature, and have a present-time focus, collateral relationships, and a Being or Doing activity orientation (Table 1-2).

Trimble (1981) and DuBray (1985) concluded from reviews of the literature on Native American values that although research instruments and methodologies have been varied, the similarities across studies were greater than the differences. There was also a remarkable consistency in values across tribes and a persistence of core values in spite of acculturation. Nonetheless, it cannot be taken for granted that differences in value orientations between tribes do not exist.

For example, in comparing the small Kluckhohn-Strodtbeck Navajo and Zuni samples with DuBray's 36 social workers from 28 different tribal origins, similarities are found only in collateral relationships and orientation to the present time. Moreover, the social workers presented a Being activity orientation and harmony-with-nature orientation; the Zuni shared a mastery-over-nature orientation with Anglo-American samples, and both Navajo and Zuni samples preferred a Doing activity orientation. It is important to add that DuBray's Anglo-American social workers also displayed individualistic relationships, a present/future time orientation, emphasis on mastery over nature, and a Being activity stance.

Beliefs

Spirituality It may be neither possible nor desirable for an individual Native American to conceive of an egocentric self or a self-contained individualism, since his or her self-concept is composed not only of mind and body but of spirit as well. Spirit is the most important of these elements and constitutes the essence of being. Carol Locust (1988) described mind as the link between body and spirit; spirit is expressed by the physical body and exists both before and after the body. The spirit world includes a supreme creator, lesser spirit beings, and also animals, rocks, and plants. The lesser spirit beings are exemplary models, and the spirit helpers (e.g., Hopi Kachinas, Apache Ghan, Navajo Yei) provide guidance and assistance. The spirit beings and helpers may appear to people in special states of awareness that are believed to be more real and hence more credible than ordinary visual perception. These states include intuitive perceptions, emotional responses to what remains unseen, dreams, and spirit or vision quests.

Nelson, an anthropologist with a long history of living among Athabascan and Eskimo people, has used his exploration, isolation, and immersion on an uninhabited island on the Pacific Northwest coast to convey something of the sense of altered consciousness required to share a world that is filled with spirit and power. The island became meaningful because "of the special way it buries itself inside the heart" and "is elevated by the love and respect shown toward it, and by the way its bounty is received" as a gift (Nelson, 1989, p. xii).

When Nelson says, "I am the island and the island is me" (p. 250), he addresses the continuity of all life, reverence for the gifts of nature, and a profound sense of awe that is experienced by the interconnectedness of past and present, spirit and flesh, man and nature. In this view, human beings are not distinct entities, existing apart from nature, with ultimate control over nature, but are simply a tiny part of a larger ecological unity.

The Native American world-view conceptualization of spirituality is so different from beliefs in the dominant society that it is difficult to render it credible to persons with a Eurocentric world view. I am reminded here that the prevailing criticism of Carlos Castañeda's Don Juan books was that they were essentially fraudulent. In this instance, a Native American world view does not include belief in a model of science that accepts physical monism but prefers a self that can be extended in time, place, and composition. Belief or disbelief in Don Juan's credibility is grounded in perceptions of the nature of reality.

Health/Illness   Health and illness have to be translated as wellness and unwellness in order to be applicable to many Native Americans. Wellness/un-wellness and spirituality are intertwined and inseparable. Since the self for many Native Americans is essentially tripartite, incursions into any of the elements of the self may be disruptive to physical and/or mental health as these terms are understood in the dominant society. As a result, healing and worship, religion and medicine, or church and hospital may be fused and have similar connotations. The practices of spirituality in the service of wellness may be tribe-specific, but the nature of the cultural beliefs concerning health, in the sense of wellness, are pan-Indian.

Wellness implies harmony in spirit, mind, and body. This harmony entails a holistic sensing of the state of continuous fusion among the elements of self with all life, including the creator. Life owes its existence to a spiritual energy or power, originally from the creator, that is suffused into spirits, persons, plants, animals, and inanimate objects. Each person thus has an energy aura or protective barrier. When this energy is positive and intact and surrounds the extended self, there is power to ward off unwellness. With some help from spirits, there can be a dignified and graceful coping with physical illness, emotional distress, and the experiences of living with injury, disaster, and death.

Unwellness, or disharmony, comes about either by natural causes in the form of violations of taboos or from unnatural causes such as witchcraft. Each individual is ultimately responsible for her or his own wellness in the sense of having the power to create harmony or disharmony. This responsibility implies maintaining strong spiritual energy so that the self, the environment, and the universe are so attuned as to preclude violation of taboos and intrusions of negative energy from witchcraft. Figure 5-1 expresses the wellness/unwellness cycle in terms of sources of disharmony and restoration or reconstitution of harmony.

FIGURE 5-1 • *The Wellness/Unwellness (Health/Illness) Cycle for Native Americans*

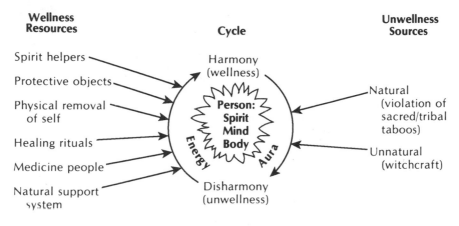

Perceptions

Services Underutilization of mental health services by Native Americans is a complex phenomenon in which perceptions are constantly invoked. Mental health services are often not available, especially in reservation communities (LaFromboise, 1988); the Bureau of Indian Affairs, the Indian Health Service, and tribal health departments are confronted with severe problems of alcohol and drug abuse, anxiety, depression, cultural conflict, and suicide (Rhoades et al., 1975). In 1983, there were only 180 Native Americans identified as holding master's or doctoral degrees in psychology (Stapp, Tucker, & VandenBos, 1985) and most of them were involved in research or education, in addition to providing services.

The Indian Health Service has only recently decided that a national plan for culturally competent services is necessary; tribal priorities have been for medical and legal services (LaFromboise, 1988). Although Anglo-American professional mental health service providers are present on reservations, some of these individuals are disadvantaged by approaching their clients from a typical medical model, or doctor-patient stance. Such practice is often devoid of the informal, equalitarian character of relationships on the reservation. As a result, many of the role prerogatives so esteemed by Anglo-American mental health professionals may serve only to preclude the establishment of trust. Similarly, the use of established professional methods of assessment and intervention are based on objective ways of obtaining knowledge. Since subjective perception and knowledge derived from such perception continue to be more powerful for traditional people, the use of objective professional technology may also subvert the process.

In addition, services that originate in the dominant culture, even if available and well-intentioned, may not correspond to the perceived needs for services because of how problems are defined. Historically, Native Americans had a limited range of labels for causes of distress. Torrey (1970) cited five Eskimo theories of etiology that included breach of taboo, soul loss, object intrusion, spirit intrusion, and sorcery; another source listed windigo psychosis, arctic hysteria, soul loss, spirit intrusion, taboo breaking, and ghost sickness (Trimble, Manson, Dinges, & Medicine, 1984). For traditional Native Americans at least, who conceptualize their problems in such terms, there can be no fit whatever with the diagnostic terminology of the *Diagnostic and Statistical Manual* (DSM) currently used by professional service providers.

A cogent example of what may occur as a result of such poor fit is provided by a study of recall for descriptions of illness and treatment among Anglo-American and polylingual Australian Aborigine women (Steffensen & Colker, 1982). Descriptive passages were prepared that contrasted Western and Aboriginal cultural practices. The Western account described a boy who became ill from eating spoiled food and indicated the reaction of his mother and the treatment received. The Aboriginal passage presented a Walbiri account of illness from bones placed in the boy's body by the spirit of a sacred site, indicated the treatment he received from a bush doctor aided by others, and described the attitudes of patient and practitioner. The American and polylingual Aboriginal women, matched for age and education, had these accounts read to them and then were asked to tell the stories again. Each group of women was unable to remember accurately or in adequate detail the account that was alien to their own world view. There were extreme differences in the total numbers of words recalled, memory for the gist of the account, and magnitude of distortions. This study indicates that world-view differences can prevent any sharing of a common conceptual framework between caregivers and patients, simply as a result of failure to communicate.

To make matters worse, there are now relatively few traditional helpers, including medicine people and herbalists. There were fewer than 500 healers on the Navajo reservation in the 1970s, and the process of training for this doctor/counselor/priest/historian role is both long and arduous (Hadley, 1976). Traditional healers must undergo what Katz (1981) has described as a transformation of consciousness in order to experience a sense of connectedness that fuses spiritual healing power, themselves, and their community into a potential for healing others. Since healers remain in the context of daily living, there is always a struggle to continue being a conduit of this power to the community without using the power for personal benefit.

As a result of the small number of traditional medicine men and Native American professional mental health providers, most persons with mental health problems must rely on indigenous helpers or paraprofessionals in their own communities, who may or may not have any professional training, and/or see

Anglo-American professionals who may or may not be culturally competent. However, tribal colleges are beginning to develop undergraduate programs for training human service providers in areas of mental health, chemical dependency, and criminal justice. The program at Sinte Gleska University in Rosebud, South Dakota provides a model for the development of culturally competent counseling skills (Hornby, Klein, & Dana, 1990).

When services are available, however, there may be no conflict between usage of traditional or modern services. For example, Trimble's discussion of a paper on effects of labeling behavior (Levy, 1988, p. 234) reported a Seattle study in which Salish clients used different labels for the same complaint in different settings. Thus, a stomach complaint may be called a spirit residing in the abdomen for a shaman or be labeled an anxiety reaction for a mental health service provider.

Service Providers Violations of trust by Anglo-Americans have historically been the hallmark of Indian-White relationships (Lockart, 1981). As a result, it is difficult for Native Americans to trust any Anglo-American service provider. This fact is especially poignant because trust is the most important quality of a helping person for Native American high school students, regardless of tribe or school context. The survey by LaFromboise, Dauphinais, and Rowe (1980) also indicated that cultural knowledge and practical information are both requirements for providers.

In addition to trust, the human qualities of providers, as displayed in behavior and sensed by the client, will also determine whether or not services are acceptable, especially over time in the same setting or with the same provider. Native Americans expect other persons, including providers, to be respectful, tolerant, accepting of life and of other people, family-oriented, generous, cooperative, flexible, and with a sense of humor (Kemnitzer, 1973). They do not respond favorably to authoritarian postures, aggressiveness, or affect that is overly intense. Members of some tribes may even become apathetic and withdrawn in social situations where mistrust is experienced (Honigmann, 1967).

The role models of service providers for Native Americans traditionally were their medicine men, who shared the crises of illness and death, provided psychological support, and were in positions of responsibility, power, and leadership, although their leadership was perceived as informal (Officer, 1963). These spiritual advisors continue to be respected for the kinds of persons they are, the quality of their values, and the genuineness of their orientation to other persons rather than for their specific skills, task orientation, or material possessions (Lewis & Gingerich, 1980).

However, these traditional healers have been generally misunderstood, caricatured, pathologized, and dehumanized by a Eurocentric world view (Dinges, Trimble, Manson, & Pasquale, 1981). To the extent that such attitudes have been communicated by Anglo-American providers and others, this history of derogation has not made it easier for Native Americans to receive mainstream mental health services and may have made unfortunate incursions into their belief systems as well.

Service-Delivery Style   Rodger Hornby (1985) described a service-delivery style that mirrors the Plains Indian sequence of talk. This sequence begins with informal chit-chat on topics of mutual interest and shared understanding. There is also a context for the service-delivery contact in an enduring social relationship with the client in other life settings. An acceptable style often involves meeting outside of the provider's office, considered an important precondition for a helping person by Native American high school students (La-Fromboise et al., 1980). Gustafson (1976) found that empathy was ineffective because his patients needed to belong to a new and powerful group and wanted the therapist literally to become a guardian. Thus, a desire for involvement in the life of the therapist and therapist involvement in the life of the client can become a condition for continuation of services.

In some tribal and village settings, the granting of permission to provide services by a relative or friend is considered by the Native American or Alaska Native service provider to be a signal honor that is not lightly bestowed. Such consent for services indicates that the service provider is deemed trustworthy and able to use this relational and spiritual power with other persons in an impeccable manner, similar to the traditional behaviors of a medicine person (Alberts & Bill, 1990).

By contrast, any services whatsoever to friends or relatives by providers in the dominant Anglo-American society would be antithetical to ethical professional requirements. These requirements emphasize impersonality, distance, and non-involvement with clients before, during, and following the application of treatment methods. Extra-therapeutic involvement with a client has always been considered by Anglo-American service providers to be not only professionally undesirable but dangerous personally, ethically, and legally for the therapist. Traditional Native American ideas of appropriate attitudes and behaviors for persons providing mental health services were the product of a perception of reality that was distinctly different from the Anglo-American world view.

References

Alberts, R., & Bill, D. (1990, October). *Cross-cultural communication and psychotherapy.* Workshop conducted at the meeting of the Alaska Chapter, National Association of Social Workers, Anchorage, AK.

Covington, B. (1990, June). *A bicultural mental health program.* Paper presented at the Second Annual Washington Statewide Mental Health Conference, Yakima, WA.

Dinges, N. G., Trimble, J. E., Manson, S. M., & Pasquale, F. L. (1981). Counseling and psychotherapy with American Indians and Alaskan Natives. In A. J. Marsella & P.

B. Pedersen (Eds.), *Cross-cultural counseling and psychotherapy* (pp. 243–276). New York: Pergamon.

DuBray, W. H. (1985). American Indian values: Critical factor in casework. *Social Casework: The Journal of Contemporary Social Work, 66,* 30–37.

Forbes, J. D. (1988). Undercounting Native Americans: The 1980 Census and the manipulation of racial identity in the United States. *Storia Nordamericana, 5,* 1–35. (Torino, Italy)

Fuchs, E., & Havighurst, R. I. (1973). *To live on this earth: American Indian education.* Garden City, NY: Anchor.

Gladwin, T. (1957). Personality structure in the Plains. *Anthropological Quarterly, 30,* 111–124.

Gustafson, J. P. (1976). The group matrix of individual therapy. *Contemporary Psychoanalysis, 12*(2), 227–239.

Hadley, L. (1976, Winter). Folk healing for the wounded spirit: II. Medicine men: Purveyors of an ancient art. *Innovations,* pp. 12–18.

Honigmann, J. (1967). World view and self-view of the Kaska Indians. In R. Hunt (Ed.), *Personalities and cultures: Readings in psychological anthropology* (pp. 33–48). Garden City, NY: Natural History Press.

Hornby, R. (1985, May). Mental health services delivery to the Rosebud Sioux. In R. Dana (Chair), *Cross-cultural services for Native Americans.* Symposium conducted at the meeting of the Southern Anthropological Society, Fayetteville, AR.

Hornby, R., Klein, S., & Dana, R. H. (1990, April). *Human services for non-traditional students.* Symposium conducted at the American Indian Higher Education Consortium, Ninth Annual Conference, Bismarck, ND.

Katz, R. (1981). Education as transformation: Becoming a healer among the !Kung and Fijians. *Harvard Educational Review, 51*(1), 57–78.

Kelso, D. R., & Attneave, C. L. (1981). *Bibliography of North American Indian mental health.* Westport, CT: Greenwood.

Kemnitzer, L. S. (1973). Adjustment and value conflict in urbanizing Dakota Indians measured by Q-Sort technique. *American Anthropologist, 75,* 687–707.

Kluckhohn, F. R., & Strodtbeck, F. L. (1961). *Variations in value orientations.* Homewood, IL: Dorsey.

LaFromboise, T. D. (1988). American Indian mental health policy. *American Psychologist, 43,* 388–397.

LaFromboise, T. D., Dauphinais, P., & Rowe, W. (1980). Indian students' perception of positive helper attitudes. *Journal of American Indian Education, 111,* 11–15.

LaFromboise, T. D., & Low, K. G. (1989). American Indian children and adolescents. In J. T. Gibbs & L. N. Huang (Eds.), *Children of color: Psychological interventions with minority youth* (pp. 114–147). San Francisco: Jossey-Bass.

Levy, J. E. (1988). The effects of labeling on health behavior and treatment programs among North American Indians. In S. M. Manson & N. G. Dinges (Eds.), *Behavioral health issues among American indians and Alaska Natives: Explorations on the frontiers of biobehavioral sciences* (pp. 211–244). (Volume 1, Monograph 1). Denver, CO: National Center for American Indian and Alaska Native Mental Health Research.

Lewis, R. G., & Gingerich, W. (1980). Leadership characteristics: Views of Indian and non-Indian students. *Social Casework: The Journal of Contemporary Social Work, 61*(8), 494–497.

Linkages for Indian Child Welfare Programs (1990, April). 1980 census estimated to have undercounted Indians by 50%. *7,*(3), 4.

Lockart, B. (1981). Historic distrust and the counseling of American Indians and Alaska Natives. *White Cloud Journal, 2*(3), 31–34.

Locust, C. (1988). Wounding the spirit: Discrimination and traditional American Indian belief systems. *Harvard Educational Review, 58,* 315–330.

Lurie, N. O. (1971). The contemporary American Indian scene. In E. B. Leacock & N. O. Lurie (Eds.), *North American Indians in historical perspective* (pp. 418–481). New York: Random House.

Malan, V. D. (1963). The value system of the Dakota Indians: Harmony with nature, kinship, and animism. *Journal of American Indian Education, 3*(1), 21–25.

Manson, S. M., & Trimble, J. E. (1982). American Indian and Alaska Native communities. In L. R. Snowden (Ed.), *Reaching the underserved: Mental health needs of neglected populations* (pp. 143–163). Beverly Hills, CA: Sage.

Medicine, B. (1981). American Indian family: Cultural change and adaptive strategies. *Journal of Ethnic Studies, 8*(4), 13–23.

Mohatt, G., & Blue, A. W. (1982). Primary prevention as it relates to traditionality and empirical measures of social deviance. In S. P. Manson (Ed.), *New directions in prevention among American Indian and Alaska Native communities* (pp. 91–118). Portland, OR: Oregon Health Sciences University.

Mowat, F. (1975). *People of the deer.* Toronto: Seal Books.

Nelson, R. (1989). *The island within.* San Francisco: North Point.

Officer, J. E. (1963). Informal power structures within Indian communities. *Journal of American Indian Education, 3,* 1–8.

Rhoades, E. R., Marshall, M., Attneave, C., Echohawk, M., Bork, J., & Beiser, M. (1975). Mental health problems of American Indians seen in outpatient facilities of the Indian Health Service. *Public Health Reports, 95*(4), 329–335.

Rotenberg, K. J., & Cranwell, F. R. (1989). Self-concept in American Indian and white children. *Journal of Cross-Cultural Psychology, 20,* 39–55.

Stapp, J., Tucker, A. M., & VandenBos, G. R. (1985). Census of psychological personnel: 1983. *American Psychologist, 40,* 1317–1351.

Steffensen, M. S., & Colker, L. (1982). Intercultural misunderstandings about health care: Recall of descriptions of illness and treatment. *Social Science and Medicine, 16,* 1949–1954.

Thornton, R., Sandefur, G. D., & Grasmick, H. G. (1982). *The urbanization of American Indians; A critical bibliography.* Bloomington, IN: Indiana University Press.

Torrey, E. F. (1970). Mental health services for American Indians and Eskimos. *Community Mental Health Journal, 6,* 455–463.

Trimble, J. E. (1981). Value differentials and their importance in counseling American Indians. In P. B. Pedersen, J. G. Draguns, W. J. Lonner, & J. E. Trimble (Eds.), *Counseling across cultures* (pp. 203–226). Honolulu, HI: University Press of Hawaii.

Trimble, J. E. (1987). Self-perception and perceived alienation among American Indians. *Journal of Community Psychology, 15,* 316–333.

Trimble, J. E. (1988). Stereotypical images, American Indians, and prejudice. In P. A. Katz & D. A. Taylor (Eds.), *Eliminating racism: Profiles in controversy* (pp. 181–202). New York: Plenum.

Trimble, J. E., Manson, S. M., Dinges, N. G., & Medicine, B. (1984). American Indian concepts of mental health. In P. B. Pedersen, N. Sartorius, & A. J. Marsella (Eds.), *Mental health services; The cultural context* (pp. 190–220). Beverly Hills, CA: Sage.

Weyler, R. (1984). *Blood of the land; The government and corporate war against the American Indian movement.* New York: Vintage.

CHAPTER SIX

Assessment Issues

Introduction

A recent *Annual Review of Psychology* chapter (McReynolds, 1989) described clinical assessment as "the process of systematically learning about a patient or client" (p. 84), including diagnosis of psychopathology per se, as well as a detailed understanding of the person or personality description. McReynolds affirmed that both the process and the diagnostic labels for psychopathology are societal professional judgments that constitute the anticipated outcomes of assessment.

In European and American contexts, these societal judgments make several assumptions that have consequences for individuals who do not participate exclusively in the dominant society's culture. Disorders are assumed to be within the person, caused by genetic predisposition, brain chemistry, and/or early learning rather than being produced, for example, by a societal or environmental context for life experiences. In addition, frequently there is neither a definite pathogenic agent nor any clear demarcation between behaviors/symptoms that are psychiatrically labeled as psychopathological and personality characteristics/behaviors indicative of problems-in-living that are shared by many persons.

Personality and psychopathology become available for study and labeling by using psychological assessment procedures. Historically, assessment preceded intervention and provided a database for subsequent intervention as an integral part of professional practice. This order of professional activities probably stems from the assumption of determinism, represented in training by a cause-and-effect relationship between assessment and intervention. Recently, however, the use of personality assessment has been truncated or omitted entirely, for reasons of cost efficiency and also because of the conviction that personality description per se may not, in fact, be a necessary precursor to intervention. Nonetheless, diagnostic information has been increasingly desired and considered to be mandatory because attention is being focused on the goodness-of-fit between an assessment diagnosis and specific interventions (Meyer, 1989).

It has been assumed that these assessment procedures provide reliable and valid measures for all assessees, regardless of their cultural origins. However, the derivative psychometric assumptions used in the development of these procedures, including rank ordering of stimuli, psychosocial judgments, and self-evaluation of cognitive processes, may not be appropriate cross-culturally (Trimble, Lonner, & Boucher, 1983). Moreover, the procedures themselves, the methods of conducting the assessment process, and the interpretive judgments involved, as well as the theoretical model of personality, are all consistent with the Eurocentric world view and model of science described in Chapter 1.

As a consequence of using these procedures, it is inevitable that clients who do not share a Eurocentric world view are at risk of having their presenting problems inadequately identified or entirely obscured. They are at risk for pathologization, caricature, or dehumanization, probably in proportion to the magnitude of their differences in world view from the dominant Anglo-American society. Thus, for example, the degree of potential distortion for bicultural Hispanic Americans would be less than for reservation Native Americans who were primarily Lakota speakers. Even when the outcomes of culturally unsophisticated assessment are not so extreme, there will always be a possibility for confounding culture and psychopathology. Moreover, there is also likelihood of confounding psychopathology with deviance, a larger classification of behavior. Psychopathology constitutes a residual deviance or that portion of deviance not readily explained on the basis of information available in the cultural context (Scheff, 1966).

Instruments developed in this country have been adapted for use in other countries, but assessors have not been as willing to adapt these same instruments for use with multicultural populations in the United States. As a consequence, imposed etic measures have been used instead of new emic measures, although a few extant measures may be universal in application—genuine etics (see Chapter 9). Imposed etic measures erroneously assume that European and American emics are indeed universal and therefore constitute genuine etics (Berry, 1980). Implicit in this assessment process is the propaedeutic step of having moderator information that delineates the individual resolution of the demand for acculturation by the dominant society (see Chapter 7). Whenever feasible, this information should include bilevel estimates of the extent to which the original culture remains intact, as well as the extent to which the values and behaviors of the dominant society have been adopted. However, the use of moderators per se may indicate that there has been a failure to consider the use of available emic measures for major cultural groups in the United States. Moderator data is clearly a less desirable long-range alternative than use of emic measures, because any so-called "correction" for culture does not question the assumption that an imposed etic is appropriate for multicultural populations. Emic measures, however, have neither been readily available nor favored by Anglo-American assessors.

Multicultural assessment literature has not been emphasized in recent books primarily devoted to counseling issues with Hispanic populations (Marín & Marín, 1991; Ponterotto & Casas, 1991; Rogler, Malgady, & Rodriguez, 1989), although several journal articles and book chapters have provided assessment models and applications for multicultural populations (Dana, 1990; Lonner, 1985; Lonner & Ibrahim, 1989; Sundberg & Gonzales, 1981). These selected publications are representative of a current focus on counseling/psychotherapy research and/or practice with multicultural populations. Assessment research and assessment practices have generally been underreported, or the available descriptions are incomplete and omit detailed discussions of underlying issues and specific assessment instruments.

This chapter will examine several issues for assessors of multicultural populations, including purposes of assessment, interpretation of assessment findings, procedures for adapting emic measures developed in this country for non-Anglo-American cultural groups, and etic and/or emic measures.

This chapter will not consider culturally appropriate service-delivery styles, because these styles have been described in Chapters 2–5. However, the administration of assessment devices can only be accomplished in the context of an acceptable etiquette for the professional relationship. Culturally competent assessment techniques without concomitant use of a culturally acceptable style of service delivery cannot yield valid personality/psychopathology findings, in spite of the good intentions of Anglo-American assessors who may be kind, warm, well-meaning, and accepting of other persons.

Purposes of Assessment

The first set of concerns pertains to the purposes for assessment, especially with instruments developed in the United States and used with multicultural populations in this country. These purposes are clinical diagnosis and/or personality description, including the delineation of problems-in-living that may not be generally considered as pathological in nature. Symptoms of psychopathology and personality characteristics/behaviors, including problems-in-living, constitute the kinds of behavior observed during assessment.

Clinical Diagnosis

Diagnostic assessments of individuals who do not share a Eurocentric world view should make reliable distinctions between psychopathologies that occur in Anglo-American society and psychopathologies that may or may not be defined by similar behaviors/symptoms in other cultures. Idioms of distress and the subjective experience of distress differ markedly as a function of culture.

Each cultural group has indigenous concepts or culture-specific concepts of disorders (see Chapters 2–5). It has been erroneously assumed that the diagnostic categories used in the United States and published in the *Diagnostic and Statistical Manual* (DSM-III-R) (American Psychiatric Association [APA], 1987) are culture-general and therefore valid for individuals who do not represent Anglo-American culture.

However, as López and Núñez (1987) discovered, the only cultural reference in the DSM is the recognition that religious and subcultural beliefs may be difficult to distinguish from schizophrenic delusions or hallucinations and should not be used as evidence of psychosis. It is also important to remember that in the most recent *Diagnostic and Statistical Manual* (DSM-III-R), aside from organic brain disorders, there is worldwide distribution for only "schizophrenia, manic-depressive (bipolar) disorder, major depression, and a group of anxiety disorders including panic anxiety, obsessive compulsive disorder, and certain phobias" (Kleinman, 1991, p. 5). It has been recommended that a cultural axis be added to DSM in order to require attention to culture (Kleinman & Good, 1985).

Epidemiological studies of prevalence rates of psychiatric disorders among indigenous people have failed to examine the cultural or psychiatric significance of the *general* finding of severe disturbance (O'Nell, 1989). The DSM does not provide the only available nomenclature for multicultural groups. In addition to the DSM, there is an international classification of mental disorders developed by the World Health Organization that has been used in many different cultural settings (World Health Organization [WHO], 1978).

The failure to establish cultural validity due to the assumption that diagnostic categories are valid cross-culturally has been called the category fallacy (Kleinman, 1977). Nonetheless, in order to use DSM diagnostic categories for individuals from other cultures, it is necessary to establish the validity of each diagnostic category for that culture. In order to avoid the category fallacy, Marsella (1978) suggested that emic categories be described by using ethnoscience methodology, followed by baseline and interrelationship data for frequency, intensity, and duration. After these preliminary data become available, techniques can be used to establish objective symptom patterns by using multivariate techniques.

Finally, comparative studies using culturally relevant definitions can be completed. The development of culture-specific population databases by using emic strategies constitutes a necessary prerequisite to cross-cultural comparisons. However, research that follows Marsella's proposal has not been done for standard assessment instruments. In the absence of comparable cross-cultural data, there has been a tendency to use imposed etic assessments. These measures have served to minimize and obscure cultural differences across populations and/or to attribute such differences to psychopathology.

Diagnostic categories do not necessarily have the same composition of symptoms in different cultures. For example, depression in the Standing Rock

Dakota Sioux cuts across conventional DSM categories and appears as a syndrome that has been translated as "totally discouraged" (Johnson & Johnson, 1965). This syndrome contains alcohol abuse, present deprivation, and a nostalgic orientation to the past that includes preoccupation with thoughts of spirits, ghosts, and death; thought travel to the ghost camp where dead relatives reside; and an active wish to join these relatives by willing death or threatening/committing suicide. This depression syndrome also illustrates a set of symptoms that is clearly culture-specific and perhaps even tribe-specific and/or reservation-specific.

Problems-in-Living

In addition to the identification of culture-general and culture-specific psychopathologies, it is necessary to distinguish between pathology per se, or genuine deviance, and residual deviance that may be understood only within its cultural setting. Residual deviance refers to less functional behaviors, or those problems-in-living that are not necessarily pathological but are derived from specific and unique cultural experiences. There may be no clear distinction between culture-specific pathological disorders and residual deviance or conditions that may be more adequately described as problems-in-living, so base rates for disorders in different cultural settings are necessary.

An example of acculturation as a problem-in-living is found in a comparison of acculturated and traditional Hopi villages (Levy, Kunitz, & Henderson, 1987). In this study, the more extreme symptomatology in the acculturated village (i.e., suicide and homicide) presumably occurred because greater deviance was tolerated. A second Hopi example of a common problem-in-living occurs during mourning, especially in women, and includes depression and hallucinations of the recently deceased family member (Matchett, 1972). These mourning behaviors are recognized and accepted by the Hopi but are not openly discussed.

Problems-in-living occurring in different cultures should be given greater attention in descriptions in the DSM nomenclature. There is already general information for different cultural groups concerning the presence and prevalence of specific problems-in-living as part of the current DSM (e.g., alcohol and drug abuse, antisocial behavior, anxiety, damaged sense of self, depression, difficulties in human relationships, physical and emotional violence, etc.). These psychopathologies often have different meanings and/or differing at-risk populations in different cultural settings.

There are additional problems-in-living, relevant for minority cultural groups in this country, that are not included in the current diagnostic nomenclature. These problems need to be identified for each of the major cultural groups. Some examples would include cultural confusion, damage as a result of racism by the dominant society, and deficits in skills required for functioning in the dominant society. It is necessary to distinguish between these culture-specific problems-in-living and diagnosable psychopathologies for clients in this society who do not have Anglo-American origins.

Description of Personality

Another set of concerns focuses on interpretations of assessment findings. Interpretation includes dimensions of content and process. The content basis for interpretation consists of discrete personality constructs or global personality theories. It is necessary for interpretation to take the cultural context into account and to make use of culture-specific theories of personality, whenever available, to avoid a confounding of culture and personality.

The process of interpretation will also be affected by assessor bias. This bias has several forms, beginning with the usually unconscious ethnocentric attempt to render all assessees similar—homogenization. This bias was referred to in Chapter 1 as Stage 3 of an ethnocentrism-ethnorelativism continuum and constitutes a minimization or trivialization of differences. Other indicators of potential bias include an unquestioning use of science and method that stems from a Eurocentric world view, and a potential for positive and negative stereotyping of persons from other cultures.

Personality assessment began with global personality theory and used broad-bandwidth projective techniques in measures such as the Rorschach. Recently, there has been an increasing preference for atheoretical measurement of discrete constructs by using self-report instruments of relatively narrow bandwidth, particularly for behavioral assessment (Dana, 1984). Whenever inkblot techniques are used, their scoring systems are now focused primarily on psychopathology instead of personality description (e.g., Exner Comprehensive Rorschach and Holtzman Inkblot Technique). There has been a preference for factor analysis as the method for establishing construct validity. Both broad- and narrow-bandwidth measures will be discussed in this book, because they share a common construct validation paradigm.

Constructs   Personality constructs have been developed from empirical methods or personality theory. The constructs themselves frequently constitute the building blocks for objective personality measures and are of European and American derivation. Different languages and cultures will not necessarily employ the same constructs. As a result, it is always necessary to determine whether or not a particular construct exists in another language or culture, prior to any use for cross-cultural personality description. Even if the construct is present, it may not have the same meaning. Moreover, there must be construct equivalence in any personality test used with members of another culture. Translation difficulties often signal a lack of construct equivalence, especially if there is no vocabulary in the target group for a particular construct.

Whenever the client does not share the Eurocentric world view that prevails in the dominant society, a cultural context for interpretation of these constructs will be required. For example, as a direct result of world-view differences, there will be distinct differences in the boundaries of the self-concept, the desirability of certain value orientations, the conceptualizations of phenomena, and feelings of personal control and responsibility for one's own behavior. Constructs of self, values, definition of phenomena, responsibility, and control may have diagnostic significance and may also be relevant for personality description. Whenever discrete personality constructs are associated with these cultural differences, the presence, importance, and/or meaning of these constructs may be culture-specific as well. The mediation of these personality constructs by imposed etic measures can result in distortions in the description of personality due to a confound of culture and personality.

Since diagnosis per se at this time does not inevitably result in a determination of cost-effective and relevant interventions, it may be of primary importance for assessors to be able to provide culturally relevant descriptions of personality. Such descriptions are often more detailed than any aggregation of specific problems-in-living and constitute a necessary assessment database for individual or group interventions.

To provide culturally relevant descriptions, personality characteristics and behaviors must be interpreted within their living contexts. Are these characteristics and behaviors functional in the sense of fostering the coping with the life events and the problem-solving necessary for survival, adaptation, and personal well-being? The use of culture-specific personality theories is also necessary for such descriptions, since personality theory developed for Europeans and Americans cannot be assumed to be relevant in other cultural contexts. Moreover, the use of new emic instruments may be required, to provide adequate and meaningful personality descriptions that use culture-specific theories.

Assessor Bias   Bias in interpretation exists in the form of unacknowledged and unquestioned Anglo-American cultural beliefs in assimilation, the use of theory and methods that are Eurocentric in origin, and as a result of stereotyped expectations for behaviors for minority group members.

The assumption by therapists—and presumably by assessors as well—of greater similarity than dissimilarity between culturally diverse groups provides evidence for unstated Eurocentric beliefs in assimilation (B. A. Greene, 1985; Turner & Armstrong, 1981). Ethnocentrism includes not only a minimization of differences but, for example, the labeling of African-American group differences as deficits by Anglo-American service providers (Wyatt, Powell, & Bass, 1982).

Although theory and method bias in assessment, particularly using the MMPI, has been reviewed elsewhere (Dana & Whatley, 1991), it is pertinent here to outline the sources of bias. First, Eurocentric science, as exemplified by positivist, empiricist method, has been applied only imperfectly. Comparative MMPI research studies of Anglo-American and other cultural groups have typically not only used inappropriate statistics but also failed to equate groups adequately on socioeconomic criteria or even to define ethnicity (R. L. Greene, 1987). As a result, there is an inadequate research basis to justify using interpretations from existing tests in original or translated adaptations for the multicultural groups in this country. Overconfidence in method has served to minimize any discomfort on the basis of poorly applied methodology alone.

Ultimately of greater importance is bias in the explanatory system used as a frame of reference. The prevailing explanatory systems have been personality theories as developed by males of European and American origins. These theories have been applied to all assessees in American society, regardless of their cultural identities. Moreover, this bias has been expressed by personality theorists in the form of a deficit hypothesis that now includes "cultural deprivation" and "social pathology" (Mays, 1985).

Inappropriate conceptualizations of psychopathology can also stem from a Eurocentric male bias. Such conceptualizations have resulted in pejorative DSM labels of Histrionic Personality Disorder, Dependent Personality Disorder, and Masochistic Personality Disorder, for Anglo-American women. At best these labels may be patronizing and at worst they are pathologizing; an inevitable end result is that the "patient is not understood or cared about" (Stiver, 1985).

Multicultural clients are especially vulnerable to misdiagnosis as having Dependent Personality Disorder and Paranoid Personality Disorder, for example. The DSM description of Dependent Personality Disorder includes criteria of granting others the prerogative of assuming responsibility for major life decisions and a subordination of one's own needs to those of other persons.

In some cultural groups, particularly Asian Americans, others are expected to assume such responsibilities, not as a result of an individual's inability to function independently, but because the self-concept places these responsibilities on designated family members. Similarly, a subordination of needs occurs on a voluntary basis—not as a result of avoiding responsibility, but because the welfare of others is believed to be synonymous with the best interests of the individual. These diagnostic issues can become even more complex whenever, for example, a son or daughter is in process of adopting a bicultural or dominant-society orientation within a traditional family context.

For a second example, African-American test data showing psychopathology may lack equivalent component behaviors, due to differing behavioral contexts that occur as a function of culture and/or social class. This is particularly apparent in diagnoses of paranoia or schizophrenia and failure to diagnose depression, which may be evidenced by multiple somatic symptoms (Carter, 1974). Paranoia, especially when identified as Paranoid Personality Disorder, may not necessarily be pathological, since paranoia is a common, reality-based byproduct of African-American experience with prejudice and discrimination, and a healthy cultural paranoia often represents a legitimate coping skill (Newhill, 1990). If African Americans with comparable cultural biases were to construct a DSM, there might well be an Overly Naive, Gullible Personality Disorder instead of or in addition to Paranoid Personality Disorder.

African Americans continue to be predictably misdiagnosed as schizophrenics by use of interview data from the Schedule for Affective Disorders and Schizophrenia (SADS) and the Global Assessment Scale (GAS), for example (Pavkov, Lewis, & Lyons, 1990). Misdiagnosis affects the choice of intervention system—criminal justice versus mental health (Lewis, Shanok, Cohen, Kligfeld, & Frisone, 1980)—and the choice of particular interventions within the mental health system. Moreover, there are inadvertent stigmatizing social effects that include an increase in the likelihood of subsequent employment in the secondary job market and/or eventual welfare status, as well as fostering social isolation. This isolation has resulted in a permanent underclass and also can influence diagnosis and treatment during any future hospitalizations.

An example of inappropriate operationalism may be found in the construction of both versions of the Minnesota Multiphasic Personality Inventory (MMPI-1 and MMPI-2). The empirical item selection procedures used were deliberately unrelated to item content in predominantly Anglo-American standardization samples. However, subsequent item-answering behaviors in African-American and Anglo-American groups have differed as a function of the magnitude of the cultural differences between groups. African Americans who are similar on a range of demographic variables that serve to minimize cultural differences from their Anglo-American counterparts produce similar MMPI profiles (Dahlstrom, Lachar, & Dahlstrom, 1986). However, the indices for demonstrating group similarity are themselves suspect in the absence of group matching on the basis of homogeneity in cultural orientation.

Bias also can occur in expectations for particular personality characteristics or behaviors. These expectations may represent the unverbalized fears of assessors. For example, Chinese clients may be misperceived by Anglo-American clinicians (as compared with Chinese-American clinicians) as anxious, confused, or reserved (Li-Repac, 1980). African-American clients are also perceived to have inappropriate sexuality (Wyatt et al., 1982), or their grossly disturbed behaviors are rationalized as culturally appropriate by Anglo-American service providers (Lewis et al., 1980). Although these examples of diagnostic errors may result from a confound of psychopathology with culture, there is also an element of stereotypy present.

Adapting European-American Emics

A third set of concerns is the examination of procedures for adapting an assessment device of Anglo-American origin for assessees in this country who are culturally different. In other words, how is an emic measure that was designed for the dominant-culture population in the United States transformed into a measure that is valid for other specific cultural populations in this country?

Adaptations are required for construct equivalence, functional equivalence, and metric or scale equivalence. Functional equivalence pertains to different behaviors developed to cope with similar problems in different cultural contexts. Metric equivalence pertains to the formats for presentation of scales, questionnaires, and personality measures. The formats that have become commonplace for the majority of persons in European-American societies are artifacts of modernization. Metric equivalence is therefore only at issue in American society for nonliterate persons and some persons who do not speak English.

In spite of an awareness of established procedures for translation whenever standard measures are to be applied in another country or culture, adaptations have typically not been perceived by assessors as essential considerations for assessment measures when used in this country with minority populations. Linguistic equivalence should be coupled with construct equivalence and should include culturally appropriate affect or emotional responses.

This section provides a description and critique of procedures for adapting construct-referenced tests for use with persons from non-Anglo-American cultural backgrounds. This discussion has been separated from interpretation because understanding some of the problems with the process of assessment interpretation requires a method-oriented supplementation. Although construct equivalence, functional equivalence, and metric or scale equivalence are all necessary procedures, the emphasis here will be on construct equivalence, including construct validation, translations, culturally determined response sets, and willingness to self-disclose. Factor analysis has frequently been used as a construct validation method; it provides one possible means of transforming imposed etic measures into measures that may be considered to represent genuine etics.

Construct Validation

One aspect of interpretation is focused on construct-referenced tests that represent personality or cognitive characteristics. Construct validation is required whenever the criterion, or universe of content, is not adequate to define whatever is being measured (Cronbach & Meehl, 1955). As a consequence, cross-cultural validation of the constructs used in these measures becomes mandatory in order to discover whether or not the interpretations from a test developed in the United States can validly be used in another country or culture (Loevinger, 1957). Cross-cultural construct validation necessitates a systematic extension of the Campbell-Fiske paradigm (Campbell & Fiske, 1959), because cross-cultural use or adaptation of culture-alien tests is ultimately dependent on validation using culture-syntonic measures of the same construct (Irvine & Carroll, 1980).

In spite of this caveat, the method generally used has been cross-cultural replication of factor analytic dimensions that are interpreted as theoretical constructs. Replication using other factor analytic models has been infrequent. Moreover, an examination of distributions is necessary prior to replication in order to detect range restrictions and outliers (Ben-Porath, 1990). If the factor dimensions resulting from different factor analytic methods are stable, and therefore present an invariant structure across cultures, then cross-cultural validity may be inferred. Nonetheless, the definition of "stable" has not been precise, and many authors have suggested that there is also a need to establish the boundaries of factor invariance before cross-cultural comparisons of factor levels are attempted. At a practical level, only a small number of scales may be invalid (Ben-Porath, 1990), or scale items may have different loadings (Eysenck & Eysenck, 1983). These scale problems can be corrected by omission of invalid scales, changes in the scoring keys, or revisions in picture-story cards to allow for variability within a particular group (Costantino, Malgady, Casullo, & Castillo, 1991).

Factor analysis alone is not believed to be sufficient for an unequivocal demonstration of construct validity (Irvine & Carroll, 1980), although this psychometric approach has been used with tests of abilities and personality. In addition to a psychometric model in which factor analysis is prominent, Irvine and Carroll also evaluated Piagetian approaches, field differentiation, anthropological cognition, and cognitive information processing as alternative models. They suggested that cognitive information processing offers a theory-based, process-oriented model in which the components can be operationalized. For an intelligence test example using this approach, see Carroll (1974).

It is necessary to ask several questions about each construct prior to any empirical work. Does the construct exist in the language/culture of application? If the answer is yes, then it is necessary to determine whether or not the construct is identical or different in its components. A final question pertains to the cross-cultural similarity of the subjective experience in which the construct is enmeshed.

Translations

A process for answering questions about linguistic and construct equivalence is provided by (a) translations and translation attempts; (b) the format for

exposure to the educational system in this country. As a result, it would be helpful to know prior to a particular assessment process how the assessor, the relationship, the setting, or the test format can influence self-disclosure.

Self-disclosure is a multidimensional concept that has been carefully researched in Anglo-American culture (Chelune, 1978). It is feasible to measure self-disclosing behavior per se as well as discloser or observer perspectives on this behavior. One self-report instrument, the Self-Disclosure Situations Survey (SDSS) (Chelune, 1976), provides a means of examining self-disclosure that potentially has special relevance for increasing knowledge of multicultural assessment and/or therapy relationships with service providers. The SDSS consists of a variety of social situations that sample common interactions with a friend or friends and with a stranger or strangers at different intimacy levels. It is not suggested that SDSS be used as a moderator variable, but research findings on multicultural populations would provide information on the culturally relevant parameters of self-disclosure.

Emic and Etic Measures

A fourth set of issues pertains to etic and emic measures. The potential for misuse of emic measures in the form of imposed etics, as described above, provides a major contribution to the confounds of psychopathology with deviance and/or with culture. Assessors have underused emic measures because they have generally failed to recognize that both etics and emics are essential levels of analysis and/or that an imposed etic theoretical framework has been supplemented concurrently by an exclusively etic methodology (Irvine & Carroll, 1980).

The historic controversies over idiography or nomothesis and clinical or actuarial/statistical prediction are related to current attitudes toward emic and etic measures. Idiography describes a preoccupation with one person, while nomothesis refers to general laws of group behavior (Dana, 1966). Clinical and actuarial prediction provided human and mechanical ways to process assessment data (Sarbin, 1986). These controversies erroneously equated a study of the person with methodologies that were considered "soft," or non-scientific, and as a consequence, the use and development of clinical prediction has been discouraged in many Boulder Model training programs. As a result, the use of methods such as life history and projective techniques, as well as early cross-cultural studies by anthropologists using these methods, were largely ignored by assessors.

These controversies were also false dichotomies, as DuMas (1955) has indicated. He described parallel nomothetic and idiographic domains by emphasizing the data accruing from each domain and the interrelations between domains. DuMas concluded that idiography was more effective for the study of the individual case after specified nomothetic data became available and that both controversies were thereby amenable to resolution. Similarly, there is no absolute demarcation between emic and etic measures. Both need to be used for personality description, identification of problems-in-living, and diagnosis of psychopathology. The relevant question is *how* imposed etics are to be used.

Emic measures are culture-specific by definition. Historically, many of these measures were concerned with a single case. Examples include the identification of individualized traits and central life themes; patterning, correlation, or causal relationships among variables; subjective meanings of events/circumstances; and descriptive generalizations or predictions (Runyan, 1984, pp. 168–169). Other emic methods include matching, content analysis of the frequencies of associated ideas in verbal material (i.e., personal structure analysis), individualized questionnaires based on extensive interviewing of one person, essential characteristics or major structural foci in a life, self-anchoring scales, and peak experiences. These measures have not been widely used, in spite of an early advocacy by Gordon Allport (1937). Quantitative method approaches that are emic in nature also include single-case experimental designs, ipsative ordering of responses to provide for intra-individual comparisons, and inverse factor analysis to enable identification of major dimensions of individual personality.

Etic measures are ostensibly culture-general or universal, although they are more typically Anglo-American emics that have been previously described and labeled as imposed etics. These imposed etic measures include objective measures of achievement, interest, intelligence, personality, and psychopathology. These measures have all been developed within Anglo-American culture, and some of them have subsequently been adapted by translation for people who do not speak English, or used with major cultural groups in this country without modification or special norms. All of these measures consider deviations from normative standards as content that is descriptive of the individual. As a result, for the test results to be applicable, individuals who are assessed by these measures should be similar in all relevant aspects, including culture, to the original standardization populations.

A unique cross-cultural measurement opportunity is found in the attempt to create genuine etic instruments. Genuine etic measures may indeed be feasible, and the development of such instruments will not only enhance the validity of cross-cultural assessment but can foster the search for constructs that have cross-cultural or universal stability. There is a growing consensus that at least five broad factors may constitute a basic human personality structure (Digman, 1990). These five factors have appeared in more than five languages, and one of these factors is believed to represent culture. If some factor analytic theories of personality have universal application, the process of cross-cultural assessment will be simplified and clarified as a result.

Points on an etic/imposed etic versus emic continuum of measures may be represented by translations, enlarged norms for standard instruments, new norms, emic adaptations of etic measures, and new emic measures. Translations aspire to be genuine etics, although most translations at present are imposed etics. Somewhat enlarged norms for culturally distinct groups are now available in the MMPI-2. However, the numbers of culturally diverse persons in the MMPI-2 standardization were negligible; as a result, its representativeness is suspect, especially with the positive skew for affluence. This difference between the MMPI-2 strategy and the actual outcome of normative development provides a strong argument for limiting the use of the MMPI-2 to middle-class multicultural persons who can be presumed to be at least similar in demographic variables to their Anglo-American counterparts, a caution invoked earlier by Jones and Zoppel (1979). Examples for projective techniques include the availability of culture-specific norms for the TEMAS (Tell-Me-A-Story) and the Holtzman Inkblot Test (HIT).

Any development of new norms has been criticized for categorizing multi-cultural persons in this country by using a static view of society (Jones & Thorne, 1987). Since society and the groups within a society are in a process of constant change, it may be misleading to freeze constituent groups at any point in time. Evidence has already been presented that major changes often occur by genera-tion, as a result of education/occupation, English language fluency, and other variables, including political events in the countries of origin. The development of new norms could also result in a proliferation of many sets of norms for each group, due to the extreme variability within groups.

These arguments notwithstanding, tests developed in one culture are of limited use with culturally different populations without the development of new, culture-specific norms. The caveat here is that it is necessary to define "culturally different" by using moderator variables, prior to any consideration of culture-specific norms for standard tests.

Emic measures do not necessarily have to be designed for a single cultural group if their stimulus materials, administration procedures, and scoring/inter-pretive formats can be focused on one individual. However, it is necessary to demonstrate that both stimulus materials and scoring variables are culturally appropriate.

There are several emic measures that focus on individuals. For example, the Role Construct Repertory Test describes the constructs used in perceiving the self and others (Kelly, 1955). This ipsative test has promise for cross-cultural construct validity, as it was derived from established object-sorting techniques and embodies the act of construing, or Kelly's theory of human experience (Irvine & Carroll, 1980). Since literacy is not required, there is no potential bias in sampling (DuPreez & Ward, 1970). Another example, the Q-Sort Method (Stephenson, 1953), also emphasizes the relative salience of standard or personal sets of descriptive statements. Similarly, the Semantic Differential has been used to measure subjective culture (Osgood, May, & Miron, 1975).

At the onset of any cross-cultural assessment, a decision should always be made concerning the appropriateness of emic or imposed etic measures. In general, emic measures are desirable for clients who have non-European origins and demonstrate cultural intactness in their world views, self-concepts, and behaviors, although exceptions to this recommendation will be described.

A choice between emic or imposed etic measures may not be difficult for a particular client. Nonetheless, selection or construction of new emic measures may not always be feasible, for several reasons. Emic measures have received only infrequent research attention in the assessment literature. These measures have not been emphasized in assessment training, and few assessment practitioners are experienced in their application. As a result, there has been an undue reliance on existing imposed etic measures.

Measures that have been used with the four populations described in this book are interviews/interview schedules, checklists or ratings, and psychological tests, including questionnaires, projective techniques, and standard tests of intelligence. Often these measures are used without regard to their cross-cultural validity, although some of them have included small samples of persons who are ostensibly of non-Anglo-American cultural origin, or culturally diverse, in standardization samples and norms. A number of existing measures have been translated or otherwise modified for use with multicultural populations subsequent to construction and validation. Finally, the original stimuli used in some measures have not been modified, but attempts have been made to render the interpretations of findings culturally congruent. Many of these measures will be described and evaluated in Chapters 8 and 9.

References

Allport, G. W. (1937). *Personality.* New York: Holt.

American Psychiatric Association. (1987). *Diagnostic and statistical manual of mental disorders* (3rd ed., rev.). Washington, DC: Author.

Ben-Porath, Y. S.(1990). Cross-cultural assessment of personality: The case for replicatory factor analysis. In J. N. Butcher & C. D. Spielberger (Eds.), *Advances in personality assessment* (Vol. 8, pp. 27–48). Hillsdale, NJ: Erlbaum.

Berry, J. W.(1980). Introduction to methodology. In H. C. Triandis & J. W. Berry (Eds.), *Handbook of cross-cultural Psychology: Methodology* (Vol. 2, pp. 1–28). Boston, MA: Allyn & Bacon.

Brislin, R. W.(1970). Back-translation for cross-cultural research. *Journal of Cross-Cultural Psychology, 1,* 185–216.

Brislin, R. W. (Ed.). (1976). *Translation; Applications and research.* New York: Wiley.

Campbell, D. T., & Fiske, D. W.(1959). Convergent and discriminant validation by the multitrait-multimethod matrix. *Psychological Bulletin, 56,* 81–105.

Carroll, J. B.(1974). *Psychometric tests as cognitive tasks: A new structure of intellect.* (Research Bulletin 74–16). Princeton, NJ: Educational Testing Service.

Carter, J. H. (1974). Recognizing psychiatric symptoms in black Americans. *Geriatrics, 29,* 95–99.

Chelune, G. J.(1976). The Self-Disclosure Situations Survey: A new approach to measuring self-disclosure. *Catalog of Selected Documents in Psychology, 6,* 111–112.

Chelune, G. J. (1978). Nature and assessment of self-disclosing behavior. In P. McReynolds (Ed.), *Advances in Psychological assessment* (Vol. 4, pp. 278–320). San Francisco: Jossey-Bass.

Chun, K., Campbell, J., & Yoo, J. (1974). Extreme response style in cross-cultural research: A reminder. *Journal of Cross-Cultural Psychology, 5,* 465–480.

Costantino, G., Malgady, R. G., Casullo, M. M., Castillo, A. (1991). Cross-cultural standardization of TEMAS in three Hispanic subcultures. *Hispanic Journal of Behavioral Sciences, 13,* 48–62.

Cronbach, L. J., & Meehl, P. E. (1955). Construct validity in psychological tests. *Psychological Bulletin, 52,* 281–302.

Dahlstrom, W. G., Lachar, D., & Dahlstrom, L. E. (1986). *MMPI Patterns of American minorities.* Minneapolis, MN: University of Minnesota Press.

Dana, R. H. (1966). *Foundations of clinical psychology: Problems of personality and adjustment.* Princeton, NJ: Van Nostrand.

Dana, R. H. (1984). Personality assessment: Practice and teaching for the next decade. *Journal of Personality Assessment, 48,* 46–57.

Dana, R. H. (1990). Cross-cultural and multi-ethnic assessment. In J. N. Butcher & C. D. Spielberger (Eds.), *Advances in personality assessment* (Vol. 8, pp. 1–26). Hillsdale, NJ: Erlbaum.

Dana, R. H., & Whatley, P. R. (1991). When does a difference make a difference? MMPI scores and African-Americans. *Journal of Clinical Psychology, 47,* 400–406.

Digman, J. M. (1990). Personality structure: Emergence of the five-factor model. *Annual Review of Psychology, 41,* 417–440.

Draguns, J. G. (1984). Assessing mental health and disorder across cultures. In P. Pedersen, N. Sartorius, & A. J. Marsella (Eds.), *Mental health services: The cross-cultural context* (pp. 31–57). Beverly Hills, CA: Sage.

DuMas, F. M. (1955). Science and the single case. *Psychological Reports, 1,* 65–75.

DuPreez, P., & Ward, D. G. (1970). Personal constructs of modern and traditional Xhosa. *Journal of Social Psychology, 82,* 149–160.

Eysenck, H. J., & Eysenck, S. B. G. (1983). Recent advances in the cross-cultural study of personality. In J. N. Butcher & C. D. Spielberger (Eds.), *Advances in personality assessment* (Vol. 2, pp. 41–69). Hillsdale, NJ: Erlbaum.

Greene, B. A. (1985). Considerations in the treatment of Black patients by White therapists. *Psychotherapy, 22,* 389–393.

Greene, R. L. (1987). Ethnicity and MMPI performance: A review. *Journal of Consulting and Clinical Psychology, 55,* 497–512.

Irvine, S. H., & Carroll, W. K. (1980). Testing and assessment across cultures: Issues in methodology and assessment. In H. C. Triandis & J. W. Berry (Eds.), *Handbook of cross-cultural psychology: Methodology* (Vol. 2, pp. 181–244). Boston, MA: Allyn & Bacon.

Johnson, D. L., & Johnson, C. A. (1965). Totally discouraged: A depressive syndrome of the Dakota Sioux. *Psychiatric Research Review, 2,* 141–143.

Jones, E. E., & Thorne, A. (1987). Rediscovery of the subject: Intercultural approaches to clinical assessment. *Journal of Consulting and Clinical Psychology, 55,* 488–495.

Jones, E. E., & Zoppel, C. L. (1979). Personality differences among blacks in Jamaica and the United States. *Journal of Cross-Cultural Psychology, 10,* 435–456.

Kelly, G. A. (1955). *The psychology of personal constructs.* New York: Norton.

Kleinman, A. (1977). Depression, somatization, and the new cross-cultural psychiatry. *Social Science and Medicine, 11*, 3–10.

Kleinman, A. (1991, July). The psychiatry of culture and the culture of psychiatry. *Harvard Mental Health Letter, 8*(1), 4–6.

Kleinman, A., & Good, B. J. (Eds.). (1985). *Culture and depression.* Berkeley, CA: University of California Press.

Levy, J. E., Kunitz, S. J., & Henderson, E. B. (1987). Hopi deviance in historical and epidemiological perspective. In J. Jorgensen, & L. Donald (Eds.), *Themes in ethnology: Essays in honor of David F. Aberle* (pp. 261–294). Berkeley, CA: Folklore Institute.

Lewis, D. O., Shanok, S. S., Cohen, R. J., Kligfeld, M., & Frisone, M. (1980). Race bias in the diagnosis and disposition of violent adolescents. *Psychiatry, 137*(10), 1211–1216.

Li-Repac, D. (1980). Cultural influences on perception: A comparison between Caucasian and Chinese-American therapists. *Journal of Cross-Cultural Psychology, 11*, 327–342.

Loevinger, J. (1957). Objective tests as instruments of psychological theory. *Psychological Reports, 3*, 635–694.

Lonner, W. J. (1985). Issues in testing and assessment in cross-cultural counseling. *The Counseling Psychologist, 13*, 599–614.

Lonner, W. J., & Ibrahim, F. A. (1989). Assessment in cross-cultural counseling. In P. B. Pedersen, J. G. Draguns, W. J. Lonner, & J. E. Trimble (Eds.), *Counseling across cultures* (3rd ed., pp. 299–334). Honolulu, HI: University of Hawaii Press.

López, S., & Nuñez, J. A. (1987). Cultural factors considered in selected diagnostic criteria and interview schedules. *Journal of Abnormal Psychology, 96*, 270–272.

Marín, G., & Marín, B. V. (1991). *Research with Hispanic populations* (Applied Social Science Research Methods Series, Volume 23). Newbury Park, CA: Sage.

Marsella, A. J. (1978). Thoughts on cross-cultural studies on the epidemiology of depression. *Culture, Medicine, and Psychiatry, 2*, 343–357.

Matchett, W. F. (1972). Repeated hallucinatory experiences as part of the mourning process. *Psychiatry, 35*, 185–194.

Mays, V. M. (1985). The Black American and psychotherapy: The dilemma. *Psychotherapy, 22*, 379–387.

McReynolds, P. (1989). Diagnosis and clinical assessment: Current status and major issues. *Annual Review of Psychology, 40*, 83–108.

Meyer, R. G. (1989). *The clinician's handbook: The psychopathology of adolescence and adulthood.* Needham Heights, MA: Allyn & Bacon.

Newhill, C. E. (1990). The role of culture in the development of paranoid symptomatology. *American Journal of Orthopsychiatry, 60*(2), 176–185.

O'Nell, T. D. (1989). Psychiatric investigations among American Indians and Alaska Natives: A critical review. *Culture, Medicine and Psychiatry, 13*, 51–87.

Osgood, C. E., May, W. H., & Miron, M. S. (1975). *Cross-cultural universals of affective meaning.* Urbana, IL: University of Illinois Press.

Pavkov, T. W., Lewis, D. A., & Lyons, J. S. (1990). Psychiatric diagnosis and racial bias: An empirical investigation. *Professional Psychology: Research and Practice, 20*, 364–368.

Ponterotto, J. G., & Casas, J. M. (1991). *Handbook of racial/ethnic minority counseling research.* Springfield, IL: Thomas.

Rogler, L. H., Malgady, R. G., & Rodriguez, O. (1989). *Hispanics and mental health: A framework for research.* Malabar, FL: Krieger.

Rorer, L. G. (1965). The great response style myth. *Psychological Bulletin, 63*, 129–148.

Runyan, W. M. (1984). *Life histories and psychobiography: Explorations in theory and method.* New York: Oxford University Press.

Sarbin, T. R. (1986). Clinical and statistical inference: Forty years later. *Journal of Personality Assessment, 50,* 362–369.

Scheff, T. J. (1966). *Being mentally ill: A sociological theory.* Chicago: Aldine.

Stephenson, W. (1953). *The study of behavior.* Chicago: University of Chicago Press.

Stiver, I. P. (1985, June). Psychotherapy's uncaring language. *APA Monitor, 16*(6), 5.

Sundberg, N. D., & Gonzales, L. R. (1981). Cross-cultural and cross-ethnic assessment: Overview and issues. In P. McReynolds (Ed.), *Advances in psychological assessment* (Vol. 5, pp. 460–541). San Francisco: Jossey-Bass.

Trimble, J. E., Lonner, W. J., & Boucher, J. D. (1983). Stalking the wiley emic: Alternatives to cross-cultural measurement. In S. H. Irvine & J. W. Berry (Eds.), *Human assessment and cultural factors* (pp. 259–271). New York: Plenum.

Turner, S., & Armstrong, S. (1981). Cross-racial psychotherapy: What the therapists say. *Psychotherapy: Theory, Practice and Research, 18,* 375–378.

Wagatsuma, H. (1977). Problems of language in cross-cultural research. *Annals of the New York Academy of Sciences, 285,* 141–150.

World Health Organization. (1978). *Mental disorders: Glossary and guide to their classification in accordance with the ninth revision of the International Classification of Diseases.* Geneva: World Health Organization.

Wyatt, G. E., Powell, G. J., & Bass, B. A. (1982). The Survey of Afro-American Behavior: Its development and use in research. In B. A. Bass, G. E. Wyatt, & G. T. Powell (Eds.), *The Afro-American family: Assessment treatment, and research issues* (pp. 13–33). New York: Grune & Stratton.

CHAPTER SEVEN

Moderator Variables and Assessment

Introduction

The assessment of culturally diverse persons can only be accomplished competently by clearly delineating the contribution of culture to the presenting problems and symptomatology. An initial step in the process of assessment in the United States and other nations is knowledge of the extent to which original culture has been retained, as well as the extent to which acculturation to the dominant society and world view has occurred.

Information concerning level of acculturation is believed to be related to treatment philosophies, psychotherapy styles, and community intervention (D. W. Sue, 1981; S. Sue & J. K. Morishima, 1982). This information would partially satisfy the ethical necessity for appraisal of the client as a cultural entity prior to use of any other assessment strategy (Ibrahim & Arredondo, 1986). Acculturation levels also may affect the nature of symptoms, client understanding of symptom origins, presenting complaints, and reactions to intervention by the family (Gaw, 1982).

This chapter has two major purposes: to provide information on the acculturation process and mental health, especially as it pertains to refugees; and to examine moderator variables that can be used to assess the extent of acculturation for each cultural group and/or the extent to which the original culture has been retained.

Acculturation

Acculturation has been defined as changes in the original cultural patterns of groups that have continuous, first-hand contact with one another (Redfield, Linton, & Herskovits, 1936). Group-level acculturation is accompanied by changes in individual, or psychological acculturation (Graves, 1967). The stress that often accompanies acculturation has been examined during the precontact, contact, conflict, crisis, and adaptation phases of the process (Berry, Kim, Minde, & Mok, 1987). New stressors begin to appear in the contact phase, and acculturative stress typically increases during the conflict phase. However, the degree of cultural/behavioral change is often greatest during the crisis phase, and it is during this phase that homicide, suicide, family violence, or substance abuse may accompany the attempted adaptation (Berry & Kim, 1988).

The adaptation phase has several possible modes of resolution, including assimilation to the dominant society, previously referred to as a non-traditional outcome because the original culture has been lost or relinquished. A bicultural solution exists when an integration occurs that permits both retention of the original culture and acquisition of dominant-culture behaviors. Retention of the original culture and separation from the dominant-society emphasizes a traditional outcome of the acculturation process. Marginality will often occur when the traditional culture is not retained and the dominant society culture is not accepted. Marginality will almost always include some admixture of traditional culture and dominant-culture characteristics. Some authors have described a fifth orientation for Native Americans—transitional—in which individuals are bilingual but question traditional values and religion (LaFromboise, Trimble, & Mohatt, 1990).

Since there are many motives for acculturation, it is important to determine whether the process has been voluntary or involuntary and whether the process has been undertaken in a context of traditional resources and support networks. Social supports refer to existing social and cultural institutions, including ethnic associations, shelters, extended families, and availability of original-culture group members. Obviously, refugees often lack the resources that would have been provided within their own cultural communities, resources particularly lacking in smaller cities and rural areas where there is no intact cultural community. These persons may experience mental health problems and subsequent needs for services as a result of an absence of social supports. This condition will be especially critical for persons from cultures in which social support is the conventional and primary approach to problem-solving.

Berry and Kim (1988) suggested that mental health problems will be least intense with biculturality and progressively increase in severity with assimilation, traditionality, and marginality outcomes of acculturation. In this connection, Berry and Kim provided a framework of the major variables that may affect the relationship between acculturation and mental health. This framework includes the phases and modes of individual acculturation previously described. There are also different types of acculturating groups, including indigenous peoples, immigrants, refugees, ethnic groups, and sojourners. Moreover, the dominant society may accept pluralism or be relatively tolerant or prejudiced, and thus facilitate the acculturation process or render it even more difficult. In societies where pluralism is accepted, there will be established social support networks to facilitate acculturation in an atmosphere that is accepting of diversity. However, in a prejudiced society, there may be discriminative policies with regard to employment, housing, medical care, and political rights.

This framework also includes group and individual characteristics. Sociocultural group characteristics include traditional settlement patterns (i.e., nomadic, pastoral, urban) and social stratification or status (i.e., departure versus entry, mobility, educational and occupational resources). Individual psychological characteristics are those conventionally considered by assessors. However, some psychological characteristics are unique to acculturating persons. These include characteristics present prior to contact and those developed during the acculturation process. For example, prior knowledge of the host language and culture, voluntary motives for contact, and positive attitudes toward acculturation all contribute to reduced stress.

This framework has been modified here for presentation in checklist form as a systematic aid in assessment (Table 7-1). The checklist is included here to suggest the complexity of the acculturation process and to indicate the variety of group and individual resources that may or may not be available to particular individuals. The first section in this table indicates "willingness to acculturate," which depends on personality components that will discussed later in this chapter. The second section contains cues for locating an individual within classes of general categories. Information contained in this section may be used to identify some of the conditions responsible for acculturative stress and to predict the severity of stressors. The third section lists individualizing characteristics that provide evidence for areas in which to look for strengths and liabilities related to the negotiation of acculturation experiences. Individual data provided in this section may be used to suggest resources that are available for intervention, including the strengths or assets of the individual as well as potential community resources.

Moderator Variables

Rationale

A moderator variable may be defined as a correction for cultural differences—one that is applied informally as part of an interview or more formally in a questionnaire. The purpose of any moderator variable is to obtain a reliable estimate of the potential contribution of cultural variance to an assessment procedure. This information may be particularly useful in understanding a cultural contribution that can minimize distortions in pathology indices that often occur in the MMPI. Moreover, moderator data can provide a culturally relevant context for interpretation of interview or projective technique data. Moderators

TABLE 7-1 • *Checklist of Acculturation Information*

Willingness to Acculturate

___ Yes ___ No

Phase	*Mode*	*Type of Group*
___ Precontact	___ Assimilation	___ Native peoples
___ Contact	___ Bicultural	___ Immigrants
___ Conflict	___ Traditional	___ Refugees
___ Crisis	___ Marginal	___ Ethnic groups
___ Adaptation		___ Sojourners

Group Sociocultural	*Individual Psychological*
___ Settlement pattern	___ Prior knowledge
___ Status	___ Intercultural encounters
___ Status mobility	___ Prior motives/attitudes
___ Support network	___ Education
___ Group acceptability	___ Employment
	___ Age
	___ Gender
	___ Marital status
	___ Contact experience
	___ Acquisition: Knowledge
	___ Acquisition: Skills
	___ Cognitive control
	___ Congruence: Expectations and actuality

Source: Adapted in part from content in Berry and Kim (1988), using their Table 9.1 (p. 219) as a general guide for format.

are often helpful and may be necessary, because almost all assessment of culturally different persons in this country proceeds from an imposed etic stance.

An imposed etic is applied whenever assessment is accomplished by using instruments and techniques developed in the dominant society on the basis of the prevailing Eurocentric model of science. The use of an imposed etic assumes that culturally different assessees are, in fact, not culturally different but have been willing to assimilate and have acquired a world view and value system similar to individuals in the dominant society. However, many culturally different persons opt for biculturality or retention of an original culture almost exclusively, and still others will have a marginality orientation.

One generally unacknowledged outcome of using an imposed etic has been to magnify the differences among groups, by using a standard developed in one culture as a basis for comparisons across many cultures. Moreover, the Eurocentric beliefs of many Anglo-American assessors typically result in the assumption that group differences are minimal. (See Chapter 1 for a description of Stage 3 in the ethnocentric-ethnorelative continuum.) Often the result of this assumption is a double bind for many assessees who have non-European cultural origins. First, the MMPI scores, for example, of some African Americans, Hispanic Americans, and Native Americans are often significantly higher, especially on clinical scales, than scores for Anglo-Americans on whom the MMPI-1 was standardized. Second, since the implicit expectation is for minimal group differences on the MMPI, there is always a potential for pathologization of culturally different persons in the absence of culture-specific norms for them, or independent measures that can serve as correction factors.

As a result, culturally competent assessment seeks to provide a fair appraisal of these differences whenever imposed etic methods are used. The use of moderator variables to permit a fair appraisal of the impact of culture on assessment procedures should not be construed as acceptance of the deficit hypothesis. The purpose of using moderator variables is to prevent genuine differences from being ignored, disregarded, or minimized, while still being able to employ measures that have been designed for and standardized on Anglo-Americans.

A distinction will be made between monolevel and bilevel moderator variables. Monolevel moderator variables have been designed primarily to provide information concerning retention of the original culture. Monolevel measures, which are based on specific criteria, generally include at least three major dimensions of psychological acculturation: (a) language and customs, including dialect proficiency and preference; (b) culture-specific attitudes and value orientations, especially concerning family roles; (c) socioeconomic and educational status (Olmedo, 1979).

Bilevel measures examine the acquisition of dominant-society values and behaviors as well as characteristics of an original or traditional culture. These bilevel measures should be used whenever available, particularly for individuals who must interact on a daily basis with Anglo-Americans. The current status of monolevel and bilevel moderators for each cultural group will be reviewed, with suggestions for use of these moderators.

African Americans

Need for Moderator Variables   The literature on potential cultural variance in the MMPI-1 profiles of African Americans and MMPI group differences between African Americans and Anglo-Americans documents a need for moderator variables (Dana, 1988; Dana & Whatley, 1991; Greene, 1987). This literature suggested caution in any group comparison, because of pervasive statistical errors, an absence of criteria for ethnic group membership, and a lack of social class or socioeconomic comparative criteria. For example, Greene found statistical errors in 85 percent of the cited group comparison studies, and ethnic group membership criteria were omitted in 77 percent of these studies.

There has been consistent confusion with regard to the criteria for social stratification. The lack of similarity between social class designations for African Americans and Anglo-Americans for income, occupation, and educational representation has already been described in Chapter 2. Moreover, the percentages of persons in each social class are dissimilar, and neighborhood of residence fails to indicate social class homogeneity of residents, as there is a mixture of lower- and middle-class persons in segregated urban neighborhoods (Myers, 1982).

For these reasons, there has been no consensus on how to operationalize social class, and there can be no comparability across studies on social status. As a result, researchers in this area have used a variety of different socioeconomic status measures (Dana & Whatley, 1991). However, it has been demonstrated that the control of sociodemographic variables does reduce the number of group item differences (Bertelson, Marks, & May, 1982; Dahlstrom, Lachar, & Dahlstrom, 1986; Greene, 1987), especially as reflected in elevated scores for scales F, 8, and 9. Nonetheless, group item differences will always remain, because this control is inevitably faulty and haphazard in spite of good intentions. There are, for example, no less than 289 items in three studies with a consistent response direction for African Americans (Dahlstrom et al., 1986; Erdberg, 1970; White, 1975).

There have been many explanations for these persistent group differences in MMPI item responses, including distinctive cultural values, perceptions, and expectations (Gynther, 1981). An independent measurement of these cultural variables can be accomplished by using moderator variables for Nigrescence and/or Afrocentrism.

Nigrescence   At present, there are a variety of moderator variables that may be used to measure Nigrescence, or the process of becoming aware of African-American identity. Two major instruments for assessing Nigrescence, the Developmental Inventory of Black Consciousness (DIB-C) and the Racial Identity Attitude Scale (RIAS) have benefited from careful construction and availability of published descriptive data.

The DIB-C was developed by Milliones (1980) prior to 1974 as a doctoral dissertation, by using the Thomas and Cross models described in Chapter 2. Four stages of racial consciousness were measured (Table 7-2): Stage I (Preconsciousness), Stage II (Confrontation), Stage III (Internalization), and Stage IV (Integration). Items from an item pool were assigned to stages on the basis of consensus among three judges. A sequentially organized psychometric strategy for subsequent item selection included item discrimination and tests of homogeneity, social desirability, and divergent validity. Milliones found an inverse relationship between the internalization of white racial stereotypes and progressive DIB-C scores; Taylor (in press) has reported additional validity and normative data.

Helms (1986) defined racial identity as the portion of world view that is shaped by societal attributions of value to the ascribed ethnic group. The RIAS was designed to assess the first four stages in the Cross model (Table 7-2): Stage I (Preencounter); Stage II (Encounter); Stage III (Immersion-Emersion); Stage IV (Internalization). The DIB-C items were adapted from earlier Q-sort items (Hall, Cross, & Freedle, 1972) by Parham and Helms (1981). Reliability and validity data by stage have been reported in separate studies (Helms, 1990). As Table 7-2 suggests, the DIB-C and RIAS measure both Stages I and II of the Cross and Thomas models. (See Table 2-1 for a description of these stages.) However, the DIB-C omits Stage III, and the RIAS omits Stage V. As a result, the two measures are not directly comparable across all stages.

As one approach to an examination of the potential influence of the cultural variance represented by the item differences, these measures were administered with the MMPI-1 to male African-American college students (Whatley & Dana, 1989). It was anticipated that these moderator or independent variables would be related to elevations on MMPI-1 scales F, 6, 8, and 9. In particular, it was predicted that the process of becoming Afrocentric, as indicated by Nigrescence Stages II and III, would be associated with higher MMPI-1 scores on these same scales. Relationships were also hypothesized between these consistently endorsed items and the selected MMPI-1 scales.

Intercorrelations were obtained between moderator variables and selected MMPI-1 scales. All of the DIB-C stages were significantly related to the MMPI-1 scales, positively for Confrontation and Internalization, and negatively for Preconscious and Integration stages. For RIAS, only the Preconscious correlations were all positive, and Internalization correlations were negative. The results of multiple regression analyses, with K-corrections, between moderator stages and MMPI-1 dependent variables suggested that the DIB-C Confrontation and Internalization stage scores were associated with elevations on F, 6, 8; RIAS Pre-encounter was associated with F and 8, Immersion-Emersion with 9, and Internalization with 6 (Table 7-3). The DIB-C Internalization and RIAS Immer-

TABLE 7-2 • *DIB-C and RIAS Stages Compared with Cross/Thomas Stages of Nigrescence*

Thomas/Cross	*DIB-C*	*RIAS*
I. Negromachy/pre-encounter	Preconsciousness	Pre-encounter
II. Withdrawal-testifying/ encounter-reinterpretation	Confrontation	Encounter
III. Information processing/ immersion-emersion	(None)	Immersion-emersion
IV. Activity/internalization	Internalization	Internalization
V. Transcendence/ internalization-commitment	Integration	(None)

TABLE 7-3 • *Significant Variance by Stage Associated with MMPI-1 F, 6, 8, 9, and Items for African Americans*

DIB-C	RIAS
Preconscious: None	Pre-encounter: F, 8
Confrontation: F, 6, 8	Encounter: None
(No comparable stage)	Immersion-emersion: 9, Items
Internalization: Items	Internalization: 6
Integration: None	(No comparable stage)

sion-Emersion stages were associated with endorsement of a greater number of MMPI-1 race-related items than were other stages.

The DIB-C appeared to be the better instrument for significantly explaining variance on MMPI scales F, 6, and 8, and the RIAS Immersion stage taps scale 9. However, the RIAS has received more research attention as well as more criticism. For example, Ponterotto and Wise (1987) found little statistical support for the Encounter stage, and the items for this stage did not align themselves in any definitive pattern. These authors suggested that either the attitudes themselves were questionable or the transitional nature of the stage rendered measurement difficult. Parham and Helms (1985) have also recognized the difficulty of constructing items to capture the essence of any stage.

Afrocentrism   Afrocentrism, or Africentricism as it is labeled by Baldwin (1984), has been measured by one instrument, the African Self-Consciousness Scale (ASC) (Baldwin & Bell, 1985). This scale was developed from Baldwin's Africentric theory of Black personality structure. For Baldwin, African self-consciousness consists of (a) awareness of Black identity; (b) recognition of survival priorities and affirmative practices, customs, and values; (c) active participation in defense of survival, liberation, development, dignity, and integrity; and (d) recognition of racial oppression and active opposition to this oppression.

On the basis of this definition, the 42-item ASC questionnaire was developed to assess the construct of African self-consciousness on the basis of judges' ratings of a large pool of items for construct fidelity, competency, and expressive dimensions. The ASC demonstrated adequate test-retest reliability. Internal validity was evidenced by comparison of subjects having extreme ASC scores with their checklist ratings of ASC construct behaviors and on the basis of correlations with an independent measure of African-American personality. Studies of college students conducted in predominantly African-American and Anglo-American college environments found that ASC scores were higher for junior and senior students (Baldwin, Duncan, & Bell, 1987; Cheatham, Tomlinson, & Ward, 1990).

Recommendations for Use of Moderator Variables with African Americans At present, it is recommended that the DIB-C be used in preference to the RIAS to estimate the variance due to culture in MMPI-1 scale elevations. The DIB-C, although it has been less well reported in published literature, appears not only to be a more robust instrument with careful psychometric construction, but is more useful in explaining variance on those MMPI scales that have consistently pathologized African Americans.

Nonetheless, both the DIB-C and RIAS are sorely in need of norms for different populations of African Americans, with breakdown by age, gender, urban-rural residence, education/occupation, and dominant-society versus predominantly African-American educational institutions. Additional studies of these moderator variables are needed to demonstrate the variance due to culture in the MMPI-2. Finally, it would be helpful to have Rorschach and MMPI case studies of African Americans who are high and low in Afrocentrism. Such studies could illuminate some of the individualized culture-specific contributions to elevated MMPI scores. An increased understanding of African-American Rorschach interpretation should result from disentangling the potential confound of culture and psychopathology.

The ASC was developed to be used in concert with Baldwin's Africentric personality theory. Validation studies to date have been meager and somewhat contradictory in findings of educational setting effects on scores. The ASC can be used most effectively with the accompanying Africentric personality theory. Although there are other measures of African-American group consciousness (e.g., Banks, 1970; Terrell & Taylor, 1981), these measures do not have any published construct validation literature and therefore cannot be recommended.

Asian Americans

Need for Moderator Variables Although the 1980 census identified 32 distinct ethnic or cultural groups of Asian Americans in the United States, Chapter 3 provided cultural descriptions only of Chinese Americans, Japanese Americans, and Southeast Asian refugees, including Vietnamese, Laotians, Cambodians, Hmong, and ethnic Chinese. There is a paucity of published literature on other Asian groups, especially Asian Indians, Filipinos, and Koreans, and the numbers of groups with different cultural and language origins is great. In addition, Asian immigrants and refugees often speak excellent English, which obscures the fact that their understanding of services and service delivery may be limited. For example, although Filipino immigrants are typically well-educated, speak fluent English, and may be health service professionals, they are often astounded that our services neither recognize nor include many expected (in their culture) interventions and use an impersonal service-delivery style (Anderson, 1983). As a result of the number of Asian groups and the deceptive nature of English-language fluency, moderator variables for these populations are both necessary and, at the present time, largely unavailable.

Acculturation of Chinese Americans The history of Chinese immigrants in the United States has included ghetto living and retention of traditional culture by many individuals. In fact, changing perceptions of assimilation among Chinese Americans have been related to phases of their history (Kuo,1982). Prior to World War I, racism prevented assimilation. Between World Wars I and II, a new class of assimilated Chinese professionals appeared. More recently, an end to racially discriminatory immigration policy has resulted in a large increase in immigrants from China. The National Coalition of Americans of Pacific-Asian Ancestry became a focus for awareness of educational, political, and mental health goals. This historical sketch has been introduced to indicate the complexity of acculturation within one Asian group.

One bilevel moderator variable for Americans of Chinese descent consists of two brief questionnaires in five-point Likert-type scale format (Yao, 1979). Intrinsic cultural traits, or traditional culture, were measured by 24 items in a list entitled "What do I believe?" These items include attitudes toward family relations; interpersonal relations; sex education; women's status; social, economic, and political issues; America; and the American people. Extrinsic cultural traits, or the extent of acculturation, were measured by 16 items on a list entitled "How do I feel about living in the United States?" These items include areas of social isolation, English proficiency, adaptation to the American lifestyle, and future perspectives. The majority of those surveyed were Taiwanese men with an average education of 19.4 years and a median income of $32,589. Only 13.3 percent of the sample was cooperative, although the instruments were developed by sampling from the Houston telephone directory and five local Chinese organizations.

Acculturation of Japanese Americans A monolevel measure, the Ethnic Identity Questionnaire (EIQ), has 50 items composed of preferences for Japanese things, personality characteristics, child-rearing customs, family kinship, community social relationships, discrimination, Japanese cultural heritage, sex roles, interracial attitudes, and other areas, presented on five-point scales (Masuda, Matsumoto, & Meredith, 1970). The EIQ has been used to differentiate among the issei, nisei, and sansei generations in Seattle and Hawaii (Matsumoto, Meredith, & Masuda, 1970) and to examine acculturation and coronary heart disease in Japanese Americans (Marmot & Syme, 1976).

Acculturation of Other Asian Americans An existing acculturation scale for Hispanic Americans (Cuellar, Harris, & Jasso, 1980) was modified for Asians in order to cover several ethnic heritages, including Chinese, Japanese, and Korean, in a bilevel format (Suinn, Rickard-Figueroa, Lew, & Vigil, 1987).

Language, identity, friendship choice, behaviors, generation/geographic history, and attitudes are covered in 21 multiple-choice questions; the items are worded appropriately to recognize the major ethnic groups. The scoring of the Suinn-Lew Scale also permits classification of individuals as bicultural. Validation has included the finding of significant differences in acculturation by generation and length of residence in the United States.

Acculturation of Asian Refugees and Immigrants   Although there are no formal instruments to measure acculturation among refugees, there is one discussion of problems (Matsuoka, 1990) and some case histories for various Asian groups presented in cultural-historical contexts (Ablon, 1971; Hastings, 1977; Shepherd, 1987).

For Asian Indians, Sodowsky and Carey (1988) have developed a 92-item questionnaire that includes demographics, language use, preference in food and clothing styles, and national identity. These items were based on a literature review and earlier tests. The sample consisted primarily of married Hindu men who were professionals and students, predominantly of high income. Rather than being a measure of acculturation per se that has promise as a moderator variable, this instrument provides a means of collecting an array of data that may be used to make some inferences regarding acculturation.

Recommendations for Use of Moderator Variables with Asian Americans   A potpourri of measures was described for specific Asian-American groups. However, due to a paucity of validation information, this literature only has value as background reading for assessors who have clients from one or more of these groups in their practices. For Asian Americans, the Suinn-Lew scale is a possible choice, at least in preference to other measures at the present time. However, without further validation it may be preferable to use non-group-specific moderator variables, especially one of the world-view measures discussed later in this chapter.

Hispanic Americans

Need for Moderator Variables   Interest in the measurement of acculturation may be dated from a discussion by Olmedo (1979) that delineated multidimensional aspects of acculturation. Three dimensions were identified: (a) language proficiency/preference, knowledge of culture-specific traditions/customs, and identification preferences; (b) culture-specific value orientations; (c) socioeconomic status, including educational level and occupation. Olmedo argued for a full measurement model to encourage an "examination of relationships between multidimensional sets of quantitatively defined cultural and behavioral variables" (Olmedo, 1979, p. 1069). Since Hispanic Americans, with the exception of many Cuban Americans born in this country, are likely to speak Spanish as a first language and to be either bicultural or to retain a traditional Hispanic identity, measurement of acculturation status and orientation outcome are mandatory.

The prevailing historic practice, however, has been to overlook within-group differences among Hispanic Americans and to apply psychological tests, especially the MMPI-1, as if there were no major cultural differences between Hispanic Americans and Anglo-Americans. Velásquez (1984) reviewed the literature on the use of MMPI-1 with Mexican Americans and suggested that acculturation accounted for the greater part of the variance in test scores. A conclusion that special norms were necessary has gone unheeded, perhaps as a result of the magnitude of within-group differences among Hispanic Americans or because of the more persuasive argument that more adequate sampling of minority-group persons in the MMPI-2 standardization would suffice to reduce between-group differences. In fact, Gonzales and Roll (1985) suggested that, at least for intelligence tests, there will be no score differences among persons acculturated to Anglo-American society, regardless of culture of origin.

Nonetheless, traditional Hispanic Americans have been pathologized by their MMPI-1 profiles, especially when their first language is Spanish. For example, Montgomery and Orozco (1985) demonstrated that Mexican-American college students were significantly different from their Anglo-American counterparts on 10 of the 13 scales, with higher scores on F, Pt, Sc, and Ma. However, when acculturation was controlled by using a moderator variable, the Acculturation Rating Scale for Mexican Americans (ARSMA) (Cuellar et al., 1980) there were differences on only two scales, L and Mf. The measurement of acculturation, therefore, has critical importance for responsible assessment of Hispanic Americans.

Acculturation Hispanic-American acculturation has been measured for adults and children by using both monolevel and bilevel instruments (Table 7-4). Moreover, measures have been developed that recognize the cultural differences among the major subgroups of Hispanic Americans. In contradistinction to measures of moderator variables for other cultural minorities, the psychometric sophistication and relative availability of these measures is noteworthy.

Monolevel instruments have developed items to tap behaviors that represent Hispanic cultural origins. For example, the 20-item ARSMA (Cuellar et al., 1980) has factors for language preference, ethnic identity and generation, ethnicity of friends, and direct contact with Mexico (Montgomery & Orozco, 1984).

Olmedo, Martinez, and Martinez (1978) included both sociocultural characteristics and affective meanings assigned to culturally potent concepts by using the Semantic Differential Technique to develop a 20-item bilevel scale with three factors: nationality-language, socioeconomic status, and semantic variables. Val-

TABLE 7-4 • *Selected Monolevel and Bilevel Acculturation Measures for Hispanic Americans*

Reference	Measure
Cuellar et al. (1980)	Acculturation Rating Scale for Mexican Americans (ARSMA)
Franco (1983)	Children's Acculturation Scale
Garcia and Lega (1979)	Cuban Behavioral Identity Questionnaire (CBIQ)
Marín et al. (1987)	Hispanic Acculturation Scale
Martinez et al. (1984)	Children's Hispanic Background Scale
Mendoza (1989)	Cultural Life Style Inventory
Olmedo, Martinez, and Martinez (1978)	Multidimensional Scale of Cultural Differences (measure of acculturation for Chicano adolescents)
Ramirez (1984)	Multicultural Experience Inventory
Szapocznik et al. (1978)	Behavioral Acculturation Scale, Value Acculturation Scale
Szapocznik and Kurtines (1980)	Bicultural Involvement Questionnaire

idation of their Multidimensional Scale of Cultural Differences with adolescents indicated that acculturation scores were correlated highly with ethnic group membership, with Anglo-Americans scoring significantly higher than third-generation Mexican Americans, who, in turn, had significantly higher scores than first-generation Mexican Americans (Olmedo & Padilla, 1978).

There are two measures of acculturation for Cuban Americans. Garcia and Lega (1979) constructed an eight-item monolevel Cuban Behavioral Identity Questionnaire (CBIQ) in a seven-point Likert scale format. This scale differentiates between Cuban Americans and non-Cuban Hispanic groups. There were no significant differences as a result of gender, occupation, income, education, or geographic location (Florida or New Jersey). Age at time of arrival, years of residence in the United States, and density of Cuban-American residents in the neighborhood were significantly differentiated.

The development of a model for the acculturation process has permitted an examination of intergenerational behavioral consequences of the different modes of acculturation among Cuban Americans (Szapocznik & Kurtines, 1980). Bilevel scales for acculturation in behavioral and value spheres (Szapocznik, Scopetta, & Aranalde, 1978) were followed by separate bicultural and cultural involvement scales, the Bicultural Involvement Questionnaire (Szapocznik & Kurtines, 1980). Subsequent research using these scales has explored relationships between behavioral acculturation and antisocial behavior and between value acculturation and drug abuse.

A Children's Hispanic Background Scale can be administered in 10 minutes and has 30 items that assess Spanish language usage, food preferences, and general cultural exposure (Martinez, Norman, & Delaney, 1984). A similar acculturation scale for Mexican-American children, designed to be completed by teachers, has 10 Likert-type items and factor loadings on language, parental occupation/education, and the child's musical preferences (Franco, 1983).

Marín, Sabogal, VanOss Marín, Otero-Sabogal, and Perez-Stable (1987) reported on a 12-item Hispanic Acculturation Scale composed of three factors: language use and ethnic loyalty, electronic media preferences, and ethnic social relations. This scale has comparable reliability to other published scales and correlates highly with validation criteria of respondents' generation, length of United States residence, age at arrival, and ethnic self-identification.

Ramirez (1984) has developed a 57-item Multicultural Experience Inventory consisting of demographics, personal history data, and multicultural participation. This inventory identifies biculturals, traditionals, and atraditionals on the basis of a large sample of Mexican Americans, and has been validated by using psychohistories and leadership behaviors.

Another instrument sophisticated in theoretical origins and construction is the Cultural Life Style Inventory, with orthogonal dimensions of interfamily and extrafamily language usage, social affiliations, cultural familiarity, and cultural identification/pride (Mendoza, 1989). This instrument was developed from a multidimensional model of acculturation that separated affective, cognitive, and behavioral adaptations; it recognizes that assimilation may be uneven across these modalities (Mendoza & Martinez, 1981). Dominant and non-dominant lifestyles are identified. Cultural resistance, cultural incorporation, and cultural shift or transmutation may be identified as a result of a distinction between degrees of assimilation and extinction of cultural practices. There is correlational evidence of construct validity that includes hypothesis testing and concordance of profiles with profiles generated by relatives.

Recommendations for Use of Moderator Variables with Hispanic Americans   This potpourri of described instruments represents only a sampling, using selection criteria that included recency and adequacy of psychometric development, publication history (especially the use of an instrument in related research), availability of both Spanish and English versions, and population specificity (e.g., adolescents, children, Cuban Americans).

The more complex instruments such as the Cultural Life Style Inventory and the Multicultural Experience Inventory are potentially the most useful. Either of these instruments includes a context for usage as a moderator variable. This context demands an immersion on the part of the assessor in Mexican-American culture, history, and research literature in order to understand the proper use of the instrument to explore acculturation. For assessors who work with predominantly Mexican-American populations, an understanding of these different contexts will be more helpful than the use of a score that only permits classification of an assessee as assimilated, bicultural, traditional, or marginal. However, if classification per se is the only information desired, or Hispanic-American assessees are infrequently evaluated, then a brief instrument such as the Hispanic Acculturation Scale, which will probably continue to be used in published research, is an acceptable choice.

Native Americans

Need for Moderator Variables The use of moderator variables in the assessment of Native Americans is essential because their culture does influence psychological test performance. Anthropologists recognize that the amount of contact between native peoples and Europeans can be measured, for example, by exposure and adaptation moderator variables that quantify the impact of European culture (de Lacey, 1970). However, the complexity of the contact-acculturation paradigm has increased dramatically over time because of differences among native cultures, differences in their willingness to acculturate, and differences in histories of contact and the extent of coercion to acculturate. Moreover, generations of Anglo-American assessors have applied their imposed etic measures to these peoples and found them to be deficient in psychiatric health status as well as intelligence and personality. This legacy of invidious comparisons resulted from the use of tests that had been developed and normed on Anglo-American populations and also from minimization of differences between Native Americans and Anglo-Americans. As a result, there is a need for use of moderator variables as an accompaniment to assessment of Native Americans in mental health settings.

The MMPI-1, which has been routinely used with Native Americans, provides a clear example of the need for moderator variables. An early study (Pollack & Shore, 1980) demonstrated that culture overrides psychopathology, at least for Northwest Coast, Plateau, and Plains Indians. In this study, regardless of diagnosis, the MMPI profiles were all similar, with significant elevations on F, 4 (Pd), and 8 (Sc) scales.

As the dissimilarity between the traditional culture and the dominant Anglo-American culture increases, it may become necessary to collect culture-specific MMPI norms (Charles, 1988; LaDue, 1982). For example, Karen Charles found that all clinical scales for Northern Ontario Ojibwa and Cree were significantly elevated when the MMPI-1 norms were used, which resulted in a 50 percent misclassification rate.

In another study, when a moderator variable, the Rosebud Personal Opinion Survey, was used with the MMPI-1 for Plains Indians, the social, values, and language subscales were correlated significantly with elevations on these scales, and with 2 (D), 6 (Pa), and Si as well (Hoffmann, Dana, & Bolton, 1985). When

F scale items were analyzed for this population by an anthropologist, deviant responses on seven items were consistent with Lakota culture, and deviant responses on seven additional items were endorsed on the basis of high levels of reservation poverty, sickness, alcoholism, and unemployment.

Nonetheless, the prevailing consensus on interpretation of MMPI-1 scale score elevations of Native Americans has been to treat these elevations in terms of normative expectations. The argument is that any and all ethnic minority group differences can be controlled/minimized by matching, and any remaining discrepancies can be accounted for by describing differences in symptoms between groups (Butcher, Braswell, & Raney, 1983). This procedure results in reducing the cultural variance by selecting persons who closely resemble the Anglo-American population, but it fails to account for an unknown number of Native Americans (and other minority groups) who are dissimilar as a result of partial or complete retention of traditional culture.

Most Native Americans identify to some extent with their traditional cultures. A recent study suggested that approximately equal percentages of Oklahoma Native American college students were bicultural, traditional, or marginal, with fewer than 9 percent being assimilated to Anglo-American culture (Johnson & Lashley, 1989), as contrasted, for example, with a figure of 77 percent of African-American college students (Whatley & Dana, 1989). As a result, prior to any etic or imposed etic assessment procedure with a Native American, it is necessary to have some information on the extent to which assimilation or biculturality has been the solution to the demand for acculturation from the larger society. Whenever the solution to the demand by the dominant society for integration has been either an evident retention of a traditional culture or marginality, some measurement of acculturation becomes mandatory.

Acculturation   Acculturation studies for Native Americans have been done primarily by anthropologists. Siegel (1955) abstracted 74 of the early empirical studies. Hoffmann (1983b) found more than 80 additional references, largely in psychology journals, and provided a careful review of this literature (Hoffmann, 1983a). Since there are hundreds of distinct tribal groups with different acculturation histories and outcomes of acculturation, no attempt will be made to review all of this literature here. Instead, studies will be selected that provide useful tribe-specific information and indices or measures that have either pan-Indian or tribe-specific usefulness.

Several different kinds of acculturation indices have been used in these studies: specific criteria, existing measures, and new measures. Studies using projective techniques as the existing measures will not be reviewed in this context because of the level of inference or interpretation required to infer acculturation.

Table 7-5 presents selected pan-Indian, bilevel acculturation indices that represent use of specific criteria or new measures. These pan-Indian indices

TABLE 7-5 • *Selected Pan-Indian Bilevel Acculturation Indices*

Source	Index
Brown (1982)	Use of case history for 4-generation chart; behavioral criteria for family/self, social, spiritual, training/education data
Chadwick & Strauss (1975)	Use of 7 stages of assimilation (Gordon, 1964)
Howe Chief (1940)	Indian Assimilation Scale; 40 Likert scale items: willingness to assimilate, attitudes, behaviors, types of affiliation, degree of Indian blood, material cultural traits

should be useful in urban settings, with individuals of mixed tribal origins, or whenever marginality is suspected, but it will be preferable to use tribe-specific indices whenever they are available. Some representative tribe-specific monolevel and bilevel acculturation indices are presented later, in Table 7-7.

Three pan-Indian bilevel acculturation indices have been selected to illustrate different approaches. Brown (1982) developed an informal process that uses the case history as a basis for documenting acculturation. This technique can be readily applied whenever there is sufficient rapport to sustain a conversation directed at eliciting information on personal life and daily activities. Table 7-6 presents a distillation of the behavioral criteria for acculturation areas of family/self, social/recreation, spiritual/religion, and training/education. The numbers 1 through 4 in this table refer to "generations," or categories of placement on what Brown refers to as a chart of world-view conflicts that she uses directly in alcohol treatment. First- and second-generation placements represent relatively traditional lifestyles; third- and fourth-generation placements refer to more dominant-society lifestyles. In order to suggest the use of this approach as an informal assessment moderator, Brown's chart has been modified to contain the criterion reference data necessary for description of an individual.

A second pan-Indian measure, the Indian Assimilation Scale (Howe Chief, 1940), provides the single best example of a pan-Indian measure. The scale was standardized with high school girls, representing a range of tribes, who were in residence at the Haskell Indian Institute in Lawrence, Kansas. This scale examines behaviors that cover the range of outcomes of acculturation, from traditional to assimilated. The items relate to social distance, desire to become assimilated, language usage, parental attitudes, marriage preferences, attitudes toward native traditions and customs, participation in organizations, material cultural traits, types of names used in the family, topics of casual conversation, and preferences in dress. Unfortunately, this scale does not appear to have been used in published studies. One reason the scale has been overlooked by assessors may be its construction in 1937–1938, prior to the availability of sophisticated test construction methodology.

TABLE 7-6 • *A Bilevel Format for Describing Native American Acculturation*

1	2	3	4
Family/Self Relationships			
Exclusive with extended family and tribe	Only with extended family. Strong identification with tribal background.	Restricted to parents, siblings, spouse/children. Identification but little contact with tribe.	With primary family. Some contact with siblings, grandparents.
Spiritual/Religious			
Regular ceremonies.	Knowledge of ceremonies.	Belief but irregular church attendance.	Regular church attendance.
Social/Recreational/Leisure			
All with Indian people.	Preference for Indian people in own community. Enjoy activity outside of own community only with Indian people.	Most outside of Indian community. Occasional powwows, etc.	Prefer time exclusively outside of Indian community.
Training/Education			
No formal education. Prefer to listen/observe elders in unstructured settings.	Some formal education. Prefer to listen/observe.	Prefer classroom with movies, speakers. Dislike written evaluation of knowledge or skills.	Prefer classroom with formal lectures, didactics, written evaluation.

Source: Adapted and modified from Brown (1982)

Prior to the development of their pan-Indian index, Chadwick and Strauss (1975) examined several behaviors of urban Indians in Seattle, to challenge the assumption that migration to cities per se resulted in assimilation. Their procedure was to measure components of structural-social and cultural-behavioral assimilation independently and in subareas of marriage, identification, attitude reception, behavior reception, and civic assimilation. Their Structural Assimilation Scale combined home ownership, employment, and marital status; cultural or behavioral assimilation was measured by modernization and assimilation scales and separatism items. Their method compared urban Anglo-Americans and Native Americans in order to highlight differences in acculturation. Although these component measures could be developed into a single scale to provide a moderator, this has not been done. This study is included here as an alternative, and more complex, empirically derived method of putting together variables relevant to pan-Indian urban populations. It should be noted that Native Americans who had lived their entire lives in Seattle were as traditional in cultural orientation as recent arrivals from reservations.

Tribe-specific monolevel and bilevel acculturation indices should be used whenever assessment is conducted within a tribal setting. For any tribe-specific assessment, it is mandatory to have a detailed and first-hand knowledge of cultural history and ethnographic information, as well as data on current reservation attitudes toward cultural and tribal identity.

Table 7-7 provides an introduction to a variety of formal and informal methods for obtaining evidence about acculturation in selected tribes, including some major tribes in terms of their numbers and their geographic areas of residence.

Recommendations for Use of Moderator Variables with Native Americans   For Native Americans in urban settings, the informal "generations" assessment as presented in Table 7-6 is recommended. However, tribe-specific measures are preferable for reservation residents because, in general, they will provide greater detail and demonstrate to the participant assessee that the assessor has some direct knowledge of a context for the presenting problems.

Non-Group-Specific Moderator Variables

A small number of moderator variables represent creative, unfinished, and provocative exemplars. These moderators include (a) willingness to acculturate; (b) a trio of measures to provide entree into the complexity of acculturative solutions by using Ethnic Identity Types; and (c) direct measures of world view. Since all of these developments have immense potential consequences for cultural competence in assessment, they will be described in some detail (Table 7-8).

Willingness to Acculturate   Although it is often assumed that refugees and immigrants are delighted to have the opportunity of living in the United States, this may be a presumption that merits careful attention in individual assessment settings. It is always important to ascertain willingness to acculturate and then to estimate whether or not personality variables that may facilitate this process appear to be present.

TABLE 7-7 • *Tribe-Specific Monolevel (M) and Bilevel (B) Acculturation Indices*

Tribe	Source	Index
Blackfeet	McFee (1968)	20-question Sociocultural Field Schedule
Chippewa	Gillin & Raimy (1940)	Three 5-point scales: Indian vs. White; religion; occupation
Cree/Carrier/Tsmishian	Berry & Annis (1974)	Scales for marginality, deviance, attitudes toward modes of relating to society
Eskimo	Chance (1965)	Intercultural Contact and Western Identification Scales
Navajo	Graves (1967)	Measures of interpersonal norms, personal control, time perspective; formal education, occupation, Acculturation Identification Index
	Weppner (1972)	Language, social interaction, locus of control; Time; Self-anchoring scale
Ojibwa	Red Horse et al. (1978)	Language, religion, social and recreational activities
Sioux	Mohatt & Redbird (undated)	Lifestyle Scale; Cultural Intactness Index
	Hoffmann et al. (1985)	Rosebud Personal Opinion Survey; Scales for social acculturation, values, blood quantum, language usage, education/occupation
Spokane	Roy (1962)	Education, level of living, occupation, social integration, blood quantum

Some of the personality factors that are predictive of successful acculturation have been identified in a study that examined personality and demographic variables in questionnaire format (Smither & Rodriguez-Giegling, 1982), using items derived from the Hopkins Personality Inventory, an instrument developed from Hogan's socioanalytic theory (Hogan, Johnson, & Emler, 1978). For example, being conscientious and likable enables Vietnamese refugees to pay con-

TABLE 7-8 • *Generic Moderator Variables*

Source	Moderator	Cultural Group*
Hui (1988)	Individualism-Collectivism Scale	1
Ibrahim and Kahn (1987)	Scale to Assess World Views	2
Pierce, Clark, and Kiefer (1972)	Acculturative Balance Scale	3
Pierce, Clark, and Kaufman (1978–1979)	Anglo Face Scale; Traditional Orientation Scale; Revised Kluckhohn Values Schedule	4
Smither and Rodriguez-Giegling (1982)	Acculturation Questionnaire; willingness to acculturate	4
Wong-Rieger and Quintana (1987)	Multicultural Acculturation Scale	5

*1 = Hong Kong Chinese
2 – Anglo-Americans
3 = Japanese Americans and Mexican Americans
4 = Vietnamese and Nicaraguan refugees
5 = Southeast Asians, Hispanic Americans, and Anglo-Americans

scious attention to the rules governing social interaction in the dominant society. As a result, these personality variables—Intellectance and Likability—were better predictors for these refugees than the demographic variables used in some moderator measures. However, for Nicaraguan refugees who were assessed during the time of a civil war in their own country and were uncertain as to location of their future residence, neither personality nor demographic variables were predictors of acculturation.

Ethnic Identity Types This typology approach began with a bilevel pictorial measurement of popular culture knowledge, using a format analogous to intelligence tests (Pierce, Clark, & Kiefer, 1972). Three sets of pictures for Japanese Americans, Mexican Americans, and Anglo-Americans were developed, with items that differentiated between generations and were subsequently used as criteria for adding highly intercorrelated new items. A single score indicated the relative balance between the traditional culture and the adopted culture, hence the title, Acculturative Balance Scale (ABS). Such a measure does not depend on educational level or facility with English.

However, the ABS only provided information about acculturation in the cognitive sphere. Acculturation also includes two additional spheres: ethnic behaviors and value orientations. The behavioral sphere was mapped by using interviews with questions about social relationships, level of ethnic group and larger community participation, and attitudes. Ten variables were used as definers and included ratios for holidays celebrated, literacy, and fluency. These ratios permitted balance scores to be obtained. Ethnic identification and attitude toward own group were also rated during the interview. Two usable dimensions emerged from this interview data by using Tryon's cluster analysis: Anglo Face (an outward behavioral adoption of Anglo-American culture) and Traditional Face (characteristics that reflect the original traditional cultural patterns.)

Values were measured using a revised Kluckhohn and Strodtbeck scale for activity, time, man-nature, and relational orientations, and although a typology could not be extracted from this data, generational and ethnic group differences were reported, and some of the results are pertinent here. For time orientation, the younger generations became increasing present-oriented, regardless of ethnic group, and increasingly concerned with mastery over nature in the man-nature relationship. Mexican Americans retained a stronger subjugation-to-nature orientation than Japanese Americans, and Japanese Americans were more oriented toward Becoming, harmony with nature, and collateral relationships.

The scales for Acculturative Balance, Anglo Face, and Traditional Orientation were used as a basis for a description of acculturation outcomes that included age, generational differences, and individual choice in the expression of ethnic identity (Clark, Kaufman, & Pierce, 1976; Pierce, Clark, & Kaufman, 1978–1979). The use of the three measures simultaneously permitted profiles of six Ethnic Identity Types to be generated. The complexity of any solution to the acculturation dilemma can be explored for individuals by using a schema that is independent of gender, acculturation solution, and education, with age and generation controlled by their representation in specific profiles.

The Measurement of World View   There have been three approaches to the measurement of world view: (a) a purported measure of world view per se (Ibrahim & Kahn, 1987); (b) separate measures of world view components, including a value orientation scale and cognitive, behavioral, and self-identity changes (Wong-Rieger & Quintana, 1987); and (c) a measure of one component of world view, individualism-collectivism (Hui, 1988).

Ibrahim and Kahn (1987) used the five Kluckhohn value orientations as a basis for the development of a new measure. This scale was carefully constructed, using expert judges to categorize statements into value orientation categories. A pilot study of these statements was examined by using a principal-components analysis to derive a multidimensional system. Revision of the scale, a larger sample, and multidimensional scaling resulted in three five-point subscales with nine items per category. Five dimensions resulted from the scaling procedure and depicted the within-group complexity of value orientations.

The results provide an indication of how the original Kluckhohn categories have changed over time, at least for the northeastern United States in a primarily Anglo-American, suburban college population. In addition, the measure could be used to examine an individual's value orientation, although this has not been done with samples of culturally different persons. World view, of course, should not be construed to be identical with Kluckhohn's value orientations, or necessarily limited to only those five constructs.

Wong-Rieger and Quintana (1987) were interested in a measure that would be useful for several different cultural groups, particularly Southeast Asians and Hispanic Americans, and would differentiate among the various modes of acculturation. Their model included measures of understanding, newly learned skills, social roles, and values. The result of using this model, the bilevel Multicultural Acculturation Scale, was factor analytically derived and includes self-report subscales for cognitive, behavioral, and self-identity changes and a values-orientation scale. Three acculturation scores are computed: (a) an Ethnic Orientation Index; (b) an Anglo-American Orientation Index; and (c) an Overall Acculturation Index. The scale discriminates between foreign-born and Anglo-American groups and provides useful information on immigrants and sojourners. The subscale scores also provide additional information on relative acculturation across the component areas.

Hui (1988) developed the Individualism-Collectivism (INDCOL) measure to tap a multifaceted syndrome of feelings, emotions, beliefs, ideologies, behaviors, and intended behaviors related to interpersonal concern as a personality construct. This construct has one polar extreme in which the self was independent, integumented in an individual, and survival was determined on the basis of one's own behavior. The other extreme described the self as an aspect of the group, interdependent, with submersion of the individual in the group, and survival of the group being paramount.

A first step in test construction was a consensus among social scientists in different parts of the world on the constituents of the syndrome of collectivism. These constituents were labeled as: (a) cost/benefit ratio of personal decisions and/or actions for other persons; (b) sharing of material and non-material resources and outcomes; (c) being susceptible to social influence; and (d) feelings of involvement in the lives of other persons (Hui & Triandis, 1986).

The INDCOL scale was constructed by using simultaneous Chinese and English versions with modifications, or decentering, to provide more accurate translation. Three bilinguals checked the equivalence of the wordings. Hong Kong and American college students provided data for item analysis, item selection, and analysis of gender and cultural differences on six subscales for spouse, parent, kin, neighbor, coworker, and friend. Six validation studies provided an array of initial validation data. Other studies have provided construct validation. The INDCOL appears to measure the construct as intended and includes the constituents of the syndrome.

Use of Moderator Variables
in Assessment Practice

Moderator variables should be applied whenever there is evidence that a client is not representative of an Anglo-American cultural background. The fact that a client is fluent in English does not mean that his or her world view is Anglo-American. Nor can it be assumed that clients who appear to be African American or Asian American will necessarily or inevitably identify with their cultures of origin rather than with the dominant Anglo-American culture.

For African Americans, it is necessary to understand the extent to which an individual may be in the process of Nigrescence, or becoming Afrocentric. Subject to the caveats presented earlier in this chapter, including my personal preference for the DIB-C, either the DIB-C or the RIAS provides an adequate measure for rough screening, especially when there is interest in being able to describe problems due to racism and discrimination. However, for clients who are dealing with issues of Afrocentric identity, there is no substitute for a direct measure such as the African Self-Consciousness Scale.

For Asian Americans, the Suinn-Lew scale, as suggested earlier, is a possible choice, at least in preference to other measures at the present time. However, without further validation, it is probably preferable to administer the INDCOL for assessee participants of Chinese origin and to use either the Scale to Assess World Views or the Multicultural Acculturation Scale for assessees with fluent English. For assessees who do not speak English fluently, formal assessment by someone who does not speak the first language of the client is not recommended.

To provide assessment services for most Hispanic Americans, competence should include familiarity with the Spanish language, in spite of the fact that many of the moderator instruments have both English and Spanish versions. Screening for traditional culture can be accomplished with brief instruments such as the Hispanic Acculturation Scale (Marín et al., 1987). However, if the purpose is to provide a detailed personality assessment as a precursor to individual or group psychotherapy, more sophisticated instruments that provide more relevant individualized information are required. Either the Cultural Lifestyle Inventory or the Multicultural Experience Inventory will then be preferable.

For Native Americans, although the necessity for information regarding cultural orientation will almost always be urgent, there are few adequately constructed instruments. In urban settings, Brown's informal generations assessment is recommended. However, this interview process will be dependent on interviewing skill that is culture-specific, and Anglo-American assessors may not readily gain the trust that permits a comfortable conversation. Tribe-specific measures for reservation residents are preferable to pan-Indian measures, because they will generally provide greater detail and demonstrate to the participant assessee that the assessor has some direct knowledge of a context for the presenting problems. However, few of these measures are adequate psychometric instruments, largely because many were developed during an early period of anthropological study. One exception is the monolevel Rosebud Personal Opinion Survey, developed primarily for Lakota Sioux, with generous assistance from tribal members and competent psychometrics. This measure should also be useful with other Plains tribes, although demonstrations of cross-tribe validity are needed.

Ultimately, however, generic moderators should be employed *in addition to* culture-specific measures, because of the complexity of the acculturation process and a necessity for assessment information concerning the outcomes of acculturation. As Clark et al. (1976) have suggested with their profiles of Ethnic Identity Types, the outcomes of traditional and bicultural acculturation for individuals are much more complex than hitherto suspected. However, to the best of my knowledge, none of the three generic instruments described herein have been applied in assessment settings. Although these measures do not have a sufficient research basis for current application, assessors should begin to do research, using these measures as a means of becoming more familiar with the complexity of the acculturation paradigm.

References

Ablon, J. (1971). Retention of cultural values and differential urban adaptation: Samoans and American Indians in a West Coast City. *Social Forces, 49*, 385–393.

Anderson, J. N. (1983). Health and illness in Pilipino immigrants. *Western Journal of Medicine, 139*, 811–819.

Baldwin, J. A. (1984). African self-consciousness and the mental health of African-Americans. *Journal of Black Studies, 15*, 177–194.

Baldwin, J. A., & Bell, Y. R. (1985). The African Self-Consciousness Scale: An Africentric personality questionnaire. *The Western Journal of Black Studies, 9*(2), 65–68.

Baldwin, J. A., Duncan, J. A., & Bell, Y. R. (1987). Assessment of African self-consciousness among Black students from two college environments. *Journal of Black Psychology, 13*(2), 27–41.

Banks, H. A. (1970). Black consciousness: A student survey. *The Black Scholar, 2*(1), 44–51.

Berry, J. W., & Annis, R. C. (1974). Acculturative stress: The role of ecology, culture, and differentiation. *Journal of Cross-Cultural Psychology; 5*, 382–405.

Berry, J. W., & Kim, U. (1988). Acculturation and mental health. In P. R. Dasen, J. W. Berry, & N. Sartorius (Eds.), *Health and cross-cultural psychology: Toward applications* (pp. 207–236). Beverly Hills, CA: Sage.

Berry, J. W., Kim, U., Minde, T., & Mok, D. (1987). Comparative studies of acculturative stress. *International Migration Review, 21*, 491–511.

Bertelson, A. D., Marks, P. A., & May, G. D. (1982). MMPI and race: A controlled study. *Journal of Consulting and Clinical Psychology, 50*, 316–318.

Brown, S. (1982, May). *Native generations diagnosis and placement on the conflicts/resolution chart*. Paper presented at the annual meeting of the School of Addiction

Studies, Center for Alcohol and Addiction Studies, University of Alaska, Anchorage.

Butcher, J. N., Braswell, L., & Raney, D. (1983). A cross-cultural comparison of American Indian, Black, and White inpatients on the MMPI and presenting symptoms. *Journal of Consulting and Clinical Psychology, 51,* 587–594.

Chadwick, B. A., & Strauss, J. H. (1975). The assimilation of American Indians into urban society: The Seattle case. *Human Organization, 34,* 359–369.

Charles, K. (1988). *Culture-specific MMPI norms for a sample of Northern Ontario Indians.* Unpublished M. A. thesis, Lakehead University, Thunder Bay, Ontario, Canada.

Chance, N. A. (1965). Acculturation, self-identification, and personality adjustment. *American Anthropologist, 67,* 372-393.

Cheatham, H. E., Tomlinson, S. M., & Ward, T. J. (1990). The African self-consciousness construct and African American students. *Journal of College Student Development, 31,* 492–499.

Clark, M., Kaufman, S., & Pierce, R. C. (1976). Explorations of acculturation: Toward a model of ethnic identity. *Human Organization, 35*(3), 231–238.

Cuellar, I., Harris, I. C., & Jasso, R. (1980). An acculturation scale for Mexican American normal and clinical populations. *Hispanic Journal of Behavioral Science, 2,* 199–217.

Dahlstrom, W. G., Lachar, D., & Dahlstrom, L. E. (1986). *MMPI Patterns of American minorities.* Minneapolis, MN: University of Minnesota Press.

Dana, R. H. (1988). Culturally diverse groups and MMPI interpretation. *Professional Psychology: Research and Practice, 19,* 490–495.

Dana, R. H., & Whatley, P. R. (1991). When does a difference make a difference? MMPI scores and African-Americans. *Journal of Clinical Psychology, 47,* 417-440.

de Lacey, P. R. (1970). An index of contact for aboriginal communities. *Australian Journal of Social Issues, 5,* 219–223.

Erdberg, S. P. (1970). MMPI differences associated with sex, race, and residence in a southern sample. (Doctoral dissertation, University of Alabama, 1969). *Dissertation Abstracts International, 30,* 5236B.

Franco, J. N. (1983). An acculturation scale for Mexican-American children. *Journal of General Psychology, 108,* 175–181.

Garcia, M., & Lega, L. I. (1979). Development of a Cuban Ethnic Identity Questionnaire. *Hispanic Journal of Behavioral Sciences, 1,* 247–261.

Gaw, A. (1982). *Cross-cultural psychiatry.* Littleton, MA: John Wright.

Gillin, J., & Raimy, V. (1940). Acculturation and personality. *American Sociological Review, 5,* 371–380.

Gonzales, R. R., & Roll, S. (1985). Relationship between acculturation, cognitive style, and intelligence. *Journal of Cross-Cultural Psychology, 16,* 190–205.

Gordon, M. M. (1964). *Assimilation in American life: The role of race, religion, and natural origins.* New York: Oxford University Press.

Graves, T. D. (1967). Psychological acculturation in a tri-ethnic community. *Southwestern Journal of Anthropology, 23,* 337–350.

Greene, R. L. (1987). Ethnicity and MMPI performance: A review. *Journal of Consulting and Clinical Psychology, 55,* 497–512.

Gynther, M. D. (1981). Is the MMPI an appropriate assessment device for Blacks? *Journal of Black Psychology, 7,* 67–75.

Hall, W. S., Cross, W. E., & Freedle, R. (1972). Stages in the development of black awareness: An empirical investigation. In R. L. Jones (Ed.), *Black psychology* (pp. 156–165). New York: Harper & Row.

Hastings, J. (1977). Adaptation problems of Asian migrants. *Australian and New Zealand Journal of Psychiatry*, *11*, 219–221.

Helms, J. E. (1986). Expanding racial identity theory to cover the counseling process. *Journal of Counseling Psychology*, *33*, 62–64.

Helms, J. E. (Ed.). (1990). *Black and white racial identity: Theory, research, and practice.* New York: Greenwood Press.

Hoffmann, T. (1983a). *Measures of Native American acculturation.* Unpublished manuscript, University of Arkansas, Fayetteville, AR.

Hoffmann, T. (1983b). *Native American acculturation bibliography.* Unpublished manuscript, University of Arkansas, Fayetteville, AR.

Hoffmann, T., Dana, R. H., & Bolton, B. (1985). Measured acculturation and MMPI-168 performance of Native American adults. *Journal of Cross-Cultural Psychology*, *16*, 243–256.

Hogan, R., Johnson, J. A., & Emler, N. P. (1978). A socioanalytic theory of moral development. *New Directions for Child Development*, *2*, 1–18.

Howe Chief, E. (1940). An assimilation study of Indian girls. *Journal of Social Psychology*, *11*, 19–30.

Hui, C. H. (1988). Measurement of individualism-collectivism. *Journal of Research in Personality*, *22*, 17–36.

Hui, C. H., & Triandis, H. C. (1986). Individualism-collectivism: A study of cross-cultural researchers. *Journal of Cross-Cultural Psychology*, *17*, 225–248.

Ibrahim, F. A., & Arredondo, P. M. (1986). Ethical standards for cross-cultural counseling, counselor preparation, practice, assessment, and research. *Journal of Counseling and Development*, *60*, 349–352.

Ibrahim, F. A., & Kahn, H. (1987). Assessment of world views. *Psychological Reports*, *60*, 163–176.

Johnson, M. E., & Lashley, K. H. (1989). Influence of Native-Americans' cultural commitment on preferences for counselor ethnicity and expectations about counseling. *Journal of Multicultural Counseling and Development*, *17*(July), 115–122.

Kuo, C. L. (1982). Perceptions of assimilation among the Chinese in the United States. In C. B. Marrett & C. Leggon (Eds.), *Research in race and ethnic relations: A research annual* (Vol. 3, pp. 127–143). Greenwich, CT: JAI Press.

LaDue, R. A. (1982). *Standardization of the Minnesota Multiphasic Personality Inventory for the Colville Indian reservation.* Unpublished doctoral dissertation, Washington State University. (DAI, *43*(9), 3033-B).

LaFromboise, T. D., Trimble, J. E., & Mohatt, G. V. (1990). Counseling intervention and American Indian tradition: An integrative approach. *The Counseling Psychologist*, *18*, 628–654.

Marín, G., Sabogal, F., VanOss Marín, B., Otero-Sabogal, R., & Perez-Stable, E. J. (1987). Development of a short acculturation scale for Hispanics. *Hispanic Journal of Behavioral Science*, *9*, 183–205.

Marmot, M. G., & Syme, S. L. (1976). Acculturation and coronary heart disease in Japanese-Americans. *American Journal of Epidemiology*, *104*, 225–247.

Martinez, R., Norman, R. D., & Delaney, H. D. (1984). A Children's Hispanic Background Scale. *Hispanic Journal of Behavioral Sciences*, *6*, 103–112.

Masuda, M., Matsumoto, G. H., & Meredith, G. M. (1970). Ethnic identity in three generations of Japanese Americans. *Journal of Social Psychology*, *81*, 199–207.

Matsumoto, G. M., Meredith, G. M., & Masuda, M. (1970). Ethnic identification: Honolulu and Seattle Japanese-Americans. *Journal of Cross-Cultural Psychology*, *1*, 63–76.

Matsuoka, J. K. (1990). Differential acculturation among Vietnamese refugees. *Social Work, 35,* 341–345.

McFee, (1968). The 150% man, a product of Blackfeet acculturation. *American Anthropologist, 70,* 1096–1107.

Mendoza, R. H. (1989). An empirical scale to measure type and degree of acculturation in Mexican-American adolescents and adults. *Journal of Cross-Cultural Psychology, 20,* 372–385.

Mendoza, R. H., & Martinez, J. J. (1981). The measurement of acculturation. In A. Baron, Jr. (Ed.), *Explorations in Chicano Psychology* (pp. 71–82). New York: Holt, Rinehart & Winston.

Milliones, J. (1980). Construction of a black consciousness measure: Psychotherapeutic implications. *Psychotherapy: Theory, Research and Practice, 17,* 175–182.

Mohatt, G., & Red Bird, S. (Undated). *Identity through traditional Lakota methods* (Rep. No. 5RO1 MH 23697-03). Rockville, MD: National Institutes of Mental Health.

Montgomery, G. T., & Orozco, S. (1984). Validation of a measure of acculturation for Mexican Americans. *Hispanic Journal of Behavioral Sciences, 6,* 53–63.

Montgomery, G. T., & Orozco, S. (1985). Mexican Americans' performance on the MMPI as a function of level of acculturation. *Journal of Clinical Psychology, 41,* 203–212.

Myers, H. F. (1982). Research on the Afro-American family: A critical review. In B. A. Bass, G. E. Wyatt, & G. J. Powell (Eds.), *The Afro-American family* (pp. 35–68). New York: Grune & Stratton.

Olmedo, E. L. (1979). Acculturation: A psychometric perspective. *American Psychologist, 34,* 1061–1070.

Olmedo, E. L., Martinez, J. L., Jr., & Martinez, S. R. (1978). Measure of acculturation for Chicano adolescents. *Psychological Reports, 42,* 159–170.

Olmedo, E. L., & Padilla, A. M. (1978). Empirical and construct validation of a measure of acculturation for Mexican Americans. *Journal of Social Psychology, 105,* 179–187.

Parham, T. A., & Helms, J. E. (1981). The influence of black students' racial identity attitudes on preference for counselor's race. *Journal of Counseling Psychology, 28,* 250–257.

Parham, T. A., & Helms, J. E. (1985). The relation of racial identity attitudes to self-actualization and affective states of black students. *Journal of Counseling Psychology, 32,* 431–440.

Pierce, R. C., Clark, M., & Kaufman, S. (1978–1979). Generation and ethnic identity: A typological analysis. *International Journal of Aging and Human Development, 9,* 19–29.

Pierce, R. C., Clark, M., & Kiefer, C. W. (1972). A "bootstrap" scaling technique. *Human Organization, 31,* 403–410.

Pollack, D., & Shore, J. H. (1980). Validity of the MMPI with Native Americans. *American Journal of Psychiatry, 137,* 946–950.

Ponterotto, J. G., & Wise, S. L. (1987). Construct validity study of the Racial Identity Attitude Scale. *Journal of Counseling Psychology, 34,* 218–223.

Ramirez, M., III. (1984). Assessing and understanding biculturalism-multiculturalism in Mexican-American adults. In J. L. Martinez, Jr., & R. H. Mendoza (Eds.), *Chicano psychology* (pp. 77-94). Orlando, FL: Academic Press.

Redfield, R., Linton, R., & Herskovits, M. J. (1936). Memorandum on the study of acculturation. *American Anthropologist, 38,* 149–152.

Red Horse, J. C., Lewis, R. Feit, M., & Decker, J. (1978). Family behavior of urban American Indians. *Social Casework, 59,* 67–72.

Roy, P. (1962). The measurement of assimilation: The Spokane Indians. *American Journal of Sociology, 67,* 541–551.

Shepherd, J. (1987). Coping in America: Contextual variables in the adaptation of female refugees and immigrants. *Social Development Issues, 11*(2), 72–86.

Siegel, B. (1955). *Acculturation.* Palo Alto, CA: Stanford University Press.

Smither, R., & Rodriguez-Giegling, M. (1982). Personality, demographics, and acculturation of Vietnamese and Nicaraguan refugees to the United States. *International Journal of Psychology, 17,* 19–25.

Sodowsky, G. R., & Carey, J. C. (1988). Relationships between acculturation-related demographics and cultural attitudes of an Asian-Indian immigrant group. *Journal of Multicultural Counseling and Development, 16*(July), 117–136.

Sue, D. W. (1981). *Counseling the culturally different: Theory and practice.* New York: Wiley.

Sue, S., & Morishima, J. K. (1982). *The mental health of Asian Americans.* San Francisco, CA: Jossey-Bass.

Suinn, R. M., Rickard-Figueroa, K., Lew, S., & Vigil, S. (1987). The Suinn-Lew Asian Self-Identity Acculturation Scale: An initial report. *Educational and Psychological Measurement, 47,* 401–407.

Szapocznik, J., & Kurtines, W. (1980). Acculturation, biculturalism and adjustment among Cuban Americans. In A. M Padilla (Ed.), *Acculturation: Theory, models and some new findings* (pp. 139–159). (American Association for the Advancement of Science Selected Symposium 39). Boulder, CO: Westview.

Szapocznik, J., Scopetta, M. A., & Aranalde, M. A. (1978). Theory and measurement of acculturation. *Interamerican Journal of Psychology, 12,* 113–130.

Taylor, J. (in press). Cultural conversion experience: Implications for mental health research and treatment. In R. L. Jones (Ed.), *Advances in Black psychology.* Richmond, CA: Cobb & Henry.

Terrell, F., & Taylor, J. (1981). The development of an inventory to measure certain aspects of Black nationalist ideology. *Psychology, 15*(4), 31–33.

Velásquez, R. (1984). *An atlas of MMPI group profiles on Mexican Americans.* Los Angeles, CA: Spanish Speaking Mental Health Research Center, University of California at Los Angeles.

Weppner, R. S. (1972). An empirical test of the assimilation of a migrant group into an urban milieu. *Anthropological Quarterly, 45,* 262–273.

Whatley, P. R., & Dana, R. H. (1989). *Racial identity and MMPI group differences.* Fayetteville, AR: University of Arkansas.

White, W. G. (1975). A psychometric approach for adjusting selected MMPI scale scores obtained by blacks. (Doctoral dissertation, University of Missouri, 1974). *Dissertation Abstracts International, 35,* 4669.

Wong-Rieger, D., & Quintana, D. (1987). Comparative acculturation of Southeast Asians and Hispanic immigrants and sojourners. *Journal of Cross-Cultural Psychology, 18,* 145–162.

Yao, E. L. (1979). The assimilation of contemporary Chinese immigrants. *Journal of Psychology, 101,* 107–113.

CHAPTER EIGHT

Assessment I: An Emic Perspective

Introduction

This chapter will describe the usefulness of a variety of assessment methods for multicultural populations from an emic perspective. These methods include (a) behavior observations; (b) life history, case study, interview; (c) accounts; (d) life events; (e) picture-story techniques and tests; (f) inkblot techniques and tests; and (g) some miscellaneous methods, including word associations, sentence completions, and drawings. It should be emphasized that any of these measures becomes emic or etic as a result of how it is used.

An Emic Perspective

Emic and etic perspectives have been artificially separated for several reasons. First, the majority of measures in this chapter are primarily idiographic and projective in origin, although there are several descriptive and behavioral measures as well. They were designed to provide intensive study of an individual. Many of these measures will be especially useful when the assessment purpose is to provide a self-consistent description of the person within a cultural context or to make inferences that are congruent with personality theory. Culture-specific personality theories, however, are still few in number and not widely used for personality assessment at this time. As a result, the major use of these instruments is to provide personality description that remains close to the data and is culture-fair and ethnically responsible.

Second, the application of these measures demands more cultural knowledge on the part of assessors, simply because the measures are not ordinarily construct-derived and depend for their use on the cross-cultural validity of specific constructs. Most of these instruments will require additional development for each of the multicultural populations. Emic instruments are necessary because personality description is often limited to an array of previously determined constructs, either theoretically or empirically derived. As a result, the personality description may be incomplete or diluted to conform to the available constructs or the cultural relevance of an underlying theory.

An emic perspective can provide an approach to more veridical and enriched assessment conceptualizations of other persons by an emphasis on understanding individuals in their cultural contexts. The meanings of human action and language that are essential to understanding behavior can be provided by contextual grounding using emic measures (Mishler, 1979).

As noted above, a primary argument for developing and using emic measures for personality description is the difficulty of establishing meaning with narrow trait or behavior categories. These narrow categories represent a nomothetic search for context-free laws, using etic methods that Mishler (1979) called "context-stripping." The construction and use of such categories to identify data may render understanding and interpretation of these data more difficult (Packer, 1985). Finally, an assessment model that values collaboration (Dana, 1985a; Fischer, 1985) as a basis for client empowerment can result in the creation of personalized assessment procedures that embody an emic approach.

Issues of context, meaning, and collaboration can be minimized by the use of introspective narratives that have a sense of authenticity (Peterson, 1979) in addition to face validity. Howard (1991) makes a credible argument for scientific meaning construction through narrative or storytelling approaches. Following this reasoning, thought is considered to be story elaboration in which preferred stories represent cultural differences. Since culture is defined as a shared world view providing the interpretations that define the nature of reality and endow life with meaning, education becomes an initiation into this meaning system by providing children with the dominant stories of their cultural group. These stories constitute the subjective culture.

The life story of each individual becomes his or her identity; the relevant roles in the story are class, ethnicity, culture, and race. These roles constitute social categories for thinking about the self and decision-making with regard to behavior (Brislin, 1988). Howard (1991) describes life as the stories we live by, psychopathology as stories gone mad, and psychotherapy as exercises in story repair. These images provide powerful incentives to recognize the usefulness of emic measures.

Behavior Observation

Observation has roots in antiquity as an approach to infer nonobservable personality traits from physical appearance. Observation, categorization, and recording are the components of ethnographic study, and naturalistic observation has been favored by anthropologists. Ethnography provides a general description of the culture and, in addition, a research-specific description. The research-specific ethnographic description is similar to observation for the assessment purpose of understanding an individual.

The selection of behaviors to observe, or control, provides a constraint that permits the observer to choose the focus of an observational procedure in advance. A second source of control lies in the manner of recording whatever is observed. Recording may be by memory or using audio and/or video assistance to provide verbatim transcripts. Observation has been used for assessment during home visits or in community contexts to help prepare clients for office visits (Wyatt, 1982). Behavior observation offers a unique opportunity to examine behavior within a cultural context, although C. L. Williams (1986) has cautioned against cultural bias in the choice of what to observe, the process of observing, and the interpretation of results.

The presence of an observer will inevitably affect whatever behaviors are being observed. Whenever the cultural differences between observer and observed are marked, adaptation may occur slowly over time, if at all. Observation as a technique also requires training to ensure representativeness of the observed behavior, or ecological validity, reliability of recording/coding, and validity of the observations. These difficulties are compounded when the observations are made by a person who is not part of the culture and/or the setting being observed. For assessors who anticipate using observation in natural settings, these caveats are presented in detail elsewhere (Longabaugh, 1980).

Life History/Case Study

Life history or case study provides an opportunity for an individual to tell his or her story to another person. The primary purpose is to describe personality. The listener/recorder can put few or many constraints on the content and manner of this storytelling. If the purpose of the study is for assessment, constraints on the storytelling will be necessary in order to have data that are relevant for intervention planning in the form of diagnosis and/or a description of problems-in-living. Although case studies have historically used qualitative data presented in narrative form, quantitative data may also be included, and data analysis may also be qualitative or quantitative. The format of these constraints will vary with the assessee's cultural origin and acculturation choice. In addition, a culturally competent style of conducting the data gathering is necessary for client cooperation. To the extent that the client likes, trusts, and respects the assessor, the storytelling will come to fulfill the intended purposes of the interaction.

Assessors should be familiar with published life histories/case studies as part of the background needed for culturally competent assessment practice. For example, there are life histories collected by anthropologists from Native American tribes, including Algonquin (Leland, 1979; Popham, 1979), Chippewa (Barnouw, 1949), and Hopi (Aberle, 1951). As there are always issues of interpretation from a Eurocentric anthropological stance (Trimble & Medicine, 1976), assessors should be aware that early and recent accounts for the same tribe, whenever available, should be juxtaposed for comparison, particularly whenever changes in observer theoretical orientation have occurred over time; for a Yurok example, see Buckley (1982).

Interviews may be distinguished from life histories/case studies by their purpose. Interviews have an explicit assessment purpose and usually have a basis in previously prepared guidelines that are affected by theoretical orientation. The orientation may be neutral or ostensibly atheoretical, psychoanalytic, or social-learning. Obviously, any imposition of theoretical structure on the guidelines will have interpretive consequences. As a result, in the absence of theory that is culturally relevant, a neutral stance is preferable. Guidelines for this stance include identifying data, reason for interview, present situation, family, early memories, development, health, education, work, recreation, sexual development, marital data, self-description, and turning points in life (Sundberg, Tyler, & Taplin, 1973).

However, even these so-called neutral topics may not be neutral from the standpoint of a particular culture. It is necessary for the assessor to examine each content area against the cultural beliefs and practices regarding self-disclosure to persons outside of the family before assuming that any topic is likely to be acceptable to the assessee.

Similarly, the contents of conventional interview stages—beginning, middle, and closing—have to be considered for their cultural acceptability (Dana, 1986a). The beginning stage usually includes making contact, establishing rapport, clarifying purposes, suggesting what is expected of the client, and reducing anxiety. A middle stage ordinarily is focused on intake, problem identification, crisis alleviation, and orientation or termination in some settings. A closing stage not only signals an imminent conclusion but provides support, reassurance, a plan for the final minutes, a recap of the session, and anticipation for future services as an outcome of the interview. All of these components should be mediated by a culture-specific behavioral style. Moreover, knowledge of the culture will suggest omission or retention of components, ordering of components, and differential time allocations to each component as a function of cultural expectations.

Accounts Method

The accounts method has been described as a hybrid of ethnography, critical incidents, and the Thematic Apperception Test (TAT). In this method, there is a recording of action, intentions, and goals, using the subject as a collaborator to enrich the study of social behavior (Harré & Secord, 1972).

This method can be applied to a culturally diverse population to identify problems, adaptive and non-adaptive coping strategies, and acceptable interventions. Crucial to this process is a provision for community input to verify accuracy of data and to relate the data to outcomes that are valued by the community. Jones and Thorne (1987) present a variety of published examples in which target group members helped to develop ecologically valid questionnaires and other instruments for specific purposes. It is also feasible to obtain post-assessment narratives whenever etic/imposed etic instruments are used. Such narratives make it possible to include client perceptions of the assessment process as well as expectations for outcomes or results of assessment. Narratives thus constitute a case study method that can be used cross-culturally in a variety of ways consistent with scientist-practitioner assessment training. The accounts method provides a systematic array of logically consistent and potentially verifiable procedures to render the life history/case study a more potent and scientifically palatable approach to the study of individuals.

Methods for Studying Life Events

Life events are central to the study of development over the life span. A typology of life events includes the probability that an event will occur for a particular person, correlation of the event with chronological age, and social distribution, or whether the event occurs for few or many persons (Brim, 1980). Events that occur for many persons can be anticipated and support systems developed to buffer their effects. Obviously, many events are related to cultural beliefs and practices and to discrimination against individuals who are culturally different.

Life events have been examined as sources of diagnostic and personality data by using the Social Readjustment Rating Scale (SRRS) (Holmes & Rahe, 1967). The numbers, kinds, and severity of stressors that are experienced and perceived as stressful differ across age and ethnic groups, urban/rural life settings, and socioeconomic status. For example, 14- to 21-year-old adolescents, described as minority youths from urban poverty-level families, reported a constellation of stressful events related primarily to school and work settings. An 80-item checklist was developed for identifying stressful life events in this population (Mosley & Lex, 1990).

The Hispanic Stress Inventory (HSI) was constructed for Hispanic immigrants and Hispanic Americans on the basis of open-ended interviews (Cervantes, Padilla, & de Snyder, 1990, 1991). The HSI and criterion measures of anxiety, depression, self-esteem, competency, and somatization were administered in the preferred language, either Spanish or English, using acceptable procedures for translation. Separate HSI versions for immigrants and Hispanic Americans were prepared on the basis of differing factor structures. The HSI immigrant version had subscales for marital status, occupational/economic stress, parental stress, family/cultural conflict, and immigrant stress. The HSI U.S.-born subscales were for marital stress, occupational/economic stress, parental stress, and family-cultural conflict. Criterion-related validity was also estimated by comparisons between the HSI and the criterion measures. Alpha reliabilities ranged from .77 to .91, and test-retest coefficients were between .61 and .86.

There is also a Spanish translation of the Behavior Problem Checklist (BPC) (Hanna, Spencer, & Quay, 1981) for Cuban-American adolescents. This translation also was done using acceptable procedures. However, additional research will be required to compare the Spanish and English versions.

Native Americans may experience a unique set of stressors. Life-stress data from Rosebud Sioux people were collected by using items from the Life Experience Survey (Sarason, Johnson, & Siegel, 1978) and the Brandenberg-West Rating Scale (Brandenberg, 1978) to provide local norms for stressors (Dana, Hornby, & Hoffmann, 1984). These Sioux norms were compared with similar life-stress data for Reno-area Native Americans (Brandenberg, 1978), Miccosukee Indians, and North Carolina rural and urban Anglo-Americans (Liberman & Frank, 1980). There were distinct differences in sources of stress among the three Native American groups and in severity of stress between the Native American and Anglo-American groups.

The documentation of specific stressors and an awareness of the dimensions of perceived stress are critical for assessment of ethnic minority/refugee groups. The development of local data not only would permit major problems-in-living to be identified but could encourage the use of problem-specific, setting-specific interventions. Life events may be identified and recorded during an interview or using checklists and questionnaires. The HSI provides an example of an instrument that may be used at the present time with Hispanic-American and immigrant groups.

Picture-Story Techniques

Picture-story techniques provide another kind of structured narratives for storytelling during assessment. The use of pictures to evoke stories from non-Anglo-American persons has frequently involved the creation of culture-specific sets of pictures based on the original Murray Thematic Apperception Test (TAT) cards developed in the 1930s (Murray, 1938). These efforts have been stimulated and enriched by an early set of criteria for designing pictures that included sharpness-vagueness, incompleteness, compression or adequacy/relevance (card-pull), symbolism, contrast in visual impact, number/appropriateness of figures/objects/physical environments presented, familiarity with human figures, appropriateness and range of relationships portrayed (including basic family relationships), and range of emotional tone (Sherwood, 1957). Many of these criteria have received explicit research attention.

Anthropologists have had a primary role in the development and use of culture-specific sets of picture-story cards for studies of non-Western peoples (Barnouw, 1963, chapter 16; Spain, 1972). Their efforts have been criticized for bias introduced by use of Eurocentric personality theory (i.e., psychoanalysis), and reliance on picture-story findings alone without verification by direct observation (Mensh & Henry, 1953). Moreover, whenever groups rather than individuals are studied, there may be problems of representative sampling and the adequacy of the statistics used to construct any "basic" or "modal" personality (Cronbach, 1949).

In addition to these concerns, the lack of any consensual TAT scoring (see review by Vane, 1981) meant that each investigator has had to adopt, adapt, or construct a system for scoring and interpretation. These scoring systems typically did not represent all of the possibilities for scoring available in the pictures, nor has any of these scoring systems enjoyed the face validity of Hermann Rorschach's system. Furthermore, none of the most widely used scoring systems described in this review benefited from any attention to minority subjects in the standardization efforts. Unless a scoring system has emerged from a deliberate culture-specific stance, the outcome will be Eurocentric in origin and applicability. As a result, assessors should be cautious when using the original Murray TAT cards for clients who are not of Anglo-American origin.

Picture-story and inkblot techniques intended for cross-cultural usage should meet some of the following desiderata, although some of these recommendations may be controversial. First, the stimuli should be culturally relevant. Second, the scoring should reflect variables that are culturally important for psychopathology and/or problems-in-living. Third, normative data should be available for the intended population(s). Fourth, the interpretation of findings should make use of information available within the living contexts of intended assessees, to amplify and verify the meanings of the scoring variables. Fifth, culturally relevant personality theory should be used to ensure that the data provided by scoring variables constitute a sufficient basis for personality study.

There should also be substantive validation literature, including case studies. However, except as noted, these techniques have not generated an appreciable research literature. The same criteria will be used to examine the relative usefulness of culture-specific picture-story tests for each group and, later in this chapter, to consider inkblot techniques (Table 8-1).

TABLE 8-1 • Comparison of Major Picture-Story and Inkblot Techniques Using Culture Relevant-Desiderata

Technique	Stimuli	Scores	Norms	Context	Theory
T-TAT	Yes	No	No	No	No
TEMAS	Yes	No	Yes	Yes	No
TCB	Yes	No	No	Yes	No
Rorschach	No	Maybe	No	No	No
Exner Comprensive					
Rorschach	No	No	No	No	No
HIT	No	Maybe	Yes	No	No

African Americans

The Thompson Modification (T-TAT) is a 10-card version of the Murray TAT, with redrawings to emphasize racial characteristics (C. E. Thompson, 1949) (Table 8-1). Kagan and Lesser (1961, pp. 247–251) concluded in a review of T-TAT literature that alteration of figures alone without simultaneous alteration of backgrounds was insufficient. T-TAT research findings documented a differential response by African Americans to skin color as a stimulus. Thompson and subsequent researchers (Bailey & Green, 1977), by selecting skin color as the critical variable, chose a racial instead of a more appropriate cultural perspective (Snowden & Todman, 1982).

On the basis of this T-TAT history, the Themes Concerning Blacks Test (TCB) (R. L. Williams, 1972) was developed, with 20 charcoal drawings to depict aspects of African-American culture and lifestyles in rural and urban settings (R. L. Williams & R. C. Johnson, 1981). The scoring includes ratings for feeling tone (Eron, Terry, & Callahan, 1950) and categories for internal control, goal setting, instrumental activity, reality perception, personal responsibility, and self-confidence (R. L. Williams, 1972). These drawings and the scoring categories pull for positive or healthy content that may be culture-specific, or Afrocentric, in nature (Table 8-1). Comparisons between the TCB and the TAT on feeling tone, story length, racial attribution of pictures, and race of examiner have indicated that the two sets of pictures are generally perceived as different tests. Case studies have documented the cultural relevance of the TCB cards and provided evidence for contextual grounding of interpretations (Petty & Robinson, 1982; Terrell, 1982).

These studies have provided a sufficient database for provisional assessment use of this set of cards with African Americans. The extent to which the scoring categories are culture-relevant has not been sufficiently documented by research. Furthermore, it is not clear whether the TCB can be used with all

African Americans or only those who are Afrocentric in personal ideology and lifestyle. If the TCB is to be more widely used by assessors, normative data are necessary. Normative data would serve not only to identify themes that emerge as a consequence of the story-telling tradition in African-based culture but would indicate their interpretive significance as well (Snowden & Todman, 1982). Additional case studies would also suggest the relationship of scoring variables to African-American personality theory. The TCB cards have not been commercially published and are not readily available. Major research articles on TCB have appeared only in journals of limited circulation.

There is an additional consideration whenever any picture-story test is administered by an Anglo-American examiner. Such an examiner, particularly if he or she is not known to the assessee, often provokes caution, vagueness, and an inhibition of storytelling. These response characteristics have been called "reticence" by Snowden and Todman (1982) and are a culture-specific response to the testing situation. An example of the consequences of reticence may be found in the Seven Squares Test, an instrument developed in South Africa. Black assessees who had been coerced into test participation by their white supervisors did as little as possible. This test behavior was compared with the test behavior of white assessees and erroneously interpreted as a racial difference in intelligence (Dana, 1965; Dana & Voigt, 1962).

Asian Americans

The Murray TAT has been used with Asian Americans, beginning with an early study by Caudill (1952) on Japanese Americans, probably because of interest in limited aspects of personality using pictures of previously determined card-pull administered by English-speaking researchers. DeVos (1973) used the TAT to study instrumental and expressive social role behavior in Japan, and later studied immigrant Koreans (DeVos, 1983). Similarly, the original cards have been used with students from Hong Kong and Taiwan (Watrous & Hsu, 1972). These scattered studies have been cited here, as authors like DeVos and Hsu should be familiar to assessors because their interpretations are culturally competent.

Hispanic Americans

The TEMAS, an acronym for "tell me a story," in Spanish literally means "themes." It constitutes a unique development in terms of the above criteria (Costantino, Malgady, & Rogler, 1988b) (Table 8-1). This test was developed for children from 5 to 18 years of age, with norms to age 13, and for bilingual administration. The authors describe differences from the TAT that include personality theory and pictures of culturally relevant and gender-balanced familiar interpersonal relationships. Chromatic pictures were created to facilitate emotional expression. These pictures are of only moderate ambiguity, in order to be consistent with research findings on the relationship between personality-revealingness and stimulus ambiguity. Adaptive and maladaptive responses have been represented in bipolar affective and cognitive/interpersonal personality functions. These representations have been explicitly designed to depict antithetical or conflictual intrapersonal and interpersonal situations requiring solutions. An inquiry is used if necessary, and there is a short form available. As a result, not only is the new test culturally appropriate, but there has been an updating of the original cards and an expansion, on the basis of research, of the personality theory that produced them.

The personality functions scored are interpersonal relations, aggression, anxiety/depression, achievement motivation, delay of gratification, self-concept, sexual identity, moral judgment, and reality testing. The cognitive functions include reaction time, total time, fluency, omissions (including a total, and also omissions of main character, secondary character, event and setting), transformations (including a total, and also transformations of main character, secondary character, event and setting), conflict, sequencing, imagination, relationship, and inquiries. The use of these scoring variables represents an attempt to recapture some of the first-generation clinical psychology interpretive wisdom, as well as to provide a rich source for data that can be used in formal diagnostic labeling (Dana, 1986b). There are limited norms available for Anglo-Americans, African Americans, Puerto Ricans, and other Hispanic Americans. Highly satisfactory alpha, inter-rater, and test-retest reliabilities have been obtained. Content, construct, and criterion validation studies provide strong evidence that the test not only measures personality constructs but also can be used for screening and prediction of therapy outcomes. However, there is less consistency in measurement with native Puerto Rican and Argentine children, a finding that suggests revision of selected cards for different Hispanic populations (Costantino, Malgady, Casullo, & Castillo, 1991).

There is a parallel, non-minority version of the TEMAS pictures (Costantino, Malgady, & Rogler, 1988a). The discriminant validity of this version suggests that it is a useful screening tool for Anglo-American children in school and mental health facilities (Costantino, Malgady, & Colon, 1991).

Native Americans

Many sets of picture-story cards have been developed for Native American tribes and other indigenous groups by using Sherwood's criteria (1957). Spain (1972) described picture simplicity, concreteness, unambiguity, and cultural specificity in sets of cards for examining of value conflicts (Goldschmidt &

Edgerton, 1961) and instrumental activities (Spindler & Spindler, 1965). Although these instruments were not designed for personality assessment per se, an assessor who was interested in Wisconsin's Menomini or Alberta's Blood Indian Reserve residents could examine data representing limited personality domains with some confidence in the culture-specificity of the pictures.

Pictures are also available for other tribes. The Indian Research Project, conducted jointly by the Bureau of Indian Affairs and the University of Chicago Committee on Human Development in the early 1940s, was primarily responsible for use of a modified Murray TAT set developed by William Henry (1947). He used 12 line drawings by an Indian artist, including two pictures adapted from their originals and 10 pictures of everyday situations experienced by children. These pictures were also used with the Navajo (Leighton & Kluckhohn, 1947) and with the Hopi (L. Thompson & A. Joseph, 1944). The pictures were redrawn for the Sioux (MacGregor, 1946). Henry's interpretive system was used with the original Murray cards for Wisconsin's Ojibwa by Caudill (1949). The original TAT cards have also been used with the Flathead tribe (Bigart, 1971) and with Eskimos (Preston, 1964). A mix of original and modified cards was used with Navajo men (Goldstine & Gutmann, 1972). Original sets of pictures have been drawn for Eskimos (Parker, 1964), Northern Cheyenne children (Alexander & Anderson, 1957), and Sioux adults (Dana, 1982).

The desiderata previously described for evaluation of picture-story tests suggest that culture-specific pictures for Native Americans, although necessary and useful, are not sufficient without interpretation that is contextualized and theoretically relevant. Culture-specific pictures do exist, although most sets are not commercially available in printed form. Nonetheless, whenever assessment is done in a reservation setting, culture-specific pictures are recommended. If no picture set is available, the assessor can design pictures for the local setting and specific client problems. A local artist would be able to provide charcoal drawings, or pictures using colored inks or paints, incorporating some of the Sherwood (1957) design criteria.

However, there are no culturally appropriate scoring systems for use with these pictures. As a result, interpretation has to rely on clinical inference alone. (For an interpretive example, see Dana, 1985b, pp. 124–131.) Such interpretation should only be attempted by assessors who are familiar with the reservation cultural setting and thus have context for interpretation. Assessors should also read whatever is available on the specific tribe, especially material written by tribal members, and including ethnologies, tribal history, and history of contact with Anglo-American society. In addition, there should be familiarity with the cultural representation in biographies, contemporary novels, and poetry by Native American authors. Finally, it is recommended that assessors in Native American settings provide some inservice training for themselves in a tribal college by studying the language, healing practices, philosophy, and tribal law.

Interpretation Guidelines   There is one set of guidelines for interpretation of ostensibly pan-Indian psychological characteristics in Native American
picture-story protocols, based on use of 20 Murray cards (Monopoli, 1984). A
format for systematic analysis of central psychological characteristics in Navajo,
Hopi, and Zuni male and female adults was used with records obtained randomly
from early sources (Kaplan, 1956; Vogt, 1951) and included previously identified
traditional and acculturated subjects. The records were examined impressionisti-
cally in order to identify 15 variables. Traditional and acculturated persons were
described on the basis of contrasting data (Table 8-2).

These data also yielded a more extended summary of TAT expectations for
traditional Native Americans (Monopoli, 1984). There is an expectation for
simple and literal stories that are generally brief and limited to the reservation
world, with hero and secondary characters of equal importance. The plots, or
action sequences, are central, and character development is used primarily as a
secondary means to advance the narrative. Actions follow one another in a direct
and stylistically unadorned manner. Abrupt organizational shifts are common
and should not be interpreted as confusion or disorientation.

Monopoli also indicated that the amount and type of emotionality was
related to the economic condition of the reservation community, with a dampen-
ing of emotional experience and expressiveness under conditions of economic
impoverishment. Additionally, whenever living conditions were not impoverished, interpretations of restraint, control, and self-containment may be due to
TAT administration by an Anglo-American assessor. Further evidence for a
relationship between poverty and expressed emotionality may be found in the
optimistic and "open," emotional picture-story style of non-impoverished Flathead students for whom traditionalism was coupled with acceptance of dominant
culture religion, education, and technology (Bigart, 1971).

However, two caveats are relevant to both of these studies. First, since this
conclusion is based on experience with the achromatic Murray cards, the use of
chromatic pictures may be as stimulating for Native Americans as for other
groups, including Anglo-Americans (Johnson & Dana, 1965). There is also the
possibility of theoretical bias and stereotyping on the basis of belief in a syndrome of personality characteristics produced by the so-called culture of poverty.

Assessors should also expect few "intraceptive" comments, or attribution
of individual needs, emotions, and desires, and many "interpretive" ones, or
description by projection of content into the picture. There may be an absence of
differentiation between human and environmental details or trivial and emotion-
ally loaded events.

On the basis of these findings, the expectation would be for explication of
an unfolding interpretation of picture details rather than any grouping of picture
features to suggest a theme or emotions. The themes only emerge gradually and
in a mosaic fashion. The protocols may be highly "extraceptive" or contain
actions motivated by events external to the characters. Within a story, the char-

acters will be related by common external activities such as eating, drinking, or working rather than through interpersonal exchanges. People are identified generically as man or woman rather than father or daughter. Kinship terms, if present, refer to external events or activities that account for the description. Intraceptive content (motivation on the basis of internal needs of characters), whenever present, would be typically negative. The self-referents may include insecurity, anxiety, hostility, or deprivation, and intraceptive remarks suggest tension in interpersonal relations. Finally, Henry's "negative content" (omission and misidentification of ordinary descriptive content or relationship) would be construed as denial/refusal of the depicted emotional problem. As a result, interpersonal tension may be addressed obliquely with partial sublimation via teasing, gossiping, jealousy, petty delinquency, minor destructive acts, or cruelty to animals.

Considerable space has been devoted to one study (Monopoli, 1984) that extrapolates from the meager protocols of a few individuals in three very different tribes. However, this study crystallizes the dichotomy between traditional and acculturated individuals by using archival records. The careful case study method was preceded by comparisons of the Murray, Tomkins, and Henry scoring systems as a basis for examination of Native American TAT stories. A major reason for inclusion of these guidelines is to alert assessors to sources of confounding culture and personality in the picture-story protocols of traditional Native Americans.

Status of Picture-Story Tests

These emic instruments have a history of use for research purposes, primarily in anthropology and personality assessment. However, only the TEMAS emerges as immediately and unequivocally useful in assessment practice. The TEMAS has culture-appropriate and gender-balanced cards that were designed to stimulate affect and to project conflictual situations. As a result, the TEMAS provides pictures that are a distinct improvement over the original TAT cards. It is preferable to the TAT, Children's Apperception Test (CAT), or the Michigan Picture Test (MPT) for Hispanic-American and African-American children and adolescents. The scoring system is eclectic and derived from several theoretical approaches to personality and from TAT research history. The TEMAS has a scoring system that attempts to delineate and represent adequately the structural and content dimensions of the protocol. In fact, it is the first scoring system for a picture-story test that compares favorably with the Rorschach or the Holtzman Inkblot Test in adequacy of conceptualization, although the stimulus representation by the scores may be incomplete and the goodness-of-fit between culturally relevant theory and derived test scores is not readily apparent. The normative data are rudimentary, but comparisons are possible across several groups that are

TABLE 8-2 • *Pan-Indian Psychological Characteristics Derived from the TAT for Traditional and Acculturated Individuals*

---

1. Economic Deprivation and Physical Suffering

Traditional. Suffering reflects reservation quality-of-life. Worst fears: economic deprivation, health problems, violence.

Acculturated. Psychological phenomena linked to suffering/alienation: introversion, lack of social skills, incompatibility.

2. Loneliness/Isolation

Traditional. Linked to economic deprivation/physical suffering. Themes: parents' abandonment of children, isolation of aged/infirm, separation via murder, physical illness.

Acculturated. Linked to psychological phenomena: introversion, incompatibility, lack of social skills.

3. Interpersonal Conflict/Violence

Traditional. Teasing, joking, gossiping more acceptable for tension release than aggression/violence. Violence viewed as inevitable and experienced passively. Occurs in confused/drunken states as result of frustration or desperation.

Acculturated. Assertiveness valued but aggression not encouraged; discounted as a means of releasing tension, resolving disputes.

4. Individualistic vs. Familistic

Traditional. Familistic. Concern with maintenance of harmony in relationships. Relationships usually warm in extended family. Work as means, not end: use white goods for survival. Respect/glory to individual who shares with family/friends.

Acculturated. Motivated for personal success and material goods via competition. Family ties warm, but achievement has priority. Self-glorification/pride.

5. Time Orientation

Traditional. Present: toward happenings, action. Present behavior based on past sanctions/traditions.

Acculturated. Future: clock time, doing things on time, staying busy.

6. Reactions to Ambiguous Stimuli

Traditional. Loss of some creativity, flexibility whenever there is focus on economic deprivation. Self-protective, constricted response to stimuli: concentration on picture details.

Acculturated. If economic/quality of life issues are acceptable, responses allow for elaboration of human interactions.

7. Conception of Experience

Traditional. Sense data fundamental: sense-broad. When clear perceptual graduations cannot be made, no distinctions. For example, types of horses may be differentiated, while religious, social, or economic distinctions may be omitted.

Acculturated. Experience viewed within framework of social, political, religious abstractions. Discriminations made within realm of nontangible/abstract.

8. Action Sequence vs. Character Development

Traditional. Action: language/thought are action-oriented, verbs predominate, few references to thoughts or feelings.

Acculturated. Character development: feelings, thoughts, beliefs, ideas, attitudes predominate.

9. View of Nature

Traditional. Personalization of natural phenomena in terms of gods/spirits. Supplication to these forces reduces cosmic disequilibrium. Humans adjust to demands of nature.

Acculturated. Nature is seen as impersonal and to be mastered for human purposes.

10. View of Disease

Traditional. Attributed to activities of ghosts/witches. Treatment via ceremonies, intervention of singers/curers/medicine men.

Acculturated. Attributed to germs. Treatment via medical technology.

11. View of Morality

Traditional. Situation/tradition bound: "right" and "wrong" depend on traditions and particular social situation. Emphasize shaming or embarrassment upon discovery.

Acculturated. Absolute morality: transcends social context. Certain acts categorically "right" or "wrong," regardless of whether others are involved or view these acts. Emphasis on guilt for social control and anxiety over transgressions.

12. Average Story Length

Traditional. Brevity and conciseness reflect inward direction and non-ostentatious emotional style. [Henry (1947)—several brief sentences.]

Acculturated. Brevity and conciseness. [For comparison, Anglo-American records: Murray (1943)—300 words; Dana (1986b)—fewer than 150 words.]

13. Range of Events/Situations

Traditional. Limited, regardless of intellectual level.

Acculturated. Variety. More dependent on intelligence/creativity.

14. Alternative Actions, Choices, Solutions by Hero

Traditional. Low number.

Acculturated. Moderate to high number. Related to intelligence/creativity.

15. Afterlife Orientation

Traditional. No individual immortality. Absorption of physical, mental, spiritual being into cosmological whole.

Acculturated. Life as preparation for immortality after death.

Source: Adapted from Monopoli (1984). Author additions to original indicated in brackets.

salient in the New York City population. The TEMAS should have computerized scoring because of the relatively large number of variables. Moreover, additional published case examples are needed to relate the scoring variables to the cultural context of life experience and to theories of Hispanic-American and African-American personality. Such studies are important because the TEMAS scoring system is Western in conceptual origin. An enlarged normative basis and a continuation of the systematic research enterprise to examine validity are mandatory if the TEMAS is to become a major assessment instrument. The nature and direction of this future research agenda is not entirely clear, because the TEMAS has potential as a diagnostic instrument and/or as a means of providing personality data in a systematic fashion.

Except for the TEMAS, and perhaps the TCB, picture-story tests for minority groups appear to meet only the recommendation for culture-specific pictures. Nonetheless, the use of culturally appropriate pictures can encourage interpretations of stories within life contexts and lead to development of scoring variables that are germane to interpretation in terms of culture-relevant personality theory.

Inkblot Techniques

Inkblot techniques used cross-culturally include the original Rorschach with Klopfer or Beck scoring, the Exner Comprehensive Rorschach and the Holtzman Inkblot Test (HIT). Hermann Rorschach was aware that cultural differences were exposed in protocols, and he studied personality differences in two Swiss cantons, Bern and Appenzeller. The original Rorschach was the projective technique of choice for many early anthropologists. Typically, a small number of Rorschach protocols were collected and analyzed to form the basis for modal or basic personality studies of Native American tribes or for personality studies of individual tribal members. Many anthropologists once believed that the inkblot stimuli and the symbolism of responses were universal. The presence of a credible scoring system for inkblots provided the illusion that interpretations could be made easily within a psychoanalytic frame of reference.

However, this inkblot scoring system and the accompanying psychoanalytic personality theory were products of what Trimble and Medicine (1976) called a Eurocentric self-action model, which, together with an interaction model, has misguided the theoretical interpretations of Native American mental health research. They propose an ecosystems analysis matrix that is interdisciplinary and has various levels of analysis of objects of study.

In addition, Lindzey (1961) suggested that the cross-cultural validity of these inkblot techniques is questionable. This criticism is especially relevant for nonliterate societies and those cultures that have markedly dissimilar codifications of reality or world view (Lee, 1950). Moreover, the basic projective data may be contaminated whenever administration is accomplished with aid from an interpreter or whenever English is a second language for the assessee. In defense of the Rorschach, Lindzey also suggested that the Rorschach had an advantage over picture-story techniques because it requires less verbal facility from assessees.

With the wisdom of hindsight, it is now apparent that interpretive fiascos have occurred from using the Rorschach cross-culturally. For example, in spite of his participation in a Rorschach study documenting community perceptions of medicine men who were either true healers or quacks (Boyer, Klopfer, Brawer, & Kawai, 1964), Boyer concluded on the basis of psychoanalytic theory that one Apache medicine man had a "character disorder, with oral and phallic fixations . . . with occasional hysterical dissociations" (Klopfer & Boyer, 1961, p. 178). This Rorschach was administered with the aid of an interpreter and published verbatim, and the responses were scored accurately. However, the record was pathologized as a result of the author's belief that the scoring was cross-culturally valid and that psychoanalytic personality theory provided an acceptable framework for interpretation of the scores. Moreover, the Rorschach findings were not placed in the context of the reservation community, including the perceptions of community peers.

In my view, the published responses document a holistic view in which everything was related to everything else (e.g., Card I: "the birds of the cloud . . . an enemy in the cloud . . . giant bat . . . he resemble the traveling star" (Klopfer & Boyer, 1961, p. 171). An alternative interpretation from these responses and their scoring would be that the assessee, as a medicine man, did not distance himself in Anglo-American fashion from the blots by providing structure and careful delineation of concepts. Instead of recognizing such boundaries, he entered the inkblot stimulus and incorporated both the blot and his perception of it into an overarching cosmology. This cosmology had both historic and worldview meaning. His own origins were suffused with symbolism, and his personal experience was presented as inseparable from nature, magic, and the supernatural. As a result, a few main characteristics of the Rorschach stimulus permeated the record. Any inference concerning the presence of psychopathology from this record would be gratuitous without additional, non-test data. This study should have included as additional data the perceptions of the medicine man by community residents, in order to document his level of functioning with regard to problems-in-living and as a healer.

Another explanation for cross-cultural difficulties in Rorschach use has been suggested by Howes and DeBlassie (1989). They believe that the abbreviated Rorschach protocols with only a small number of responses from minority-group members have restricted possibilities for interpretation. They propose that attention to acculturation, norms, and interpersonal examiner effects would increase the number of responses elicited in cross-cultural Rorschach usage. It should be noted, however, that there are differences of opinion concerning the mean numbers of responses by cultural groups, with DeVos (1979) reporting a mean of 17 for Japanese, as compared with 28 to 32 for Anglo-Americans.

My own experiences with Native American and African-American protocols suggest that the number of responses increases with educational level. However, sustained and succcessful educational achievement is often related to partial adoption of a Eurocentric world view. Moreover, there is selectivity in the willingness to be cooperative with an assessment process, and bicultural or acculturated persons may simply be more willing to be scrutinized in this manner.

Considering the alternatives available at the present time, the Rorschach appears to be usable for cross-cultural assessment. This conclusion recognizes the caveats/desiderata suggested for the picture-story and inkblot techniques. However, legitimate cross-cultural uses may be limited at the present time, as the following examples suggest.

A first example is from assessment research with Chinese students in an American university (Dana, 1959). The salient Rorschach hypotheses from this study were examined explicitly within the contexts of Chinese culture (Hsu, 1948) and earlier Rorschach findings from similar populations (Abel, 1948; Abel & Hsu, 1949). Limits to cross-cultural generality of interpretations based on specific determinants were noted. Situational specificity and examiner effects on Rorschach responses were also present in these protocols. These results suggested that whenever samples of culturally different groups are assessed, their representativeness is usually unknown. As a result, several alternative hypotheses may be made for each scoring variable regarding group personality functioning. In this manner, the assessment setting and purpose, the assessor, and knowledge of the particular culture can be used to confirm or deny each hypothesis.

A second example is Rorschach interpretation that focused not on diagnosis of psychopathology but on providing accurate understanding of patient distress (Lovitt, 1984). An African-American patient's style of responding to illness was discrepant with hospital staff expectations. The Rorschach served as a vehicle to reorient staff perception.

A third example involved using a single Rorschach determinant, FM, to resolve a discrepancy between perceptions of a child's intelligence by a preschool teacher and the child's mother (Scott, 1981). Interviews with mother and teacher were supplemented by an individually administered preschool development test and Rorschach norms. The results confirmed the mother's belief; FM was the only Rorschach scoring variable suggesting above-average intellectual potential.

Exner Comprehensive Rorschach

John Exner developed the Exner Comprehensive Rorschsach as a synthesis of available scoring systems, including Beck, Klopfer, and others (Wiener-Levy & Exner, 1981). His selected scores were intended to be comprehensive in the sense of including the entire range of previous scores, ratios, percentages, and derivations. A major purpose of the Exner Comprehensive Rorschach was to provide more reliable diagnostic information. This has been done in the form of indices for schizophrenia, depression, hypervigilance (paranoia), and a suicide constellation.

However, in spite of the reliance on norms for interpretation, there are no special norms for cultural groups in this country, although there are some unpublished norms for persons in other countries. The Exner Comprehensive Rorschach is only considered scorable if there are more than 15 responses. This restriction may be helpful with Native American and African-American assessees who provide very few responses in a record that ordinarily would be over-interpreted in the original Rorschach.

Holtzman Inkblot Test (HIT)

The HIT was developed as a result of psychometric weaknesses of the Rorschach (Cronbach, 1949). To do this, 45 blots in each of two parallel forms, with two practice blots, were selected from a pool of blots constructed to represent the potentials of the inkblot stimulus. Assessees provided only one response per blot. The 22 HIT scoring variables included all of the major Rorschach scores, and more recent variables as well. These scores are narrower and more problem-focused than the original Rorschach scores. Representative norms were obtained from 15 different populations in the United States, across the age range. A computer scoring system and norms for university students from 17 countries are available (Gorham, Moseley, & Holtzman, 1968). There had been over 650 research studies by 1982 (Swartz, Reinehr, & Holtzman, 1983), and the HIT has been applied in many different cultural settings, particularly in Latin American countries (Moseley, 1967). When the data from 17 different nationalities were factor analyzed for similarity, classification by country of origin was feasible.

In a comprehensive study with Mexican children over a six-year period (Holtzman, 1988, pp. 584–587), the five previously identified factors, or clusters of scoring variables, were verified (Holtzman, 1980). The scores that compose each factor and their interpretations are presented in Table 8-3. With intelligence and other sociodemographic variables held constant, these patterns of cultural differences supported the belief in a basic set of personality variables that could be applied in different cultural settings. However, in spite of yielding the same factors, these studies showed differences in factor loadings. To my knowledge, there have been no item weighting revisions to compensate for these cross-cultural differences, as Eysenck and Eysenck (1983) recommended.

It is possible, at least theoretically, that cross-cultural inkblot factors have been identified, although the universality of Rorschach stimuli and scores has not been unequivocally demonstrated. It is important to emphasize here that the major factors are movement and color, which Hermann Rorschach hypothesized to constitute a universal introversion-extroversion system, or "Erlebnistypus." The three major dimensions of personality discovered by factor analysis of Eysenck Personality Inventory (EPI) data (Eysenck & Eysenck, 1983) include extroversion-introversion (HIT factors I and II) and psychoticism (HIT factor III). Moreover, the HIT finding of an extraversion-introversion system concurs with an interpretation of a principal-components analysis (with Varimax rotations) of factor analytic studies using the original Rorschach (Dana, Hinman, & Bolton, 1977).

Status of Inkblot Techniques

As Table 8-1 indicates, the Rorschach and the Exner Comprehensive versions are not recommended for routine cross-cultural application. However, as the examples in the discussion suggest, there are certainly specific instances,

TABLE 8-3 • *HIT Factors: Scoring Variables and Interpretations*

Variables	*Interpretations*

I.   Integration
      Movement
      Human
      Popular
      Form definitiveness
	High = Organized ideation with imaginative capacity, differentiated ego boundaries, and conventional awareness

II. (Bipolar) Color
      Shading
      Form definitiveness
	High = Overractivity
	Low = Form concern primary

III. Pathognomic verbalization
      Anxiety
      Hostility
      Movement
	Very high = Bizarreness, psychopathology
	Moderate (U.S. only) = Affective expressivity/loose imagination

IV. Location Form appropriateness	High = Perceptual differentiation and good form

V.   Reaction time
      Rejection
      Animal (reversed)
	High = inability to see things, or criticism and rejection

with acculturated assessees and for particular assessment problems, where either the original Rorschach or the Exner Comprehensive Rorschach should be useful.

The HIT, by contrast, has a long history of cross-cultural research and application, particularly with Hispanic populations. The HIT is preferable to the Rorschach for Hispanic-American populations and probably for other cultural/national groups as well. Nonetheless, in spite of presumptive evidence, the HIT scores themselves and the derived norms or factors may not completely describe personality/psychopathology in all cultural settings, as has been assumed. As a result, although the HIT may be useful for cross-cultural assessment, contextual interpretation of scores/factors, as well as culture-specific personality theory guidelines, still appear to be necessary (Diaz-Guerrero, 1977; Holtzman, Diaz-Guerrero, & Swartz, 1975).

Other Projective Techniques

Word Association and Completion Techniques

Holtzman (1980) provided an early review of these techniques, including studies of cognitive-linguistic aspects and response sets that are culture-specific for Japanese and Mexicans. However, completion techniques have not demonstrated psychological equivalence of meaning across cultures (Manaster & Havighurst, 1972). In examples cited by Holtzman, there were problems in translating stems for oral presentation from Thai to Tagalog in studies of social norms, roles, values, and expressive emotions.

An eight-item sentence completion has also been used to facilitate counseling of Mexican Americans (Ruiz, 1984). These stems could also be used for assessment, as they deal with minority and cross-cultural experiences. For example (p. 133):

"Cross-cultural experiences make me feel . . ."
"If Anglos would only . . ."
"If I could change my ethnicity, I would be . . ."

Ruiz illustrates the power of these completions in two examples and indicates the usefulness of being able to develop other stems in a group setting. Other examples have used English stems from the Incomplete Sentences Test for Japanese students in the United States (Rychlak, Mussen, & Bennett, 1957) or used stems devised in Japan for Japanese and later translated into English and Italian (Sofue, 1979). Story completion techniques have also been used to study personality, sociocultural attitudes, and values (Anderson & Anderson, 1961; Lansky, 1968; Peck, Havighurst, & Miller, 1970). This literature should be examined by assessors interested in using sentence completions.

Expressive Techniques: Drawing

Drawings of human figures have been used for estimations of intelligence and descriptions of personality, including cognitive development and values, in many cultural groups (Barnouw, 1963, pp. 347–348 and 356–360; Holtzman, 1980).

On the basis of the existing literature, it appears hazardous to apply existing scoring systems for intelligence (e.g., Harris-Goodenough) and personality (e.g., Machover) on a cross-cultural basis. There is some available cross-cultural data, especially for Native Americans, although generalization across tribes is not feasible (Dennis, 1966). The cultural specificity of meanings invoked by any of the existing "sign" approaches to scoring drawings will be be etic/imposed etic in nature. As a consequence, cross-cultural assessment using drawings should be done without formal scoring systems, or with emic scoring that has been developed with reference to whatever is being investigated and with local norms as a basis for interpretation of individual scores.

References

Abel, T. M. (1948). The Rorschach test in the study of culture. *Rorschach Research Exchange, 12*, 79–93.

Abel, T. M., & Hsu, F. L. K. (1949). Some aspects of personality of Chinese as revealed by the Rorschach test. *Rorschach Research Exchange, 13*, 285–301.

Aberle, D. F. (1951). The psychosocial analysis of a Hopi life-history. *Comparative Psychology Monographs, 21*(1), 1–135.

Alexander, T., & Anderson, R. (1957). Children in a society under stress. *Behavioral Science, 2*, 46–55.

Anderson, H. H., & Anderson, G. L. (1961). Image of the teacher by adolescent children in seven countries. *Journal of Orthopsychiatry, 31*, 481–492.

Bailey, B. E., & Green, J. (1977). Black Thematic Apperception Test stimulus material. *Journal of Personality Assessment, 41*, 25–30.

Barnouw, V. (1949). The phantasy world of a Chippewa woman. *Psychiatry, 12*, 67–76.

Barnouw, V. (1963). *Culture and personality.* Homewood, IL: Dorsey.

Bigart, J. R. (1971). Patterns of cultural change in a Salish Flathead community. *Human Organization, 30*, 229–237.

Boyer, L., Klopfer, B., Brawer, F. B., & Kawai, H. (1964). Comparisons of the shamans and pseudoshamans of the Apaches of the Mescalero Indian Reservation. *Journal of Personality Assessment, 28*, 173–180.

Brandenberg, C. E. (1978). *Validation of the Social Adjustment Rating Scale with Mexican-Americans and Native Americans* (Doctoral dissertation, University of Nevada, Reno). Reno, NV: University of Nevada.

Brim, O. G., Jr. (1980). Types of life events. *Journal of Social Issues, 36*, 148–157.

Brislin, R. W. (1988). Increasing awareness of class, ethnicity, culture, and race by expanding on students' own experiences. In I. S. Cohen (Ed.), *The G. Stanley Hall Lecture Series* (Vol. 8, pp. 137–180). Washington, DC: American Psychological Association.

Buckley, T. (1982). Menstruation and the power of Yurok women: Methods in cultural reconstruction. *American Ethnologist, 9*, 47–60.

Caudill, W. (1949). Psychological characteristics of acculturated Wisconsin Ojibwa. *American Anthropologist, 51*, 409–427.

Caudill, W. (1952). Japanese American personality and acculturation. *Genetic Psychology Monographs, 45*, 3–102.

Cervantes, R. C., Padilla, A. M., & de Snyder, N. S. (1990). Reliability and validity of the Hispanic Stress Inventory. *Hispanic Journal of Behavioral Sciences, 12*, 76–82.

Cervantes, R. C., Padilla, A. M., & de Snyder, N. S. (1991). The Hispanic Stress Inventory: A culturally relevant approach to psychosocial assessment. *Psychological Assessment: A Journal of Consulting and Clinical Psychology, 3*, 438–447.

Costantino, G., Malgady, R. G., Casullo, M. M., & Castillo, A. (1991). Cross-cultural standardization of TEMAS in three Hispanic subcultures. *Hispanic Journal of Behavioral Sciences, 13*, 48–62.

Costantino, G., Malgady, R. G., & Colon, G. (1991). *Clinical utility of TEMAS with nonminority children.* (Unpublished paper).

Costantino, G., Malgady, R. G., & Rogler, L. H. (1988a). *Technical manual: The TEMAS Thematic Apperception Test.* Los Angeles, CA: Western Psychological Services.

Costantino, G., Malgady, R. G., & Rogler, L. H. (1988b). *TEMAS (Tell-Me-A-Story) manual.* Los Angeles, CA: Western Psychological Services.

Cronbach, L. J. (1949). Statistical methods applied to Rorschach scores. *Psychological Bulletin, 46*, 393–429.

Dana, R. H. (1959). American culture and Chinese personality. *Psychological Newsletter, 10*, 314–321.

Dana, R. H. (1965). The Seven Squares Test: Phenomenon naming vs. causal naming. *Perceptual and Motor Skills, 20*, 69–70.

Dana, R. H. (1982). *Picture-story cards for Sioux/Plains Indians.* Fayetteville, AR: University of Arkansas.

Dana, R. H. (1985a). A service-delivery paradigm for personality assessment. *Journal of Personality Assessment, 49*, 598–604.

Dana, R. H. (1985b). Thematic Apperception Test (TAT). In C. S. Newmark (Ed.), *Major psychological assessment instruments* (pp. 89–134). Boston, MA: Allyn & Bacon.

Dana, R. H. (1986a). Clinical assessment. In G. S. Tryon (Ed.), *The professional practice of psychology* (pp. 69–87). Norwood, NJ: Ablex.

Dana, R. H. (1986b). Thematic Apperception Test with children and adolescents. In A. I. Rabin (Ed.), *Projective techniques for children and adolescents* (pp. 14–36). New York: Springer.

Dana, R. H., Hinman, S., & Bolton, B. (1977). Dimensions of examinees' response to the Rorschach: An empirical synthesis. *Psychological Reports, 40*, 1147–1153.

Dana, R. H., Hornby, R., & Hoffmann, T. (1984). Local norms of personality assessment for Rosebud Sioux. *White Cloud Journal, 3*(2), 17–25.

Dana, R. H., & Voigt, W. (1962). The Seven Squares Test. *Perceptual and Motor Skills, 15*, 751–753.

Dennis, W. (1966). *Group values through children's drawings.* New York: Wiley.

DeVos, G. A. (Ed.). (1973). *Socialization for achievement: The cultural psychology of the Japanese.* Berkeley, CA: University of California Press.

DeVos, G. A. (1979). A Rorschach comparison of delinquent and non-delinquent Japanese family members. *Journal of Psychological Anthropology, 2*, 425–441.

DeVos, G. A. (1983). Achievement motivation and intrafamily attitudes in immigrant Koreans. *Journal of Psychoanalytic Anthropology, 6*(1), 25–71.

Diaz-Guerrero, R. (1977). A Mexican psychology. *American Psychologist, 32*, 934–944.

Eron, L. D., Terry, D., & Callahan, R. (1950). The use of rating scales for emotional tone of Thematic Apperception Test stories. *Journal of Consulting Psychology, 17,* 473–478.

Eysenck, H. J., & Eysenck, S. B. G. (1983). Recent advances in the cross-cultural study of personality. In J. N. Butcher & C. D. Spielberger (Eds.), *Advances in personality assessment* (Vol. 2, pp. 41–69). Hillsdale, NJ: Erlbaum.

Fischer, C. T. (1985). *Individualizing psychological assessment.* Monterey, CA: Brooks-Cole.

Goldschmidt, W., & Edgerton, R. (1961). A pictorial technique for the study of values. *American Anthropologist, 63,* 26–45.

Goldstine, T., & Gutmann, D. (1972). A study of Navaho aging. *Psychiatry, 35,* 373–383.

Gorham, D. R., Moseley, E. C., & Holtzman, W. H. (1968). Norms for the computer-scored Holtzman Inkblot Technique. *Perceptual and Motor Skills, 26,* 1279–1305.

Hanna, N. C., Spencer, F. W., & Quay, H. C. (1981). The reliability and concurrent validity of the Spanish translation of the Behavior Problem Checklist. *Hispanic Journal of Behavioral Sciences, 3,* 409–414.

Harré, R., & Secord, P. F. (1972). *The exploration of social behavior.* Oxford, England: Blackwell.

Henry, W. E. (1947). The Thematic Apperception technique in the study of culture-personality relations. *Genetic Psychology Monographs, 35* (first half), 3–135.

Holmes, T. H., & Rahe, R. H. (1967). The Social Readjustment Rating Scale. *Journal of Psychosomatic Research, 11,* 213–218.

Holtzman, W. H. (1980). Projective techniques. In H. C. Triandis & J. W. Berry (Eds.), *Handbook of cross-cultural psychology: Vol. 2. Methodology* (pp. 245–278). Boston: Allyn & Bacon.

Holtzman, W. H. (1988). Beyond the Rorschach. *Journal of Personality Assessment, 52,* 578–609.

Holtzman, W. H., Diaz-Guerrero, R., & Swartz, J. D. (1975). *Personality development in two cultures.* Austin, TX: University of Texas Press.

Howard, G. S. (1991). Culture tales: A narrative approach to thinking, cross-cultural psychology, and psychotherapy. *American Psychologist, 46,* 187–197.

Howes, R. D., & DeBlassie, R. R. (1989). Modal errors in the cross-cultural use of the Rorschach. *Journal of Multicultural Counseling and Development, 17*(April), 79–84.

Hsu, F. L. K. (1948). *Under the ancestor's shadow.* New York: Columbia University Press.

Johnson, A. W., Jr., & Dana, R. H. (1965). Color on the TAT. *Journal of Projective Techniques and Personality Assessment, 29,* 178–182.

Jones, E. E., & Thorne, A. (1987). Rediscovery of the subject: Intercultural approaches to clinical assessment. *Journal of Consulting and Clinical. Psychology, 55,* 488–495.

Kagan, J., & Lesser, G. S. (1961). *Contemporary issues in thematic apperceptive methods.* Springfield, IL: Thomas.

Kaplan, B. (1956). *Primary records in culture and personality* (Vol. 1). Madison, WI: Microcard Foundation.

Klopfer, B., & Boyer, L. B. (1961). Notes on the personality structure of a North American Indian shaman: Rorschach interpretation. *Journal of Projective Techniques and Personality Assessment, 25,* 170–178.

Lansky, L. M. (1968). Story completion methods. In A. I. Rabin (Ed.), *Projective techniques in personality assessment* (pp. 290–324). New York: Springer.

Lee, D. (1950). Lineal and nonlineal codifications of reality. *Psychosomatic Medicine, 12,* 87–97.

Leighton, D., & Kluckhohn, C. (1947). *The children of the people.* Cambridge, MA: Harvard University Press.

Leland, J. (1979). Comment on "Psychocultural barriers to successful alcoholism therapy in an American Indian patient." *Journal of Studies on Alcohol, 40,* 737–742.

Liberman, D., & Frank, J. (1980). Individuals' perception of stressful life events: A comparison of Native American, rural, and urban samples using the Social Readjustment Rating Scale. *White Cloud Journal, 1,*(4), 15–19.

Lindzey, G. (1961). *Projective techniques and cross-cultural research.* New York: Appleton-Century-Crofts.

Longabaugh, R. (1980). The systematic observation of behavior in naturalistic settings. In H. C. Triandis & J. W. Berry (Eds.), *Handbook of cross-cultural psychology,* Vol. 2: Methodology (pp. 57–126). Boston, MA: Allyn & Bacon.

Lovitt, R. (1984). Rorschach interpretation in a multidisciplinary hospital setting. *Professional Psychology: Research and Practice, 15,* 244–250.

MacGregor, G. (1946). *Warriors without weapons: A study of the society and personality development of the Pine Ridge Sioux.* Chicago: University of Chicago Press.

Manaster, G. J., & Havighurst, R. J. (1972). *Cross-national research: Socio-psychological methods and problems.* Boston: Houghton Mifflin.

Mensh, I. N., & Henry, J. (1953). Direct observation and psychological tests in anthropological field work. *American Anthropologist, 55,* 461–480.

Mishler, E. G. (1979). Meaning in context: Is there any other kind? *Harvard Educational Review, 49,* 1–19.

Monopoli, J. (1984). *A culture-specific interpretation of thematic test protocols for American Indians.* Unpublished master's thesis, University of Arkansas, Fayetteville, AR.

Moseley, E. D. (1967). Multivariate comparison of seven cultures: Argentina, Colombia (Bogota), Colombia (Cartagena), Mexico, Panama, United States, and Venezuela. In C. F. Hereford & L. Natalicio (Eds.), *Aportaciones de la psicología a la investigacíon transcultural* (pp. 291–304). Mexico City: Trillas.

Mosley, J. C., & Lex, A. (1990). Identification of potentially stressful life events experienced by a population of urban minority youth. *Journal of Multicultural Counseling and Development, 18,* 118–125.

Murray, H. A. (1938). *Explorations in personality.* Cambridge, MA: Harvard University Press.

Murray, H. A. (1943). *Thematic Apperception Test manual.* Cambridge, MA: Harvard University Press.

Packer, M. J. (1985). Hermeneutic inquiry in the study of human conduct. *American Psychologist, 40,* 1081–1093.

Parker, S. (1964). Ethnic identity and acculturation in two Eskimo villages. *American Anthropologist, 66,* 325–340.

Peck, R., Havighurst, R., & Miller, K. (Eds.). (1970). *Coping styles and achievement: A cross-national study of children.* (Technical Report, Vol. I). Austin, TX: Research and Development Center for Teacher Education, University of Texas.

Peterson, D. R. (1979). Assessing interpersonal relationships in natural settings. *New Directions for Methodology of Behavioral Science, 2,* 33–54.

Petty, D., & Robinson, G. A. (1982). Common philosophical themes in the oral history and TCB content of four Black octogenarians. *Journal of Non-White Concerns, 10*(2), 57–63.

Popham, R. E. (1979). Psychocultural barriers to successful alcoholism therapy in an American Indian patient. *Journal of Studies on Alcohol, 40,* 656–676.

Preston, C. E. (1964). Psychological testing with Northwest Coast Alaskan Eskimos. *Genetic Psychology Monographs, 69,* 323–419.

Ruiz, A. S. (1984). Cross-cultural group counseling and the use of the Sentence Completion method. *Journal for Specialists in Group Work, 9,* 131–136.

Rychlak, J. F., Mussen, P. H., & Bennett, J. W. (1957). An example of the use of the Incomplete Sentence Test in applied anthropological research. *Human organization, 16(1),* 25–29.

Sarason, I. G., Johnson, J. H., & Siegel, J. M. (1978). Assessing the impact of life changes: Development of the Life Experiences Inventory. *Journal of Consulting and Clinical Psychology, 25,* 419–428.

Scott, R. (1981). FM: Clinically meaningful Rorschach index with minority children? *Psychology in the Schools, 18,* 429–433.

Sherwood, E. T. (1957). On the designing of TAT pictures, with special reference to a set for an African people assimilating Western culture. *Journal of Social Psychology, 45,* 161–190.

Snowden, L., & Todman, P. (1982). The psychological assessment of Blacks: New and needed developments. In E. E. Jones & S. J. Korchin (Eds.), *Minority mental health* (pp. 193–226). New York: Praeger.

Sofue, T. (1979). Aspects of the personality of Japanese, Americans, Italians, and Eskimos: Comparisons using the Sentence Completion Test. *Journal of Psychological Anthropology, 2,* 11–52.

Spain, D. H. (1972). On the use of projective tests for research in psychological anthropology. In F. L. K. Hsu (Ed.), *Psychological anthropology* (pp. 267–308). Cambridge, MA: Schenkman.

Spindler, G., & Spindler, L. (1965). The Instrumental Activities Inventory; A technique for the study of the psychology of acculturation. *Southwestern Journal of Anthropology, 21,* 1–23.

Sundberg, N. D., Tyler, L. E., & Taplin, J. R. (1973). *Clinical psychology: Expanding horizons.* Englewood Cliffs, NJ: Prentice-Hall.

Swartz, J. D., Reinehr, R. C., & Holtzman, W. H. (1983). *Holtzman Inkblot Technique, 1956-1982: An annotated bibliography.* Austin, TX: Hogg Foundation for Mental Health, University of Texas.

Terrell, D. L. (1982). The TCB in clinical-forensic psychological evaluation: A case study of exceptionality. *Journal of Non-White Concerns, 10*(2), 64–72.

Thompson, C. E. (1949). The Thompson modification of the Thematic Apperception Test. *Rorschach Research Exchange and Journal of Projective Techniques, 13,* 469–478.

Thompson, L., & Joseph, A. (1944). *The Hopi way.* Chicago: University of Chicago Press.

Trimble, J. E., & Medicine, B. (1976). Development of theoretical models and levels of interpretation in mental health. In J. Westermeyer (Ed.), *Anthropology and mental health: Setting a new course* (pp. 161–199). The Hague: Mouton.

Vane, J. R. (1981). The Thematic Apperception Test: A review. *Clinical Psychology Review, 1,* 319–336.

Vogt, E. Z. (1951). *Navaho veterans: A study of changing values.* Papers of the Peabody Museum of American Archaeology and Ethnology, Harvard University (Vol. 41, No. 1). (Reports of the Rimrock Project, Values Series, No. 1.)

Watrous, B., & Hsu, F. L. K. (1972). An experiment with the TAT. In F. L. K. Hsu (Ed.), *Psychological anthropology* (pp. 309–361). Cambridge, MA: Schenkman.

Wiener-Levy, D., & Exner, J. E. (1981). The Rorschach Comprehensive System: An overview. In P. McReynolds (Ed.), *Advances in Psychological Assessment* (Vol. 5, pp. 236–293). San Francisco: Jossey-Bass.

Williams, C. L. (1986). Mental health assessment of refugees. In C. L. Williams & J. Westermeyer (Eds.), *Refugee mental health in resettlement countries* (pp. 175–188). New York: Hemisphere.

Williams, R. L. (1972). *Themes Concerning Blacks.* St. Louis, MO: Williams & Associates.

Williams, R. L., & Johnson, R. C. (1981). Progress in developing Afrocentric measuring instruments. *Journal of Non-White Concerns, 9,* 3–18.

Wyatt, G. E. (1982). Sociocultural assessment of home and school visits in psychiatric evaluation. In B. A. Bass, G. E. Wyatt, & G. J. Powell (Eds.), *The Afro-American family: Assessment, treatment, and research issues* (pp. 137–151). New York: Grune & Stratton.

CHAPTER NINE

Assessment II: An Etic Perspective

Introduction

No attempt will be made to include here all available tests and measures, as was done in Chapter 8. Instead, this chapter will examine selected measures of psychopathology, personality, and intelligence from an etic perspective. It is recognized that these tests/measures represent only a small fraction of the etic/imposed etic instruments in current usage with multicultural populations. Tests/measures that have frequent usage with one or more of the populations described in this book are included. These descriptions of selected tests/measures will focus on an evaluation of their adequacy for cross-cultural usage. In general, this evaluation will follow a consistent format that includes the intended purpose of measurement, single or multimethod validation, translation adequacy (if appropriate), and construct equivalence.

The selected measures include: (a) broad-spectrum and single-construct psychopathology as diagnosed by interview schedules, rating scales/checklists, and questionnaires; (b) personality measures that their authors believe to be genuine etics; and (c) major tests of intelligence/cognitive functions. Table 9-1 lists these tests and measures by category as an introduction to separate descriptions later in this chapter. Additional information on the rationale for inclusion of specific measures will be provided in the discussion.

An Etic Perspective

Historically, an etic perspective has provided a research-oriented and empirical approach to assessment. As a result, such measures will continue to be more extensively used than emics in the immediate future, at least by professional psychologists. However, because these measures often aspire to be genuine etics

TABLE 9-1 • *Selected Tests /Measures for Specific Purposes*

Psychopathology: Broad Spectrum

Interview Schedules
Diagnostic Interview Schedule (DIS)
Present State Examination (PSE)
Schedule for Affective Disorders and Schizophrenia (SADS)
Structured Interview for DSM-III Personality Disorders (SIDP)

Tests
Minnesota Multiphasic Personality Inventory (MMPI)

Psychopathology: Single Construct

Alcohol
Alcohol Dependency Behavior Inventory (ADBI)
Alcohol Dependence Scale (ADS) (derived from the Alcohol Use Inventory)
Michigan Alcoholism Screening Test (MAST)

Anxiety
State-Trait Anxiety Inventory (STAI)

Depression
Beck Depression Inventory
Center for Epidemiologic Studies Depression Scale (CES-D)
Depression Adjective Checklist (DACL) (Chinese version)
Depression Adjective Checklist (DACL) (Spanish version)
Inventory to Diagnose Depression (IDD)
Lao Depression Inventory (LDI)
Vietnamese Depression Scale (VDS)
Zung Scale for Depression

Personality

California Psychological Inventory (CPI)
Eysenck Personality Questionnaire (EPQ)

Intelligence/Cognitive Functioning

Kaufman Assessment Battery for Children (K-ABC)
McCarthy Scales of Children's Abilities (MSCA)
Stanford-Binet Intelligence Scale
System of Multicultural Pluralistic Assessment (SOMPA)
Wechsler Intelligence Scales

---

and not imposed etics, the burden of demonstrating comparability of assessment
findings in cross-cultural test usage lies with the advocate/researcher. Cross-
cultural validation implies a demonstrated equivalence in constructs, construct
operationalization, items, and metric. As described in Chapter 6, research has

emphasized single-strategy approaches to construct validation almost exclusively, using factor analysis as the preferred methodology.

However, this quest for equivalence has been called paradoxical, since an etic methodology emphasizes similarities while obscuring cultural differences (see Draguns, 1984, pp. 45–46). To minimize the potential effects of this paradox, a multistrategy approach has been suggested by many authors. For example, Hui and Triandis (1985) recommended a proper translation first, then establishment of conceptual/functional equivalence by using a nomological network and examining internal structure congruence. A third step involves response pattern and regression methods for item and scalar equivalence. Construct studies of authoritarianism-conservatism and locus of control provide examples (Hui & Triandis, 1983; Miller, Slomczynski, & Schoenberg, 1981).

Psychopathology: Broad Spectrum

Structured Interviews: Checklists/Rating Scales

Checklists and rating scales have been used since the 1950s for description of abnormal behaviors, especially in inpatient settings by nurses, trained technicians, or service providers. They can be formatted for self-ratings by the patients themselves or by direct observer ratings of patient behaviors, and for completion by service providers on the basis of interviews. These instruments are used for diagnosis as well as for description of psychopathology. However, there are unresolved problems in the use of DSM-III for non-Anglo-Americans (Alarcon, 1983; Loring & Powell, 1988). Nonetheless, DSM-III descriptions have been used routinely as the diagnostic criteria for multicultural groups in the United States.

DSM-III criteria and the interview methods of data collection used by service providers have been reviewed for recognition and inclusion of cultural factors (López & Núñez, 1987). These authors reported that DSM-III merely mentions a potential role of culture in schizophrenic delusions and hallucinations. Similarly, the interview methods reviewed only minimally acknowledge cultural influences.

For example, the Present State Examination (PSE) (Wing, Cooper, & Sartorius, 1974) assumes that a transcultural description of disorders is feasible. Certain phenomena are believed to be universal, and clinical judgment regarding subcultural components in reaction to events is recommended. For schizophrenia, a caveat was included that specifies a requirement for two or more interview sentences in order to infer the rate of non-affective verbal hallucinations. Pathological delusions are defined as unexplained or non-shared false beliefs, and subcultural delusions are specified as idiosyncratically held only by small subgroups and include recognizable subcultural delusional states (e.g., koro, windigo, etc.).

For an additional example from López and Núñez (1987), the Schedule for Affective Disorders and Schizophrenia (SADS) (Spitzer & Endicott, 1978) does not consider shared cultural and/or religious beliefs to be delusions in any disorder. In schizophrenia, speech and thinking disturbances are not considered to be evidence for formal thought disorder if explainable on a cultural basis. In schizoaffective disorders, delusions and hallucinations occurring within a shared religious or subcultural belief system are not considered to be pathological. In major depression, bereavement is not included if all features are usually expressed under similar circumstances within the cultural reference group.

The Lifetime (L) version of the SADS was used with Hopi people by psychiatrists actively providing services to Native Americans and Alaska Natives (Manson, Shore, & Bloom, 1985). Agreement was high: 74 percent for occurrence of major diagnoses and 100 percent for major affective disorders as rated from videotapes. The SADS-L has also been used to establish criterion validity with Plains, Plateau, and Pueblo Indians (Shore, Manson, Bloom, Keepers, & Neligh, 1987). Modifications in administration procedures were suggested because patients had difficulty with subtleties in probe questions. There also appeared to be uncertain reliability of symptom recall as a result of cultural differences in time perception.

The Structured Interview of DSM-III Personality Disorders (SIDP) (Stangl, Pfohl, & Zimmerman, 1983), and the Diagnostic Interview Schedule (DIS) (Robins, Helzer, Croughan, & Ratcliff, 1981) omitted cultural references entirely (López & Núñez, 1987). Manson, Ackerson, Dick, Baron, and Fleming (1990) attempted to translate the DIS into Hopi by using standard back-translation procedures because English is the Hopi people's second language. This proved unfeasible because Hopi is an unwritten language, with at least five different orthographic systems used by anthropologists and others. As a result, in order to retain the intended DIS meanings, a sociolinguistically appropriate version approximating local English was used for portions of the DIS specific to depression, somatization disorder, and alcohol-related behavior (Manson et al., 1990). As an example of the consequences, a single DIS item combining guilt, shame, and sinfulness concepts was seen as three separate concepts by all 23 bilingual Hopi informants. Some items referring to sexual behavior were deleted due to cultural prohibitions.

The DIS has also been translated into Spanish, using initial translation and back-translation by Mexican Americans, and expert review by Puerto Rican and Cuban consultants (Karno, Burnam, Escobar, Hough, & Eaton, 1983). Pretesting of both versions was done with Mexican-American outpatients. A second draft was then prepared. Finally, a third draft was prepared, incorporating suggestions from independent outside reviewers. Subsequent research has supported the use of the Spanish DIS in Puerto Rico (Canino et al., 1987) and Los Angeles

(Burnam, Hough, Karno, Escobar, & Telles, 1987). The factorial stability of DIS scales has been demonstrated with Mexican Americans, Puerto Ricans, and Anglo-Americans (Rubio-Stipec, Shrout, Bird, Canino, & Bravo, 1989; Shrout, Bird, Canino, & Bravo, 1989).

Bilingual patients whose first language is Spanish are more reticent to disclose information in English and provide more paralinguistic responses that are misinterpreted as psychopathology (Marcos & Trujillo, 1981), so a strong argument can be made for use of a Spanish version of the DIS within the United States. There has been concern, nonetheless, with DIS translations, and concurrent validation of the English version has been attempted by using comparisons of Mexican-American and Anglo-American schizophrenics (Randolph, Escobar, Paz, & Forsythe, 1985). This study examined instances in which the DIS was not in agreement with a clinician and concluded that Hispanics were more open in talking about their symptoms, at least with Hispanic health professionals, perhaps as a result of respeto.

Evaluation   The PSE or the SADS are the preferred structured interviews when used by clinicians who are experienced with culturally diverse clients. It should be noted that this recommendation is based primarily on reliable analyses of materials and manuals. However, the Spanish translation of the DIS appears to be a better choice for bilingual Hispanic Americans whose first language is Spanish; there is continuing research on use of the SADS and DIS in Native American languages. Whenever these structured interviews are used for formal diagnosis, it should be recognized that the DSM was developed for Anglo-Americans.

Self-Report Tests: MMPI

The Minnesota Multiphasic Personality Inventory (Hathaway & McKinley, 1967) was constructed to assess major dimensions of psychopathology and thereby provide information necessary for diagnosis. In addition, the MMPI is used for personality description in conjunction with diagnosis. The MMPI has the widest international application of any test (Butcher, 1985), with translations into 150 languages and applications in 50 countries. Many of these translations were not controlled for accuracy or linguistic equivalence (Williams, 1986). Using the same scales, the items were often translated without revisions, restandardizations, or validity checks of the translated form (Guthrie & Lonner, 1986). As a result, these literal translations, even with back-translation to English and adequate test-retest reliability, would not necessarily have equivalent meaning. As a consequence, inferences from cross-cultural profile comparisons are not feasible, and the interpretations of profiles/configurations used in the United States will not be useful, for example, in Chile (Rissetti & Maltes, 1985).

Similarly, in a Japanese example, only two of the three factors obtained were similar to the factor structure in the United States (Clark, 1985).

Since the MMPI scales were constructed independently without use of factor analysis, there are limitations to the use of replicatory factor analysis to establish cross-cultural validity. Ben-Porath (1990) described research attempts to approximate cross-cultural validity. Factorial studies have assessed scale inter-correlations and discovered loadings on two major factors (general psychopathology and repression) and two additional minor factors (social introversion and masculinity-femininity), although the presence of overlapping items among the scales may be largely responsible for these factors. As a result, replicatory factor analysis demonstrating cross-cultural stability of these factors does not necessarily contribute to the construct validity of the scales.

Ben-Porath (1990) suggested ideal and compromise solutions. An optimal solution would be to factor analyze all MMPI items. Agreement on the item structure in the United States would then precede cross-cultural applications. As there have been contradictory results for factor analyses of all items, a compromise solution would be to factor analyze the items by scale, using intra- and inter-scale comparisons to ensure maintenance of the internal structure. Replicatory factor analyses on both single-scale elevations and configural relations would then be done.

However, the research enterprise to examine cross-cultural validity has been done primarily in countries outside of the United States, including Spanish translations for use in Chile, Cuba, Mexico, and Spain. At least two Spanish versions of the MMPI are available for use in the United States, one published by the Psychological Corporation (Bernal et al., 1959) and the García-Azan translation published by the University of Minnesota Press. Nonetheless, the English version generally has been used with bilingual Hispanics in the United States, although Hispanic-American psychologists have been aware that inappropriate MMPI use has occurred as a result. For example, A. M. Padilla and R. A. Ruiz (1975) indicated that norms for Hispanic Americans differ from Anglo-American norms. Moreover, deviations from Hispanic norms should not always be interpreted in terms of psychopathology or personality constructs, but instead may represent culture-specific response styles.

A Puerto Rican translation of the MMPI, by Diaz, Nogueras, & Draguns (1984) will be described in detail. Translation was done by the first two authors, with independent back-translation into English identifying 24 items that were different from the original. The committee approach was used to reconcile Spanish and English versions of these items. At this point, two Spanish-language professors in Puerto Rico provided an independent evaluation for linguistic appropriateness, which included correctness, accuracy, and readability. Six Puerto Rican psychologists then identified 19 items whose content and psychological meaning required modification. After all of these preliminary analyses were completed, reliability coefficients with K-corrected scales were moderate to high. Scale intercorrelations were generally consistent with the English version. This culture-specific MMPI was then administered to normal, clinical, and migrant students who had returned to Puerto Rico from the mainland. There were significant differences on K and seven clinical scales between students in the clinical and normal groups. Return migrants were different from both normal and clinical students.

An earlier Spanish MMPI translation (reported in Butcher & Pancheri, 1976) has little empirical evidence for validity. This translation appears to be markedly different from the English form, because the mean scores on F, K, Hs, Pa, and Sc scales have been found to be significantly elevated in a small sample of Hispanic-American high school women (Fuller & Maloney, 1984). Similarly, the Puerto Rican translation (Bernal et al., 1959) has been found to be different from Mexican-American Spanish in El Paso. As a result, the words and phrases sufficiently different to affect interpretation were changed and the revised version was administered to bilinguals, who back-translated it into an English version that was said to be virtually identical with the original MMPI (Whitworth, 1988). This El Paso MMPI provides significantly higher scores for Mexican Americans than did the English version.

Evaluation The MMPI professional community has not assumed that cross-cultural validation is required for MMPI use with Asian-American, Hispanic-American, and Native American populations in this country. Similarly, African Americans are assumed to be identical to Anglo-Americans in MMPI-1 item responses whenever matching has occurred using major sociodemographic variables (Dahlstrom, Lachar, & Dahlstrom, 1986; Johnson & Brems, 1990). This logic has been coupled with use of small and nonrepresentative samples of these ethnic minority groups in the MMPI-2 standardization (Butcher, Dahlstrom, Tellegen, & Kaemmer, 1989) and in research on the MMPI-1 (Butcher, Braswell, & Raney, 1983). The argument made here is somewhat similar but includes some caveats.

First, the MMPI can only be used if the assessee is similar on relevant demographic variables to the standardization population and speaks English as a first language. In practice, this means upper-middle-class status as defined by occupation, education, and a world view that is essentially Anglo-American. Whenever Spanish, for example, is the first language, clients generally will prefer the assessment process to be in Spanish. However, it is not entirely clear which Spanish version is to be preferred, although it appears that Puerto Ricans should be administered the Puerto Rican version and Mexican Americans should also receive a local translation specific to their area.

Second, for African Americans, even if there is similarity on the relevant demographic variables, an additional issue concerns the presence of an active engagement with Afrocentric identity formation. The use of moderator variables to determine similarity to the Anglo-American standardization population and norms is mandatory. However, this recommendation only addresses Afrocentric identity and still leaves open the question of possible racial bias. In the absence of Afrocentricity, underinterpretation of MMPI profiles, especially of F, 8, and 9, continues to be an appropriate recourse, as the issue of racial bias remains unsettled (Gynther, 1989).

Third, if the assessee is not African American but is an ethnic minority person of other origins, it is mandatory to use moderator variables prior to assessment whenever there are reasonable grounds for believing that the assessee may have a relatively intact cultural identity that has Asian, Hispanic, or Native American origins. For example, immigrants and refugees may be presumed to have a relatively intact cultural identity, but a third-generation Japanese American may have very little residual Japanese culture, and a third-generation Chinese American may speak Chinese as a first language and/or have a pan-Asian identity formation.

Fourth, the MMPI is the most frequently used instrument by the Indian Health Service (Silk-Walker, Walker, & Kivlahan, 1988). Its utility for screening purposes with Native Americans is unknown, and tribe-specific norms are rare (McAndrew & Ceertsma, 1964). Nonetheless, there are tribe-specific norms available, for example, for the Colville Reservation and ten reserves in the Ontario region north of Lake Superior (Charles, 1988; LaDue, 1982).

Of course, these issues need to be examined by research designed to demonstrate the empirical correlates for scale elevations and configurations for clearly defined groups of ethnic minority persons. Only as a result of such research can the MMPI-1 or MMPI-2 be applied with cultural appropriateness to members of ethnic/racial minorities in this country.

Psychopathology: Single Construct

Alcohol

Alcohol abuse and alcohol dependence are worldwide problems. In the United States, approximately one-third of the population have been heavy drinkers; 10 percent of the people consumed 50 percent of the alcohol (Department of Health and Human Services [DHHS], 1983). There is wide variation among racial/ethnic groups in patterns of alcohol use, and factors that promote, maintain, or diminish drinking problems in these groups have not been systemically identified (Lex, 1987).

Although lifetime prevalence rates do not differ in comparisons of African Americans and Anglo-Americans (Robins et al., 1984), African-American men may be at relatively reduced risk with age, in spite of familial history (Russell, Cooper, & Frone, 1990); African-American women are more frequently abstainers, and Anglo-American women are heavier drinkers (Herd, 1988). Asian-

American groups consume less alcohol than Anglo-Americans (Akutsu, Sue, Zane, & Nakamura, 1989) because of physiological reactions and attitudes. Asian groups also differ from one another in alcohol consumption, with the lowest rates for Chinese Americans (Chi, Kitano, & Lubben, 1988). Hispanic-American men, except for Cuban Americans, use more alcohol than the general population (Page, Rio, Sweeney, & MacKay, 1985). However, there are differences in values and beliefs that contribute to differences in normative drinking practices among different Hispanic-American groups (Caetano, 1989), as well as differences due to generation and degree of acculturation (Gilbert, 1987).

For Native Americans, there has been more limited incidence data and overreporting of "events" rather than "cases" or persons involved in these "events" (Silk-Walker et al., 1988). However, Silk-Walker and colleagues concluded that not only were alcoholism percentage rates for Native Americans at least twice the rates in the dominant Anglo-American society, but that higher rates of relapse, recidivism, cirrhosis, accidents, suicide, and homicide were typical.

This section will focus on instruments for description and/or diagnosis of alcoholism. Many self-report instruments have been used with the general population (Davidson, 1987). Three measures will be described that have been used with ethnic/minority populations. These are the Alcohol Dependence Scale (ADS) (factorially derived from the earlier Alcohol Use Inventory), the Michigan Alcoholism Screening Test (MAST), and an Alcohol Dependency Behavior Inventory (ADBI).

The ADS is a 25-item self-report scale that measures behaviors linked to reports of compulsive drinking, loss of control, and physical/perceptual disturbances associated with withdrawal. A separation is made between primary alcohol-related dependence and the resulting alcohol-related disabilities, in accord with DSM-III-R. Silk-Walker and colleagues (1988) reported a history of studies with Native Americans, using the Alcohol Use Inventory, that suggested tribe-specific patterns as well as differences from other ethnic groups.

The MAST contains 25 items to assess drinking behavior, negative consequences of drinking, and help-seeking efforts (Selzer, 1971). The MAST has been described as the most commonly used first-generational scale (Davidson, 1987). A short form, the BMAST (Pokorny, Miller, & Kaplan, 1972), modified by omission of the first two questions, has been used for screening Native Americans in a Seattle study (Silk-Walker et al., 1988).

The ADBI contains 36 items and was designed to tap for frequencies in Native Americans of four symptom categories—dependency, physical ailments, interpersonal relationships, and economic functioning (Peniston & Burns, 1980). Clinically defined alcoholics and non-alcoholics from tribes served by Indian Health Service hospitals and clinics in Arizona, Nevada, and Utah were differentiated. The scale had high 30-day test-retest reliability, and nondrinkers and moderate, heavy, and abusive drinkers were quantitatively distinguished.

Evaluation The multidimensional nature of alcohol use and abuse has been recognized by the existence of 15 psychometrically independent first-order factors (Wanberg & Horn, 1983). The ADS, MAST, and ADBI have provided data that suggest a limited usefulness for descriptive purposes. The evidence of intragroup and intergroup differences not only in usage but in attitudes toward alcohol and alcohol intervention indicates that new or revised instruments should be multidimensional, designed to assess attitudes, values, and beliefs as well as behaviors.

Anxiety

The State-Trait Anxiety Inventory (STAI) was developed to provide brief self-report measures of state anxiety (e.g., tension, apprehension, nervousness) and trait anxiety (e.g., description of feelings that were unaffected by stress and stable over time) (Spielberger, 1976). The STAI and a companion test, the State-Trait Anxiety Inventory for Children (STAIC) have been used in over 3,000 studies. Moreover, these instruments have been translated into more than 40 languages and dialects, including Cambodian, Chinese, Japanese, Korean, Laotian, Spanish, and Vietnamese (Spielberger, 1989). In general, these translations have followed procedures to maximize idiomatic rather than literal equivalency by examination of a large item pool for consistency (Holtzman, 1976; Spielberger & Sharma, 1976). For example, two or more items may share the same literal translation, or an item may have several different acceptable translations. As a result, synonyms or key words and alternative wordings are found that convey the underlying meaning. Similarly, an idiomatic equivalent may express the feeling connotation more faithfully than a literal translation.

The translated STAI, called IDARE (Inventário de Ansiedad Rasgo-Estado) was intended to provide general measures of anxiety for Hispanics. The preliminary translations were done by Cuban and Puerto Rican psychologists (Spielberger & Sharma, 1976) and evaluated by professionals from eight Latin American countries. The final item sets were found to have comparable test-retest reliability in Texas and Puerto Rican samples. There was evidence that Texas subjects may have experienced more stress, due to less familiarity with personality tests than other groups, and therefore had higher scores on the A-state items in both versions.

The STAIC has been translated into Spanish (IDAREN—Inventário de Ansiedad Rasgo-Estado para Niños) and validated in Puerto Rico (Bauermeister, Forestieri, & Spielberger, 1976). The IDAREN approach differed by having Puerto Rican professors compile word lists for presence and absence of anxiety. These lists were given to bilingual translators, translator-evaluators who were psychologists, and elementary school teachers. Agreement on items between translators and evaluators was required. The preliminary IDAREN was given on two occasions, and interviews were conducted after the second administration to clarify the children's interpretation of items. Concurrent validity was determined by administration of the IDARE and IDAREN to students. Construct validation was approached by test-retest, using standard and simulated test instructions.

The IDAREN yielded a two-factor solution in Spain by using the principal components method (Gomez-Fernandez & Spielberger, 1990). The Spanish children had higher mean scores than Puerto Rican or mainland samples of children who completed the STAIC. These differences were explained on the basis of special characteristics in the Spanish group (i.e., children of immigrants, moderate bilinguality, etc.).

As the STAI measures were factorially derived, confirmatory factor analysis has been appropriately used to indicate that there are no major differences in numbers of factors, loadings, and errors for men and women in the United States (Benson & Tippets, 1990). As a result, the subscales are believed to have the same meaning for both genders. Nonetheless, gender differences in the patterns of factor loadings have been found in German and Dutch studies. Factor structure invariance may therefore be questionable. However, in addition to cultural differences, there were differences in the populations studied and methodology.

Evaluation The STAI and STAIC translations into Spanish for adults and children have been carefully done, using procedures for demonstrating idiomatic equivalence. Although these tests are primarily intended for Spanish or Latin American assessees, they should also be used in this country whenever the first language of a client is not English. However, due to possible differences in interpretation of scores, local norms are required, especially for Mexican Americans. Additional research is required to clarify determinants of anxiety that result from age, gender, social class, and culture, using innovative designs that permit stress effects to be measured without endangering the research participants (as in Diaz-Guerrero, 1990).

Depression

Depression has been a frequent illness, symptom or problem-in-living, and mood for many persons throughout recorded human history. It has become clear in recent years that neurotransmitters and a set of hormones are implicated in depression. In addition, however, there are cultural differences in mood, symptom, and the expression of somatic complaints instead of affect change. In spite of numerous prevalence/incidence studies, there is no accepted cross-cultural epidemiological research strategy, although Marsella (1987) has suggested that it is necessary to use both Western and indigenous definitions of illness and sick roles, and similar case identification and sampling methods, as well as symptom frequencies, severity, and duration baselines. Symptom patterns should be derived by using multivariate analysis rather than a priori diagnostic categories (Marsella, Sartorius, Jablensky, & Fenton, 1985).

In the United States, depression as symptom has been measured by a variety of self-report measures and rating scales that sample symptoms of the Western depression syndrome; many of these instruments have been translated for cross-cultural application and applied in the United States in both English and translated versions. These instruments sample complaints that may be somatic, cognitive, existential, affective, and/or interpersonal in nature.

The remainder of this section will discuss the use of several scales to measure depression. First, the Center for Epidemiologic Studies Depression Scale (CES-D), in English and Spanish versions, is included because it has been applied to several different groups. Second, the Inventory to Diagnose Depression (IDD) will be described. Third, separate sections will be devoted to assessment of depression in Asian Americans and Hispanic Americans, using a variety of instruments. Finally, there is an evaluation of the literature for assessment practice.

CES-D   The CES-D is 20-item self-report measure of present levels of cognitive, affective, and behavioral components of depression, constructed for use in community surveys of depression. It was developed from an item pool representing previously validated depression scales and does not include some somatic features or total symptom duration contained in DSM-III. The CES-D has adequate psychometric properties, including reliability, and validity for measurement of depressive symptomatology (Devins & Orme, 1985). Four factors have been identified—depressed affect, positive affect, somatic and retarded activity, and interpersonal factors—for both Anglo-Americans and African Americans (Radloff, 1977). The CES-D has been used in a variety of studies with different ethnic populations, especially Mexican Americans, and has been found to be equally reliable for all groups (Roberts, 1980).

A Seattle-area sampling yielded Asian Americans of Chinese, Japanese, Korean, and Filipino cultural origins who differed in their CES-D factor loadings from one another and from Anglo-Americans (Kuo, 1984). These persons were examined by interviewers who were matched to respondents in ethnicity and language fluency, although it not stated whether the CES-D was administered in translation or in English. This study suggested that the CES-D did provide an adequate item pool for use with an Asian-American population.

The CES-D has been used in a Bureau of Indian Affairs boarding school with Native American adolescents representing five Southwestern tribes (Manson et al., 1990). Factor analysis yielded a three-factor solution. The dimensional structure differed from Anglo-American adults, and confirmatory factor analyses are necessary. The cutoff score of 16 used with Anglo-American adults results in a high false-positive rate and thus overpathologizes this population.

The CES-D has been used in studies with Mexican Americans in English and Spanish versions (Golding, Aneshensel, & Hough, 1991; Ring & Marquis, 1991; Salgado de Snyder, 1987; Vega, Kolody, Valle, & Hough, 1986). Some of these studies used bilingual interviewers with respondents who chose either Spanish, English, or both, and instrument formats that allowed easy language switching (Golding, 1990; Golding & Burnam, 1990). Confirmatory factor analysis suggests that the Spanish and English versions of the CES-D measure a similar underlying depression construct in Mexican Americans and Anglo-Americans (Golding & Aneshensel, 1989). However, further CES-D research is necessary, due to large differences in symptom levels between Puerto Ricans, Cuban Americans, and Mexican Americans (Moscicki, Rae, Regier, & Locke, 1987). The CES-D has consistent reliability and dimensionality and is able to detect depression among Anglo-Americans and Mexican-origin persons, regardless of language dominance. Nonetheless, the ability of the CES-D to discriminate between clinical depression and no clinical depression has been questioned (Roberts, Vernon, & Rhoades, 1989).

Inventory to Diagnose Depression (IDD) The IDD was designed as a replacement for the CES-D and other depression measures that have not fully encompassed the criteria for major depressive disorder. The IDD has high internal consistency, few gender effects, and prevalence rates that correspond to epidemiological studies more closely than the CES-D for Native American adolescents (Ackerson, Dick, Manson, & Baron, 1990). The IDD not only operationalizes all DSM-III diagnostic criteria but allows for an ongoing summary of severity of symptoms (Zimmerman, Coryell, Corenthal, & Wilson, 1986).

Asian Americans The symptoms of depression are known to vary in different Asian cultures, as the CES-D survey indicated (Kuo, 1984). Marsella, Kinsie, and Gordon (1973) reported predominantly existential complaints in Japanese and Anglo-Americans, although the Japanese also presented interpersonal symptoms. Chinese and Japanese both had cognitive symptoms, but the Chinese characteristically presented somatic complaints and did not present helplessness, guilt, hopelessness, or suicidal thoughts, which have high frequencies for Anglo-Americans (Kleinman, 1982). Since Asian-American groups would be expected to differ among themselves and from Anglo-Americans on depressive symptomatology, existing Western measures of depression may not prove to be sufficiently comprehensive.

However, a Chinese translation of the Beck Depression Inventory measures depression in Hong Kong, and there is evidence for construct equivalence with the English version (Shek, 1990, 1991). The Depression Adjective Checklist (DACL), consisting of 34 adjectives that connote some degree of depression or elation (Lubin, 1981), has been translated into Chinese, Hebrew, and Spanish versions (Lubin & Collins, 1985). The Chinese translation of the DACL has adequate reliability and concurrent validity (Chu, Lubin, & Sue, 1984).

New depression measures have also been constructed as a result of the idiosyncratic expression of depression among Asian-American populations. Two examples of such measures for Vietnamese and Laotians will be described. In a model study of how to approximate construct equivalence, Kinsie and colleagues (1982) found initially that items from existing instruments were not adequate to measure depression in Vietnamese. Moreover, the usual redundancy and contextualization of symptoms within social interactions was not reproduced in existing instruments. Somatic complaints, especially of headache, backache, and insomnia, would typically be reported at an early stage, with reluctance to be self-revealing and suppression of other symptoms.

Several stages were used in the development of a Vietnamese Depression Scale (VDS), as back-translation of an existing instrument had not been successful. An independent list of relevant words to describe depression was prepared by bilingual mental health workers. This list was examined by a review panel, using paired comparisons for nine taxonomic groupings. A three-degree format was used, because internal constraints in item presentation are not self-evident in this population. Next, this content was translated to English with back-translation to Vietnamese, using idioms. At this point, items were prepared to assess relevant somatic symptoms, depressed mood, and symptoms unrelated to lowered mood/Western depression. A pretest provided additional descriptive statements to clarify these items, as well as to eliminate some items. Finally, a 45-item preliminary Vietnamese Depression Scale was validated by using matched community and clinic samples.

By way of contrast, a Lao Depression Inventory (LDI) has been developed in a more spartan manner (Davidson-Muskin & Golden, 1989). The items were compiled from existing inventories with assistance from four refugee Lao mental health workers who also provided consultation on the interview modification for format and content. No details of the translation process are provided. Approximately one-half of a Laotian area population participated in a DSM-III-based clinical interview, to provide a diagnosis of depressed or non-depressed. Administration of the 164 LDI items in English and Lao also occurred at this time. These items were examined statistically to create a 30-item scale for optimal discrimination between depressed and nondepressed groups.

Hispanic Americans   The DACL has also been translated into Spanish. The translations of adjectives from several state lists did not use back-translation but relied instead on empirical findings to demonstrate "a high degree of similarity between the Spanish and English versions" (Lubin, Millham, & Paredes, 1980, p. 52). Other standard measures were also translated in this study, presumably in a similar manner, and used to suggest concurrent validity. Subsequent studies have suggested similarity between small groups of Mexicans and Mexican Americans on the Spanish version and bilinguals on both Spanish and English versions (Lubin, Masten, & Rinck, 1986; Lubin, Natalicio, & Seever, 1985).

Evaluation   The CES-D has been widely used with the populations considered in this book. Rather than being limited to depressive symptomatology, it provides an index for emotional distress, a more general construct (Devins & Orme, 1985). There is a Spanish version, although it is not clear at this time whether or not the two versions have construct equivalence, or even whether or not the CES-D should be used in clinical assessment.

Other depression measures have been used, including the Beck Depression Inventory, Chinese and Spanish versions of the Depression Adjective Checklist, and a Spanish version of the Zung Depression Scale. There is insufficient research to suggest that construct equivalence has been obtained in translations, and the necessary research to demonstrate utility in clinical settings has not been done.

None of the above instruments adequately reflect the expected rates for major depressive disorder suggested by epidemiological studies, due to inadequate representation of diagnostic criteria. As a result, scale score transformations have been used for diagnosis. The Inventory to Diagnose Depression was developed to overcome these shortcomings and appears to be a psychometrically sound instrument.

Personality

California Psychological Inventory (CPI)

The CPI consists of 480 items in 18 standard scales, including three scales to suggest response validity in normal persons (Gough, 1957). The scales were derived from a commonsense grouping of items. As a result, the constructs are readily understood and have face validity. The test was designed to identify persons who may be described similarly and to suggest what their behaviors will be in particular contexts. The standard scales were designed to measure "folk concepts" or culturally universal character dispositions that emerge from interpersonal behavior and social living. No cross-cultural linguistic studies were used to select the CPI traits. Contrasted groups and item homogeneity strategies were used for scale development. Three structural scales for interpersonal self-presentation or role, intrapersonal values or character, and psychological competence were developed more recently from the same item pool (Gough, 1987).

Many cross-cultural studies of the inventory scales have been done subsequent to construction. There are German, Italian, and Spanish editions and translations into Chinese and other languages. The presence of a CPI construct in another culture does not imply invariance, as the functional relationships between a construct and specific behavioral outcomes would be expected to differ in each culture. Factor analyses have generally indicated five factors (Megargee, 1972; C. H. Reynolds & R. C. Nichols, 1977), but replicatory factor analyses have found similar structures only recently. However, as Ben-Porath (1990) has indicated, the factor structure of each scale should be studied independently in replicatory factor analyses of empirically keyed instruments.

CPI item differences between Anglo-Americans and African Americans have been reported and interpreted as cultural differences (Cross & Burger, 1982). Similarly, there were differential response patterns between urban Native Americans, primarily Chippewa, who were matched for socioeconomic backgrounds and employment histories (Davis, Hoffman, & Nelson, 1990). Only a relatively small number of studies on the major cultural groups were reported in a handbook (Megargee, 1972).

Evaluation The scale development for the CPI originated in the late 1940s. As a result, sophisticated after-the-fact research has compensated for psychometric deficiencies in construction. There is evidence that this imposed ctic instrument warrants further research. At the present time, however, in spite of a cross-cultural literature suggesting applications, cross-cultural invariance is neither apparent nor believed to be necessary by CPI proponents. The CPI may be used with the multicultural populations described in this book if the logic of construction, measurement purposes, and limitations are understood.

Eysenck Personality Questionnaire (EPQ)

The EPQ was developed from earlier inventories over a relatively long time, to provide validation for a theory of human nature by using measures of the major dimensions of personality. The EPQ has 90 items and scales for extroversion-introversion (E), neuroticism-stability (N), psychoticism-superego control (P), and a lie or fakability dimension (L) (H. J. Eysenck & S. B. G. Eysenck, 1975). Three of these four scales have resulted in separate and unrelated factors for E, N, and P. Construct validity has been extensively investigated, using behavioral, therapeutic, and other criteria. Following translation, the cross-cultural research strategy has been to replicate these factors and then to assess factorial similarity separately for males and females as evidence of cross-cultural stability. There has been almost an entire replication of factors in 25 countries, including Hong Kong, Japan, Spain, and Puerto Rico, although the methodology for assessing factor similarity has been questioned (Barrett, 1986). Cross-cultural comparisons were conducted after replicatory factor analysis had demonstrated an invariant factorial structure. However, these findings have been challenged as method artifact (Bijnen, Van der Net, & Poortinga, 1986). As a result, the cross-cultural invariance of the EPQ should to be examined by a variety of methods for assessing underlying factorial similarity (Ben-Porath, 1990).

One example of EPQ use with Cree and Ojibway women alcoholics participating in Alcoholics Anonymous (AA), detoxification, and an extended treatment group has practical assessment implications (Gade & Hurlburt, 1985). The women in the detoxification and extended treatment groups were high on P or tough-mindedness, all groups were high on N or emotionality, and AA group members were more extroverted. These group scores were used to develop a rationale for treatment expectations that was in accord with previous research.

Evaluation The EPQ provides a model of the factorial approach to cross-cultural personality measurement by using what the Eysencks believe to be a genuine etic instrument. They have provided strong technical arguments for using the EPQ instead of the MMPI (H. J. Eysenck & S. B. G. Eysenck, 1982; H. J. Eysenck & S. B. G. Eysenck, 1983). The EPQ has been developed in a rigorous manner that demonstrates construct equivalence. Nonetheless, the major value of the EPQ may be in cross-cultural research predicated on genetic bias and parsimonious personality theory rather than its application as an instrument for personality study in clinical assessment settings.

Intelligence/Cognitive Functioning

The use of intelligence testing for school placement and diagnosis of mental retardation has resulted in protests from racial/cultural minority spokespersons, some of whom have had recourse to litigation. The major sources of potential bias are assessors who represent the dominant Anglo-American culture and instruments that have been constructed from a Eurocentric psychometric paradigm (see Chapter 6).

E. R. Padilla and G. E. Wyatt (1983) have described options for intelligence testing on the basis of these problems. The most frequently used option has been to use existing tests without modification. However, existing tests have also been used with direct modifications or with translation and subsequent modifications. Culture-free tests, learning-potential assessment devices, development of culture-specific tests, and criterion sampling are other options. Culture-free tests, including the Porteus Mazes, Raven Progressive Matrices, Davis-Ells Test, and Cattell Culture-Free Test, rely on perceptual skills and are influenced by cultural factors (Wyatt, 1982). The learning-potential paradigm uses pretest, coaching, and post-test and thus incorporates initial ability and effects of learning (Budhoff, 1969). Culture-specific tests such as the Black Intelligence Test of Cultural Homogeneity mistakenly assume minimal within-group variance and are not considered to be intelligence tests per se or to have predictive validity for educational purposes (Wyatt, 1982). Criterion sampling entails analyses of on-the-job performance, includes changes in what has been learned, and measures competence as a cluster of life outcomes (McClelland, 1973)

This section will summarize the usage and usefulness of the Wechsler and Stanford-Binet tests with multicultural populations. In addition, two alternative tests will be described: the System of Multicultural Pluralistic Assessment (SOMPA), and the Kaufman Assessment Battery for Children (K-ABC). The McCarthy Scales of Children's Abilities (MSCA) are also included because of the existence of a translated version and research use with Hispanic Americans.

Standard Intelligence Tests

The assessment of intelligence with standardized tests was compromised initially by homogeneous (Anglo-American) standardization samples, bias, and credibility of the deficit hypothesis among professional psychologists. Subsequent restandardizations have included some minority persons in sampling procedures that generally provide for representation on only a small number of sociodemographic variables. The standard tests are the Stanford-Binet (SB-L-M and SB-R) and the Wechsler tests, which include the Wechsler Scale of Adult Intelligence (WAIS and WAIS-R), the Wechsler Intelligence Scale for Children (WISC and WISC-R), and the Wechsler Preschool and Primary Scale of Intelligence (WPPSI).

Research has generally indicated that group differences can be minimized by careful matching on sociodemographic variables. Over time, cultural bias in intelligence tests has become difficult to document, even with more sophisticated psychometrics for reliability, including item analysis or regression lines for academic prediction (Naglieri & Hill, 1986; Ross-Reynolds & Reschly, 1983; Sandoval, 1979). However, factor invariance across cultural groups has not been demonstrated for Wechsler tests used with Hispanic Americans (McShane & Cook, 1985) or Native Americans (Dana, 1984). Not only do the numbers of factors differ for Native Americans, but the factorial structure patterns also differ. These tests apparently measure the construct of intelligence somewhat differently across cultural groups.

The fact that these tests do not have construct equivalence for all groups, or cross-cultural construct validity, has been only infrequently emphasized, in spite of a societal focus on obtained group differences in scores. In the absence of such validity, assessors can influence the outcome of individual intelligence testing by taking more time to develop rapport and by using race- or gender-appropriate examiners with children (Hanley & Barclay, 1979; Terrell & Terrell, 1983). However, even if such assessment practices do increase obtained IQ scores, these practices cannot substitute for acceptable evidence of cross-cultural construct validity in standard intelligence tests and do violence to the standardized procedures for administration.

Translations of the WISC-R and SB into Spanish have not resolved the problems due to archaisms, contaminations, Anglicisms, and alterations of word meanings. Moreover, African-American children who speak dialects may be penalized by standard English (E. R. Padilla & G. E. Wyatt, 1983), although this conclusion remains controversial. As a result, English versions of standard intelligence tests have been administered whenever possible, often with the aid of interpreters.

There is only one study that suggests the limitations of present practices and offers some suggestions for more responsible assessment of intelligence with Hispanic Americans whose primary language is Spanish or who are bilingual. López and Romero (1988) presented a comparison of the Escala de Inteligencia Wechsler para Adultos (EIWA) (a 1965 Puerto Rican WAIS adaptation) and the WAIS. These authors were not satisfied with improvisations with WAIS administration gleaned from their own experience. Test administration in English, with language difficulty taken into account during interpretation, has obscured any estimate of performance interference as a result of use of the assessee's second language. An administration of Performance subtests, without the Verbal subtests, using Spanish or English instructions also has limited legitimate inferences. Use of an interpreter, or referring test administration to a Spanish speaker, is ethically dubious, since an on-the-spot translation is invalid and unreliable.

As a second phase, López and Núñez (1987) examined EIWA and WAIS manuals, scoring sheets, materials, test item content, and administration and scoring procedures for both versions. Almost complete reliability occurred for the results of these procedures, and major differences were found between the two tests, especially in the conversion of raw to scale scores. Minor differences occurred in administration, content, and scoring of all subtests except digit span and object assembly. These authors concluded that EIWA and WAIS (or WAIS-R) scores would not be comparable. The EIWA standardization subjects were more rural, had less education, and were in low-social-status jobs. As a result, Spanish-speaking assessors should use the EIWA instead of WAIS-R only with language-impaired, rural, and minimally educated clients. Moreover, users of test data should be informed of the specific data used for interpretations of cognitive functioning and the normative data used as a basis for these interpretations. Furthermore, Wechsler tests should not be used as the sole source of data with Spanish-speaking clients. Either the English or Spanish test versions can be used appropriately if these recommendations are followed. These suggestions would apply also to Chinese translations of the WISC and WAIS that appear to have factorial equivalence (Chan, 1984; Dai, Ryan, Paolo, & Harrington, 1991). By extrapolation, these suggestions are also applicable to other Asian-American populations, especially Southeast Asian refugees.

System of Multicultural Pluralistic Assessment (SOMPA)

The SOMPA consists of an assemblage of assessment devices deriving from beliefs in Eurocentric cultural bias and cultural pluralism (Mercer & Lewis, 1978). The SOMPA uses information obtained from the child and from the child's mother/guardian. Information from the mother is used to complete the Sociocultural Scales, the Adaptive Behavior Inventory for Children (ABIC), and the Health History Inventories. Information from the child includes the WISC-R and Bender-Gestalt Test, Physical Dexterity Tasks, height and weight, and visual and auditory acuity. The Sociocultural Scales and the WISC-R are used together to derive an Estimated Learning Potential (ELP). The test authors believe that the WISC-R represents what the child has learned about the dominant Anglo-American culture, and the ELP contributes information on sociocultural status (e.g., family size and structure, socioeconomic status, and urban acculturation). As a result, two sets of norms interface simultaneously—the child's own reference group and Anglo-American norms. ELPs have been described as WISC-R scores with sociocultural scores partialed out by multiple regression, or corrected for differential learning opportunities. ELP scores are used to estimate real intelligence and to make inferences regarding learning potential. It is assumed that there are no genetic differences in learning potential and that it is necessary to have sociocultural knowledge to infer learning potential.

Reviews of the SOMPA in the *Ninth Mental Measurements Yearbook* by recognized experts have generally been scathing. The gist of these criticisms is that test bias as defined by mean score differences among groups cannot be substantiated for the Wechsler tests (C. R. Reynolds & S. M. Kaiser, 1990). Reviewers have been dismayed that neither the advocacy stance nor the test construction procedures accord with expectations for Eurocentric psychometrics. However, criticisms of greater importance have been levied: the SOMPA confuses culture and social environment, and construct equivalence, a more usual approach to cross-cultural validity, has not been examined (Snowden & Todman, 1982).

The SOMPA has been used with Hispanic-American children who are primarily of Mexican origin or descent, although there are also norms for Puerto Rican children (Ramos-McKay, undated). The Puerto Rican norms were developed in Connecticut; the Spanish version of the WISC-R had been prepared for Cuban children in Florida (Martin, 1977). This Connecticut population was significantly different from the earlier Spanish-language version SOMPA norms.

Kaufman Assessment Battery for Children (K-ABC)

The K-ABC was developed for psychological and clinical assessment; educational evaluation of exceptional children, including the learning-disabled; educational planning and placement; *minority group assessment;* preschool assessment; and limited neuropsychological assessment (Kaufman, Kamphaus, & Kaufman, 1985; Merz, 1984). There are 16 subtests that include mental processing, or problem-solving in novel situations, and achievement, or factual, school-related knowledge. Aggregated global scores are available for Sequential Processing, Simultaneous Processing, Mental Processing Composite, Achievement, and Nonverbal. Sequential Processing refers to a stepwise process, and Simultaneous Processing involves the organization/integration of many stimuli at the same time. Mental Processing is designed to tap fluid intelligence in the form of adaptable and flexible behavior in response to unfamiliar problems. The Nonverbal Scale is a short form of the Mental Processing Scale using subtests administered in pantomime with motoric responses. It should be noted that a microcomputer program is available to enter and analyze the K-ABC data.

Standardization on more than 2000 children was accomplished in 24 states, using census population reports to stratify sampling within each age group by gender, geographic region, community size, socioeconomic status, race/ethnic group, and educational placement in regular or special classes. Normalized standard scores, percentile ranks and stanines, age and grade equivalents for arithmetic and reading, and sociocultural percentile ranks were prepared. Norming for the K-ABC was more psychometrically sophisticated in numbers and selection of relevant demographic variables for race/ethnic group membership than was done for the standard intelligence tests constructed at an earlier date.

The reliability data for K-ABC compared favorably with data from the standard Wechsler tests for children. In addition, as an aid in interpretation, standard errors of measurement were used to create confidence intervals for obtained scores in the form of bands around the obtained scores. Validity was reported in 43 studies, with equal attention to construct and criterion-related validity. Construct validity included developmental changes, internal consistency, convergent and discriminant validation, and correlations with other tests, in addition to factor analysis.

The ethnic group differences between Hispanic-American or African-American children and Anglo-American children were less than the IQ differences obtained on WISC-R. Moreover, the level of parental education contributed more to ethnic group versus Anglo-American differences than did ethnicity per se. Clearly, the intention of the K-ABC is to be useful for children who have limited English language proficiency or speak a nonstandard English dialect. Moreover, a Spanish version is also available, and comparisons of test performances on both versions for Hispanic-American children with limited English language are feasible.

McCarthy Scales of Children's Abilities (MSCA)

The MSCA consists of verbal, perceptual-performance, quantitative, memory, and motor measures (McCarthy, 1972). Standardization used a nationally representative sampling that was stratified for age, gender, color, geographic region, occupation of father, and informally for urban-rural residence. The MSCA has been criticized for having a relatively low ceiling; few items for social competence, judgment, or abstract verbal reasoning; and factor analytic support primarily for three scales (Keith, 1985).

A Spanish version of the MSCA developed by Valencia (1988) has been used extensively in research with normal Hispanic-American children. These studies suggest that the scales may be used with Mexican-American children who are English-speaking, although interpretations should be made with caution. The scales should not be used with Puerto Rican children without additional research.

Evaluation   Although the evidence indicates that standard tests of intelligence are not psychometrically biased, this conclusion refers primarily to comparisons of carefully matched groups. An absence of significant group differences under research conditions does not necessarily imply that use of these tests with their original norms will not have pejorative outcomes for many individuals. The potential impact of the assessor's gender, linguistic proficiency, cultural identity, and style of test administration, especially with children, should never be minimized.

Test administration procedures, test materials, and a culturally appropriate style of interaction should be presented in the assessee's first language whenever the primary concern is an estimate of intelligence or cognitive functioning. This means that translations of standard tests are imperative. These translations should include Spanish versions, at least for Mexican Americans and Puerto Ricans, and versions for refugees from Southeast Asia, especially Chinese, Vietnamese, Laotians, and Hmong. The current practice of using translators, either to administer English tests in Asian languages or to provide a basis of communication between assessor and client, is probably unethical, as López and Romero (1988) have suggested is the case for Spanish-speakers. These authors have provided the most cogent set of recommendations available at present.

The existing Wechsler tests will continue to be used in the foreseeable future, with and without translations, especially by professional psychologists in school and mental health settings. As a result, assessors must be aware that these tests do not have factor invariance across groups, notably for Hispanic Americans and Native Americans. Factor invariance will vary with acculturation and first language for Hispanic Americans. For Native Americans, however, who have resisted destruction of their unique world view as a group, there appears to be relatively greater factorial consistency across tribes, as well as a factorial pattern that is distinctively different from the Anglo-American pattern. The Wechsler tests will not readily be displaced for multicultural populations by the MSCA and similar tests. Although the MSCA is a promising instrument with an available Spanish version, it still lacks sufficient research development.

The SOMPA has a history of usefulness in school settings in both English and Spanish versions. Nonetheless, the criticism that this test battery has social-environmental rather than cultural origins emphasizes the compensatory, and probably time-limited, nature of the SOMPA. Compensation does imply the value judgment that minority group children have to have special norms to perform as well as Anglo-American children on the WISC-R, the criterion measure of intelligence.

The K-ABC has several distinct advantages over the other tests in this section. First, it shares with the SOMPA an intention for use with multicultural populations that was expressed prior to test construction and that served as a guide in test development. Second, unlike the SOMPA, the K-ABC used conventional psychometric methodology to develop test scores to measure human intelligence, as suggested by multidisciplinary research literature. The result ensured comparability in measurement of multicultural populations with earlier standard intelligence tests, but using scores with different origins. Third, these scores included a known processing dichotomy, sequential versus simultaneous, and a measure based on nonverbal administration and response. Fourth, the test construction methodology included more sophisticated selection and sampling of demographic variables and, as a result, probably further reduced IQ differences between groups. Fifth, the construct validation studies included a variety of methods in addition to factor analysis, as recommended for unequivocal cross-cultural validity.

The continued use of intelligence tests that provide for a rank-ordering of persons against an Anglo-American criterion must be recognized as part of a societal demand for acculturation and acceptance of Anglo-American standards. This demand can only be modified or changed by political decisions that result from realignments of power following shifts in the population composition during the next century. In the interim, however, the use of these tests should be on the basis of the current multicultural research literature, an appreciation/understanding of multicultural clients, and consistent use of appropriate social interaction styles, including first languages.

References

Ackerson, L. M., Dick, R. W., Manson, S. M., & Baron, A. E. (1990). Properties of the Inventory to Diagnose Depression in American Indian adolescents. *Journal of the American Academy of Child and Adolescent Psychiatry, 29,* 601–607.

Akutsu, P. D., Sue, S., Zane, N. W., & Nakamura, C. Y. (1989). Ethnic differences in alcohol consumption among Asians and Caucasians in the United States. *Journal of Studies on Alcohol, 50,* 261–267.

Alarcon, R. D. (1983). A Latin American perspective on DSM-III. *American Journal of Psychiatry, 140,* 102–105.

Barrett, P. (1986). Factor comparison: An examination of three methods. *Personality and Individual Differences, 7,* 327–340.

Bauermeister, J. J., Forestieri, B. V., & Spielberger, C. D. (1976). Development and validation of the Spanish form of the State-Trait Anxiety Inventory for Children (IDAREN). In C. D. Spielberger & R. Diaz-Guerrero (Eds.), *Cross-cultural anxiety* (Vol. 1, pp. 69–85). Washington, DC: Hemisphere.

Ben-Porath, Y. S. (1990). Cross-cultural assessment of personality: The case for replicatory factor analysis. In J. N. Butcher & C. D. Spielberger (Eds.), *Advances in personality assessment* (Vol. 8, pp. 27–48). Hillsdale, NJ: Erlbaum.

Benson, J., & Tippets, E. (1990). Confirmatory factor analysis of the Test Anxiety Inventory. In C. D. Spielberger & R. Diaz-Guerrero (Eds.), *Cross-cultural anxiety* (Vol. 4, pp. 149–156). New York: Hemisphere.

Bernal, A., Colon, A., Fernandez, E., Mena, A., Torres, A., & Torres, E. (1959). *Inventario Multifacetico de la Personalidad.* Translation of the Minnesota Multiphasic Personality Inventory. New York: Psychological Corporation.

Bijnen, E. I., Van der Net, T. Z. J., & Poortinga, Y. H. (1986). On cross-cultural comparative studies with the Eysenck Personality Questionnaire. *Journal of Cross-Cultural Psychology, 17,* 3–16.

Budhoff, M. (1969). Learning potential: A supplementary procedure for assessing the ability to reason. *Seminars in Psychiatry, 1,* 278–290.

Burnam, M. A., Hough, R. L., Karno, M., Escobar, J. I., & Telles, C. A. (1987). Acculturation and lifetime prevalence of psychiatric disorders among Mexican Americans in Los Angeles. *Journal of Health and Social Behavior, 28,* 89–102.

Butcher, J. N. (1985). Current developments in MMPI use: An international perspective. In J. N. Butcher & C. D. Spielberger (Eds.), *Advances in personality assessment* (Vol. 4, pp. 83–94). Hillsdale, NJ: Erlbaum.

Butcher, J. N., Braswell, L., & Raney, D. (1983). A cross-cultural comparison of American Indian, Black, and White inpatients on the MMPI and presenting symptoms. *Journal of Consulting and Clinical Psychology, 51,* 587–594.

Butcher, J. N., Dahlstrom, W. G., Tellegen, A., & Kaemmer, B. (1989). *Manual for the restandardized Minnesota Multiphasic Personality Inventory: MMPI-2. An administrative and interpretive guide.* Minneapolis, MN: University of Minnesota Press.

Butcher, J. N., & Pancheri, P. (1976). *A handbook of cross-national MMPI research.* Minneapolis, MN: University of Minnesota Press.

Caetano, R. (1989). Differences in alcohol use between Mexican Americans in Texas and California. *Hispanic Journal of Behavioral Sciences, 11,* 58–69.

Canino, G. J., Bird, H. R., Shrout, P. E., Rubio-Stipec, M., Bravo, M., Martinez, R., Sesman, M., Guzman, A., Guevara Costas, L. M., & Costas, H. (1987). The Spanish Diagnostic Interview Schedule. *Archives of General Psychiatry, 44,* 720–726.

Chan, D. W. (1984). Factor analysis of the HK-WISC at 11 age levels between 5 and 15 years. *Journal of Consulting and Clinical Psychology, 52,* 482–483.

Charles, K. (1988). *Culture specific MMPI norms for a sample of Northern Ontario Indians.* Unpublished master's thesis, Lakehead University, Thunder Bay, Ontario, Canada.

Chi, I., Kitano, H., & Lubben, J. E. (1988). Male Chinese drinking behavior in Los Angeles. *Journal of Studies on Alcohol, 49,* 21–25.

Chu, C. R. L., Lubin, B., & Sue, S. (1984). Reliability and validity of the Chinese Depression Adjective Check Lists. *Journal of Clinical Psychology, 40,* 1409–1413.

Clark, L. A. (1985). A consolidated version of the MMPI in Japan. In J. N. Butcher & C. D. Spielberger (Eds.), *Advances in personality assessment* (Vol. 4, pp. 95–130). Hillsdale, NJ: Erlbaum.

Cross, D. T., & Burger, G. (1982). Ethnicity as a variable in responses to California Psychological Inventory items. *Journal of Personality Assessment, 46,* 153–159.

Dahlstrom, W. G., Lachar, D., & Dahlstrom, L. E. (1986). *MMPI Patterns of American minorities*. Minneapolis, MN: University of Minnesota Press.

Dai, X., Ryan, J. J., Paolo, A. M., & Harrington, R. G. (1991). Sex differences on the Wechsler Adult Intelligence Scale—Revised for China. *Psychological Assessment: A Journal of Consulting and Clinical Psychology, 3*, 282–284.

Dana, R. H. (1984). Intelligence testing of American Indian children: Sidesteps in quest of ethnical practice. *White Cloud Journal, 3*(3), 35–43.

Davidson, R. (1987). Assessment of the alcohol dependence syndrome: A review of self-report screening questionnaires. *British Journal of Clinical Psychology, 26*, 243–255.

Davidson-Muskin, M. B., & Golden, C. (1989). Lao Depression Inventory. *Journal of Personality Assessment, 53*, 161–168.

Davis, G. L., Hoffman, R. G., & Nelson, K. S. (1990). Differences between Native Americans and Whites on the California Psychological Inventory. *Psychological Assessment: A Journal of Consulting and Clinical Psychology, 2*, 238–242.

Department of Health and Human Services. (1983). *Fifth report to the U. S. Congress on alcohol and health*. Washington, DC: U.S. Government Printing Office.

Devins, G. M., & Orme, C. M. (1985). Center for Epidemiologic Studies Depression Scale. In D. J. Keyser & R. C. Sweetland (Eds.), *Test critiques* (Vol. 2, pp. 144–160). Kansas City, MO: Test Corporation of America.

Diaz, J. O. P., Nogueras, J. A., & Draguns, J. (1984). MMPI (Spanish translation) in Puerto Rican adolescents: Preliminary data on reliability and validity. *Hispanic Journal of Behavioral Science, 6*(2), 179–189.

Diaz-Guerrero, R. (1990). Gender and social class determinants of anxiety in the Mexican culture. In C. D. Spielberger & R. Diaz-Guerrero (Eds.), *Cross-cultural anxiety* (Vol. 4, pp. 3–10). New York: Hemisphere.

Draguns, J. G. (1984). Assessing mental health and disorders across cultures. In P. B. Pedersen, N. Sartorius, & A. J. Marsella (Eds.), *Mental health services: The cross-cultural context* (pp. 31–58). Beverly Hills, CA: Sage.

Eysenck, H. J., & Eysenck, S. B. G. (1975). *Manual for the Eysenck Personality Questionnaire*. San Diego, CA: Educational and Industrial Testing Service.

Eysenck, H. J., & Eysenck, S. B. G. (1982). Culture and personality abnormalities. In I. Al-Issa (Ed.), *Culture and psychopathology* (pp. 277–308). Baltimore, MD: University Park Press.

Eysenck, H. J., & Eysenck, S. B. G. (1983). Recent advances in the cross-cultural study of personality. In J. G. Butcher & C. D. Spielberger (Eds.), *Advances in personality assessment* (Vol. 2, pp. 41–69). Hillsdale, NJ: Erlbaum.

Fuller, C. G., & Maloney, H. N., Jr. (1984). A comparison of English and Spanish (Núñez) translations of the MMPI. *Journal of Personality Assessment, 48*, 130–131.

Gade, E., & Hurlburt, G. (1985). Personality characteristics of female American Indian alcoholics: Implications for counseling. *Journal of Multicultural Counseling and Development, 13*, 170–175.

Gilbert, M. J. (1987). Alcohol consumption patterns in immigrant and later generation Mexican American women. *Hispanic Journal of Behavioral Sciences, 9*, 299–311.

Golding, J. M. (1990). Division of household labor, strain, and depressive symptoms among Mexican Americans and non-Hispanic whites. *Psychology of Women Quarterly, 14*, 103–117.

Golding, J. M., & Aneshensel, C. S. (1989). Factor structure of the Center for Epidemiologic Studies Depression Scale among Mexican Americans and non-Hispanic whites. *Psychological Assessment: A Journal of Consulting and Clinical Psychology, 1*, 163–168.

Golding, J. M., Aneshensel, C. S., & Hough, R. L. (1991). Responses to depression scale items among Mexican-Americans and non-Hispanic Americans. *Journal of Clinical Psychology, 47*, 61–75.

Golding, J. M., & Burnam, M. A. (1990). Immigration, stress, and depressive symptoms in a Mexican-American community. *Journal of Nervous and Mental Disease, 178*, 161–171.

Gómez-Fernández, D. E., & Spielberger, C. D. (1990). Assessment of anxiety in Spanish elementary school children. In C. D. Spielberger & R. Diaz-Guerrero (Eds.), *Cross-cultural anxiety* (Vol. 4, pp. 193–203). New York: Hemisphere.

Gough, H. G. (1957). *A manual for the California Psychological Inventory.* Palo Alto, CA: Consulting Psychologists Press.

Gough, H. G. (1987). *California Psychological Inventory Administrators Guide.* Palo Alto, CA: Consulting Psychologists Press.

Guthrie, G. M., & Lonner, W. J. (1986). Assessment of personality and psychopathology. In W. J. Lonner & J. W. Berry (Eds.), *Field methods in cross-cultural research* (Vol. 8, Cross-Cultural Research and Methodology Series, pp. 231–264). Beverly Hills, CA: Sage.

Gynther, M. D. (1989). MMPI comparisons of Blacks and Whites: A review and commentary. *Journal of Clinical Psychology, 45*, 878–883.

Hanley, J. H., & Barclay, A. G. (1979). Sensitivity of the WISC and WISC-R to subject and examiner variables. *Journal of Black Psychology, 5*, 79–84.

Hathaway, S. R., & McKinley, J. C. (1967). *The Minnesota Multiphasic Personality Inventory.* New York: Psychological Corporation.

Herd, D. (1988). Drinking by Black and White women: Results from a national survey. *Social Problems, 35*, 493–505.

Holtzman, W. H. (1976). Critique of research on anxiety across cultures. In C. D. Spielberger & R. Diaz-Guerrero (Eds.), *Cross-cultural anxiety* (Vol.1, pp. 175–187). Washington, DC: Hemisphere.

Hui, C. H., & Triandis, H. C. (1983). Multistrategy approach to cross-cultural research; The case of locus of control. *Journal of Cross-Cultural Psychology, 14*, 65–83.

Hui, C. H., & Triandis, H. C. (1985). Measurement of cross-cultural psychology: A review and comparison of strategies. *Journal of Cross-Cultural Psychology, 16*, 131–152.

Johnson, M. E., & Brems, C. (1990). Psychiatric inpatient MMPI profiles: An exploration for potential racial bias. *Journal of Counseling Psychology, 37*, 213–215.

Karno, M., Burnam, A., Escobar, J. I., Hough, R. L., & Eaton, W. W. (1983). Development of the Spanish-language version of the National Institute of Mental Health Diagnostic Interview Schedule. *Archives of General Psychiatry, 40*, 1183–1188.

Kaufman, A. S., Kamphaus, R. W., & Kaufman, N. L. (1985). New directions in intelligence testing: The Kaufman Assessment Battery for Children (K-ABC). In B. B. Wolman (Ed.), *Handbook of intelligence: Theories, measurements, and applications* (pp. 663–698). New York: Wiley.

Keith, T. Z. (1985). McCarthy Scales of Children's Abilities. In D. J. Keyser & R. C. Sweetland (Eds.), *Test Critiques* (Vol. 4, pp. 394–399). Kansas City, MO: Test Corporation of America.

Kinsie, J. D., Manson, S. M., Vinh, D. T., Tolan, N. T., Anh, B., & Pho, T. N. (1982). Development and validation of a Vietnamese-language depression rating scale. *American Journal of Psychiatry, 139*, 1276–1281.

Kleinman, A. (1982). Neurasthenia and depression: A study of somatization and culture in China. *Culture, Medicine, and Psychiatry, 6*, 117–190.

Kuo, W. H. (1984). Prevalence of depression among Asian-Americans. *Journal of Nervous and Mental Disease, 172*, 449–457.

LaDue, R. A. (1982). *Standardization of the Minnesota Multiphasic Personality Inventory for the Colville Indian reservation.* (Doctoral dissertation, Washington State University, 1982). *Dissertation Abstracts International, 43,* 3033B.

Lex, B. W. (1987). Review of alcohol problems in ethnic minority groups. *Journal of Consulting and Clinical Psychology, 55,* 293–300.

López, S., & Núñez, J. A. (1987). Cultural factors considered in selected diagnostic criteria and interview schedules. *Journal of Abnormal Psychology, 96,* 270–272.

López, S., & Romero, A. (1988). Assessing the intellectual functioning of Spanish-speaking adults: Comparison of the EIWA and the WAIS. *Professional Psychology: Research and Practice, 19,* 263–270.

Loring, M., & Powell, B. (1988). Gender, race, and DSM-III: A study of the objectivity of psychiatric diagnostic behavior. *Journal of Health and Human Behavior, 29,* 1–22.

Lubin, B. (1981). *Depression Adjective Check Lists: Manual. 1981 edition.* San Diego, CA: EDITS.

Lubin, B., & Collins, J. F. (1985). Depression Adjective Check Lists: Spanish, Hebrew, Chinese and English versions. *Journal of Clinical Psychology, 41,* 213–217.

Lubin, B., Masten, W. G., & Rinck, C. M. (1986). Comparison of Mexican and Mexican American college students on the Spanish (American) version of the Depression Adjective Check List. *Hispanic Journal of Behavioral Sciences, 8*(2), 173–178.

Lubin, B., Millham, J., & Paredes, F. (1980). Spanish language versions of the Depression Adjective Check Lists. *Hispanic Journal of Behavioral Sciences, 2*(1), 51–57,

Lubin, B., Natalicio, N., & Seever, M. (1985). Performance of bilingual subjects on Spanish and English versions of the Depression Adjective Check Lists. *Journal of Clinical Psychology, 41,* 218–219.

Manson, S. M., Ackerson, L. M., Dick, R. W., Baron, A. E., & Fleming, C. M. (1990). Depressive symptoms among American Indian adolescents: Psychometric characteristics of the Center for Epidemiologic Studies Depression Scale (CES-D). *Psychological Assessment: A Journal of Consulting and Clinical Psychology, 2,* 231–257.

Manson, S. M., Shore, J. H., & Bloom, J. D. (1985). The depressive experience in American Indian communities: A challenge for psychiatric theory and diagnosis. In A. Kleinman & B. Good (Eds.), *Culture and depression: Studies in the anthropology and cross-cultural psychiatry of affect and disorder* (pp. 331–368). Berkeley, CA: University of California Press.

Marcos, L. R., & Trujillo, M. R. (1981). Culture, language and communicative behavior: The psychiatric examination of Spanish-Americans. In R. P. Duran (Ed.), *Latino language and communication behavior* (pp. 187–194). Newark, NJ: Ablex.

Marsella, A. J. (1987). The measurement of depressive experience and disorder across cultures. In A. J. Marsella, R. M. A. Hirschfeld, & M. M. Katz (Eds.), *The measurement of depression* (pp. 376–397). New York: Guilford.

Marsella, A. J., Kinsie, D., & Gordon, P. (1973). Ethnic variations in the expression of depression. *Journal of Cross-Cultural Psychology, 4,* 435–458.

Marsella, A. J., Sartorius, N., Jablensky, A., & Fenton, F. R. (1985). Cross-cultural studies of depressive disorders: An overview. In A. Kleinman & B. Good (Eds.), *Culture and depression: Studies in the anthropology and cross-cultural psychology of affect and disorder* (pp. 299–324). Berkeley, CA: University of California Press.

Martin, P. C. (1977). *A Spanish translation, adaptation, and standardization of the Wechsler Intelligence Scale for Children–Revised.* Unpublished doctoral dissertation, University of Miami, Miami, FL.

McAndrew, C., & Ceertsma, R. H. (1964). A critique of alcoholism scales derived from the MMPI. *Quarterly Journal of Alcohol Studies, 25,* 68–73.

McCarthy, D. (1972). *Manual for the McCarthy Scales of Children's Abilities.* New York: Psychological Corporation.

McClelland, D. C. (1973). Testing for competence rather than "intelligence." *American Psychologist, 28,* 1–14.

McShane, D., & Cook, V. J. (1985). Transcultural intellectual assessment: Performance by Hispanics on the Wechsler scales. In B. B. Wolman (Ed.), *Handbook of intelligence: Theories, measurements, and applications* (pp. 737–785). New York: Wiley.

Megargee, E. (1972). *The California Psychological Inventory handbook.* San Francisco: Jossey-Bass.

Mercer, J., & Lewis, J. (1978). *System of Multicultural Pluralistic Assessment.* New York: Psychological Corporation.

Merz, W. R. (1984). Review of the Kaufman Assessment Battery for Children. In D. J. Keyser & R. C. Sweetland (Eds.), *Test Critiques* (Vol. 1, pp. 393–405). Kansas City, MO: Test Corporation of America.

Miller, J., Slomczynski, L. M., & Schoenberg, R. J. (1981). Assessing comparability of measurement in cross-national research: Authoritarianism-conservatism in different socio-cultural settings. *Social Psychology Quarterly, 44,* 178–191.

Moscicki, E. K., Rae, D., Regier, D. A., & Locke, B. Z. (1987). The Hispanic Health and Nutrition Examination Survey: Depression among Mexican Americans, Cuban Americans, Puerto Ricans. In M. Gaviria & J. D. Arana (Eds.), *Health and behavior: Research agenda for Hispanics* (pp. 145–159). Chicago, IL: University of Illinois Press.

Naglieri, J. A., & Hill, D. S. (1986). Comparison of WISC-R and K-ABC regression lines for academic prediction with Black and White students. *Journal of Clinical Child Psychology, 15,* 352–355.

Padilla, A. M., & Ruiz, R. A. (1975). Personality assessment and test interpretation of Mexican Americans: A critique. *Journal of Personality Assessment, 39,* 103–109.

Padilla, E. R., & Wyatt, G. E. (1983). The effects of intelligence and achievement testing on minority group children. In G. J. Powell (Ed.), *The psychosocial development of minority group children* (pp. 417–437). New York: Brunner/Mazel.

Page, J. B., Rio, L., Sweeney, J., & MacKay, C. (1985). Alcohol and adaptation to exile in Miami's Cuban population. In L. A. Bennett & G. M. Ames (Eds.), *The American experience with alcohol: Contrasting cultural perspectives* (pp. 315–332). New York: Plenum.

Peniston, E. G., & Burns, T. R. (1980). An Alcohol Dependency Behavior Inventory for Native Americans. *White Cloud Journal, 1*(4), 11–15.

Pokorny, A. D., Miller, B. A., & Kaplan, H. B. (1972). The brief MAST: A shortened version of the Michigan Alcoholism Screening Test. *American Journal of Psychiatry, 129,* 342–345.

Radloff, L. S. (1977). The CES-D scale: A self-report depression scale for research in the general population. *Applied Psychological Measurement, 1,* 385–401.

Ramos-McKay, J. M. (Undated). *Puerto Rican norms for the SOMPA and WISC-R.* Unpublished manuscript.

Randolph, E. T., Escobar, J. I., Paz, D. H., & Forsythe, A. B. (1985). Ethnicity and reporting of schizophrenic symptoms. *Journal of Nervous and Mental Disease, 173,* 322–340.

Reynolds, C. H., & Nichols, R. C. (1977). Factor rates for the CPI: Do they capture the valid variance? *Educational and Psychological Measurement, 37,* 907–915.

Reynolds, C. R., & Kaiser, S. M. (1990). Test bias in psychological assessment. In T. B. Gutkin & C. R. Reynolds (Eds.), *The handbook of school psychology* (2nd ed., pp. 487–525). New York: Wiley.

Ring, J. M., & Marquis, P. (1991). Depression in a Latino immigrant medical population. *American Journal of Orthopsychiatry, 61,* 298–302.

Rissetti, F. J., & Maltes, S. G. (1985). Use of the MMPI in Chile. In J. N. Butcher & C. D. Spielberger (Eds.), *Advances in personality assessment* (Vol. 4, pp. 209–257). Hillsdale, NJ: Erlbaum.

Roberts, R. E. (1980). Reliability of the CES-D scale in different ethnic contexts. *Psychiatry Research, 2,* 125–134.

Roberts, R. E., Vernon, S. W., & Rhoades, H. M. (1989). Effects of language and ethnic status on reliability and validity of the Center for Epidemiologic Studies Depression Scale with psychiatric patients. *Journal of Nervous and Mental Disease, 177,* 581–592.

Robins, L. N., Helzer, J. E., Croughan, J., & Ratcliff, K. S. (1981). National Institute of Mental Health: Diagnostic Interview Schedule. *Archives of General Psychiatry, 38,* 381–389.

Robins, L. N., Helzer, J. E., Weissman, M. M., Orvaschel, H., Gruenberg, E., Burker, J. D., Jr., & Regier, D. A. (1984). Lifetime prevalence of specific psychiatric disorders in three sites. *Archives of General Psychiatry, 41,* 949–958.

Ross-Reynolds, J., & Reschly, D. J. (1983). An investigation of item bias on the WISC-R with four sociocultural groups. *Journal of Consulting and Clinical Psychology, 51,* 144–146.

Rubio-Stipec, M., Shrout, P. E., Bird, H., Canino, G., Bravo, M. (1989). Symptom scales in Diagnostic Interview Schedule: Factor results in Hispanic and Anglo samples. *Psychological Assessment: A Journal of Consulting and Clinical Psychology, 1,* 30–34.

Russell, M., Cooper, M. L., & Frone, M. R. (1990). The influence of sociodemographic characteristics on familial alcohol problems: Data from a community sample. *Alcoholism: Clinical and Experimental Research, 14,* 221–226.

Salgado de Snyder, V. N. (1987). Factors associated with acculturative stress and depressive symptomatology among married Mexican immigrant women. *Psychology of Women Quarterly, 11,* 477–488.

Sandoval, J. (1979). The WISC-R and internal evidence of test bias with minority groups. *Journal of Consulting and Clinical Psychology, 47,* 919–927.

Selzer, M. L. (1971). The Michigan Alcoholism Screening Test: The quest for a new diagnostic instrument. *American Journal of Psychiatry, 127,* 1653–1658.

Shek, D. T. L. (1990). Reliability and factorial structure of the Chinese version of the Beck Depression Inventory. *Journal of Clinical Psychology, 46,* 35–43.

Shek, D. T. L. (1991). What does the Chinese version of the Beck Depression Inventory measure in Chinese students—General psychopathology or depression? *Journal of Clinical Psychology, 47,* 381–390.

Shore, J. H., Manson, S. M., Bloom, J. D., Keepers, G., & Neligh, G. (1987). A pilot study of depression among American Indian patients with research diagnostic criteria. *American Indian and Alaska Native Mental Health Research, 1*(2), 4–15.

Shrout, P. E., Bird, H., Canino, G., & Bravo, M. (1989). Symptom scales of the Diagnostic Interview Schedule: Factor results in Hispanic and Anglo samples. *Psychological Assessment: A Journal of Consulting and Clinical Psychology, 1,* 30–34.

Silk-Walker, P., Walker, R. D., & Kivlahan, D. (1988). Alcoholism, alcohol abuse, and health in American Indians and Alaska Natives (Mongraph No. 1). *American Indian and Alaska Native Mental Health Research, 1,* pp. 65–93.

Snowden, L., & Todman, P. (1982). The psychological assessment of Blacks: New and needed developments. In E. E. Jones & S. J. Korchin (Eds.), *Minority mental health* (pp. 193–226). New York: Praeger.

Spielberger, C. D. (1976). The nature and measurement of anxiety. In C. D. Spielberger & R. Diaz-Guerrero (Eds.), *Cross-cultural anxiety* (Vol. 1, pp. 1–11). Washington, DC: Hemisphere.

Spielberger, C. D. (1989). *State-Trait Anxiety Inventory: A comprehensive bibliography.* Palo Alto, CA: Consulting Psychologists Press.

Spielberger, C. D., & Sharma, S. (1976). Cross-cultural measurement of anxiety. In C. D. Spielberger & R. Diaz-Guerrero (Eds.), *Cross-cultural anxiety* (pp. 13–25). Washington, DC; Hemisphere.

Spitzer, R. L., & Endicott, J. (1978). *The Schedule for Affective Disorders and Schizophrenia* (3rd ed.). New York: New York State Psychiatric Institute, Biometrics Research Division.

Stangl, D., Pfohl, B., & Zimmerman, M. (1983). *A structured clinical interview for DSM-III* (2nd ed.). Iowa City, IA: University of Iowa College of Medicine, Department of Psychiatry.

Terrell, F., & Terrell, S. L. (1983). The relationship between race of examiner, cultural mistrust, and the intelligence test performance of Black children. *Psychology in the Schools, 20,* 367–369.

Valencia, R. R. (1988). The McCarthy Scales and Hispanic children: A review of psychometric research. *Hispanic Journal of Behavioral Sciences, 10,* 81–104.

Vega, W. A., Kolody, B., Valle, R., & Hough, R. (1986). Depressive symptoms and their correlates among immigrant Mexican women in the United States. *Social Science Medicine, 22,* 645–652.

Wanberg, K. W., & Horn, J. L. (1983). Assessment of alcohol use with multidimensional concepts and measures. *American Psychologist, 39,* 1055–1069.

Whitworth, R. H. (1988). Anglo- and Mexican-American performance on the MMPI administered in Spanish or English. *Journal of Clinical Psychology, 44,* 891–897.

Williams, C. L. (1986). Mental health assessment of refugees. In C. L. Williams & J. Westermeyer (Eds.), *Refugee mental health in resettlement countries* (pp. 175–188). New York: Hemisphere.

Wing, J. K., Cooper, J. E., & Sartorius, N. (1974). *The measurement and classification of psychiatric symptoms.* London: Cambridge University Press.

Wyatt, G. E. (1982). Alternatives to the use of standardized tests with Afro-American children. In B. A. Bass, G. E. Wyatt, & G. J. Powell (Eds.), *The Afro-American family: Assessment, treatment, and research issues* (pp. 119–135). New York: Grune and Stratton.

Zimmerman, M., Coryell, W., Corenthal, C., & Wilson, S. (1986). A self-report scale to diagnose major depressive disorder. *Archives of General Psychiatry, 43,* 1076–1081.

CHAPTER TEN

Multicultural Assessment Practice

Introduction

This book has provided background information on the four major culturally distinct populations in the United States (Chapters 2–5), in order to document their world-view differences and the need for culture-specific styles of assessment service delivery. Summaries of current research on specific measures for several multicultural assessment purposes were contained in Chapters 6–9. Although there were suggestions for use of each assessment instrument in those chapters, a heuristic device to assist in application of assessment materials to specific multicultural groups is necessary because of the unfamiliarity of some content.

This chapter begins by describing a current Anglo-American format for assessment services. This format has limitations for assessment practice with multicultural clients and requires modifications to be acceptable to clients of diverse cultural origins. These format modifications for multiculturally sensitive assessment practice incorporate several new components: (a) the use of moderator variables to provide information on cultural orientations or cultural identities within each of the four groups; (b) an awareness of potential confounds and other problems in assessment for purposes of clinical diagnosis, personality description, and evaluation of intelligence; (c) an emphasis on cultural validity in selection of instruments and interpretation of findings.

A process description and flow chart for this modified multicultural assessment format is presented, to facilitate the development of cultural competence in practice. To provide a context for the modified assessment format, there will be a discussion of assessor cultural sensitivity and cultural competence that includes professional ethics.

Limitations of a Contemporary Format for Assessment Services

A format for assessment services that has been used in the past without modification for culture will be examined as an introduction to multicultural assessment practice. This format involves the client directly with the assessment process during each of the following steps:

1. Conference with a referral source person (if there is one) to define problems and assessor responsibilities during feedback.
2. A rationale for the assessment process, specific assessment procedures, roles of the participants, and potential usages of findings are discussed with the client.
3. The assessor sees the client to administer tests.
4. The assessor, assessee, and referral source person (if any) meet to discuss the findings.
5. Copies of written reports are provided to client and referral source person.
6. The assessor and referral source person maintain communication in order to inform the assessor about subsequent utilization of assessment findings. (See Dana, 1982, chapter 10.)

However, it is evident that these steps are appropriate only for assessees who believe that the loci of power and responsibility must eventually reside in themselves. For these persons, assessment becomes a route toward self-efficacy. It is necessary to recontextualize the steps in this format for persons who have retained a traditional culture with beliefs, values, and perceptions that differ from middle-class Anglo-Americans.

Several levels of assessment service delivery provide an opportunity to modify the above format for multicultural use. These levels include information, emotional contingencies, transfer of power, and a contextualization of assessment services within the biopsychosocial systems that impinge on the client (Dana, 1985). Table 10-1 presents these levels and the desired outcomes of assessment services for multicultural clients. Tests of achievement, aptitude, holistic health, intelligence, personality, and psychopathology provide a variety of information relevant to presenting problems and intervention resources (Level 1).

However, this information can neither be readily understood nor made use of unless the emotional messages (Level 2) received by the client from the assessor initially foster a relationship of trust and eventually lead to the task orientation necessary for compliance with test administration procedures. For this relationship to occur, the assessor must use a culturally appropriate service-delivery style or social etiquette. As a result, these emotional messages can convey acceptance, reassurance, support, shared feelings, and empathy.

TABLE 10-1 • *Assessment Service-Delivery Components and Desired Outcomes for Multicultural Clients*

Level/Component	Desired Outcome
1. Information	Tests of achievement, aptitude, holistic health, intelligence, interest, personality, psychopathology, etc. are administered.
2. Emotional contingencies	Acceptance of service provider is due to demonstrated knowledge of and respect for appropriate social etiquette, clients' culture and history of relationship to dominant society, as well as awareness of culture-specific information (e.g., problems of discrimination/racism).
3. Transfer of power	Family members and/or advocates are involved in discussion of results that includes understanding of assessment process and knowledge of how results can be used.
4. Systems	Health/illness beliefs, perception of own symptoms/behavior/presenting problems, and expectations for interventions are examined in context of available intervention resources (e.g., health/mental health, learning, vocation, resettlement). Family members/community persons may facilitate, authorize, or take responsibility for interventions.

Source: Adapted from Dana (1985), p. 601.

Schwartz (1984) suggested that services provided in a relaxed, affiliative manner with warmth and caring will facilitate self-healing by the client. The inherent potentials for self-healing that are believed to be triggered by this service-delivery process include self-attention, relaxation, and positive emotions.

The assessor's ability to provide services by using expected etiquette for the assessor-assessee relationship typically permits a task orientation during test administration. In addition, this style contributes to a focus of attention during the feedback of findings that enables the information to be understood and subsequently remembered. If the emotional contingencies that precede, accompany, and follow test administration are perceived as genuine, then the quality of information provided will be determined primarily by the appropriateness of the tests and their cultural validity for a particular individual.

At a level of empowerment, as a result of processing this information and understanding the available intervention resources, there will be cultural differences in the extent to which the assessee and her or his family may be comfortable with ownership of the feedback contents (Level 3). This comfort often will depend not only on the contents of feedback but the goodness-of-fit with existing cultural beliefs about illness/health and symptoms/behaviors that may be acknowledged and with whom they may be discussed.

The systems level implies that the client may become a full partner in the entire assessment process (Level 4). In order to be such a partner, however, the client must assume responsibility for the outcome of the assessment and the use of the information obtained. This kind of power may be illusory for persons who believe in external control and external responsibility and for whom a medical model is culturally acceptable. As a result, family members and/or advocates from their own communities may need to be present and able to assume responsibility for implementation of any subsequent interventions.

For information and a shared feedback process to be helpful with multicultural clients, several conditions must be present. These conditions include a desire for feedback on the part of the assessee, an adequate style for communication, and access to resources that permit use of this feedback in ways that are congruent with cultural beliefs (Dana, 1985).

Multicultural Assessment Practice

This section describes several major components of an assessment format for multicultural clients. Within each of these components, there will be a dovetailing of selected tests/measures with specific cultural groups. This narrowing of focus is designed to provide a transition from the overview of available tests/measures in Chapters 8 and 9 to a group-specific format for assessment practice.

Moderator Variables for Assessment of Group Identity

Regardless of the purpose of assessment, the extent to which an original Asian, Hispanic, or Native American culture has been retained constitutes priority information for the assessor. For African Americans, this critical moderator information pertains to the extent to which an historic identity (Afrocentricity) has been incorporated into the self-concept, world view, everyday activities, and behavior, or whether this identity formation (Nigrescence) is in the process of development.

There are at least four solutions to the group identity dilemma or crisis that occurs as a result of relative willingness or unwillingness to be absorbed/assimilated by the dominant society and/or to retain a traditional cultural identity. These solutions include retention of the original or traditional culture, identification with the dominant Anglo-American culture, identification with both an original and an adopted culture (biculturality), and rejection of both original and Anglo-American identities (marginality). For Native Americans, a fifth orientation—transitional—has been suggested, in which individuals are bilingual but question traditional values and religion (LaFromboise, Trimble, & Mohatt, 1990). Obviously, many persons from all four cultural groups may be in the process of transition, especially toward a bicultural identity. Since moderator data will suggest or document the presence of a transitional orientation, this fifth alternative was not included separately here.

Group identity will suggest the parameters of individual identity and, to some extent, the world view as embodied in beliefs, values, language, and perceptions of service providers, services, and service-delivery styles (Figure 1-1). An exploration of group identity as a precursor to assessment has never been a routine part of the background data collected on prospective assessment clients. Nonetheless, in a multicultural society, such information is imperative for the provision of culturally competent services. Bilevel measures should be used whenever feasible to describe both the original culture and the Anglo-American cultural contributions to group identity. Although moderator variables were reviewed in Chapter 7, only a small number of these moderators have a research basis commensurate with practical assessment applications.

Assessment of Cultural Orientation   For African Americans, Nigrescence can be measured independently by using the Developmental Inventory of Black Consciousness (DIB-C) or the Racial Identity Attitude Scale (RIAS), and Afrocentricity can be measured by using the African Self-Consciousness Scale (ASC). The DIB-C and RIAS are instruments that should be improved psychometrically and are in need of available norms on different African-American populations. Nonetheless, the stages tapped by these instruments can elucidate the cultural contribution to significantly elevated MMPI clinical scales. As a result, it is necessary to use one of these instruments whenever an MMPI-1 is administered to an African American. For MMPI-2, unless there is both clinical and sociodemographic information that indicates comparability of the assessee to normative subjects, the use of either instrument (DIB-C or RIAS) is recommended. The ASC should be used even more cautiously. However, when there is collateral information that an assessee has an Afrocentric orientation, the ASC can be used to provide additional information on group identity, especially with regard to implications for culture-specific interventions.

For Asian Americans, there are no acceptable instruments for specific groups. As a result, it is necessary to use a general measure of world view and to extrapolate the results from available norms to the particular assessee. The most acceptable instruments for this purpose are the Scale to Assess World Views, the Individualism-Collectivism Scale, and the Multicultural Acculturation Scale (see Table 7-8). It may be argued that it might be preferable to wait for the development of group-specific moderators for Asian Americans. However, these existing instruments can provide information now that is relevant to the cultural orientation category and on cultural content that may be helpful in avoiding diagnostic error. Any test information on cultural identity that can be evaluated independently by the assessor is preferable to no information whatsoever.

For Hispanic Americans, the majority of available measures are for particular Hispanic subgroups, and Spanish-language versions of these measures are available. For Mexican Americans, the Multicultural Experience Inventory and the Cultural Lifestyle Inventory (see Table 7-4) not only provide orientation data but also contribute considerable relevant cultural information. It is important to note here that only the monolevel Acculturation Rating Scale for Mexican Americans (see Table 7-4) has been used with the MMPI-1 in the same way that the DIB-C and RIAS have been used with African Americans. Thus, an exception to the recommended moderator usage for Mexican Americans would occur in conjunction with MMPI-1. For Cuban Americans, either the Bicultural Involvement Questionnaire or the Cuban Behavioral Identity Questionnaire (see Table 7-4) may be used, although the questionnaire materials and scoring keys are more readily available for the latter instrument. Also, measures for children—Children's Hispanic Background Scale and Children's Acculturation Scale—and one general measure—Hispanic Acculturation Scale (see Table 7-4)—are available for use at the present time.

For Native Americans, the only available bilevel pan-Indian measure is the Conflicts/Resolution Chart, in case history/interview format. Although this device is not psychometrically derived, it does provide information on family/self relationships, spiritual/religious practices, social/recreational/leisure activities, and training/educational style that contributes to group identity. Inferences regarding cultural orientation can be made by using this information. Table 7-6 describes this device in a format that can be applied directly during an interview. A small number of tribe-specific moderators were presented in Table 7-7. Whenever a tribe-specific moderator is available, whether monolevel or bilevel, it can be used in conjunction with the Conflicts/Resolution Chart.

For refugees of Hispanic or Asian origins, the moderators suggested above should be used. However, in most instances translations into the first languages of assessees will be necessary. Although Spanish-language versions of Hispanic moderators are readily available, the world-view measures of group identity listed above that could be used with Southeast Asian refugees have not been translated. Although it would be feasible to use an interpreter for the administration of these measures, this practice would further dilute the usefulness of results that already must be taken out of a more general world-view measurement context and applied to specific Asian groups. Since the cultural orientation of most of these persons will be traditional, due to their refugee status, it would be preferable to use the translator in order to complete the information contained in Table 7-1, rather than for administration of any moderator measure. This information can be used to alert the assessor to some of the unique and severe problems faced by these persons.

Usefulness of Group Identity Information Once this information is available, certain implications for assessment decisions need to be considered as a result of sensitization to cultural preferences for services. This sensitization also permits an awareness of some issues that may arise during the assessment process.

Table 10-2 provides for an examination of some implications of group identity. Either formal measures or an informal evaluation can suggest group identity. In addition to the group identity information, the initial interview can suggest the locus of control and locus of responsibility stance. Existing measures of these variables have proven to be inadequate for most non-Anglo-Americans (see Chapter 1), although there is some consistency to the general EC-IR focus of these multicultural groups.

An inference concerning the preferred service model may also be made at this time on the basis of the group identity classification. Dominant-culture services are appropriate and acceptable for persons of multicultural origin who actively desire to assimilate and have already adopted, or are in the process of adopting, dominant-culture values and behaviors. A need for culture-specific services is indicated for clients who have retained a traditional culture, either because they are immigrants/refugees or are resident in traditional culture enclaves. These persons may or may not be fluent in English. For persons whose second language is English, or who have no English whatsoever, services should be provided in their original language, using translations of standard tests or new emic tests when available. For persons who are bicultural, services may be provided in either mode, but the client should have the option to choose, since the presenting problem may be of a nature that requires culture-specific services (e.g., discrimination, family problems, or problems stemming from bicultural identity).

Although only a relatively small number of issues have been suggested in Table 10-2, each one of these issues should be considered prior to assessment procedures. Obviously, whenever the client's language of preference is not shared by the assessor, the assessment findings are likely to be incomplete, superficial, and only minimally representative for that client. Moreover, the assessor should be aware that his or her familiarity and comfort with a culture-specific style of service delivery will be important to the client.

Several questions may arise after test administration has been completed. Does the client express an interest in the assessment findings as a result of understanding the purposes and procedures included? Will the client be able to understand conventional Anglo-American feedback that includes intrapsychic content, attribution of personal responsibility for symptoms, or imputation of an autonomous self? There also may be a preference for feedback that indicates exactly what is required for compliance with an externally imposed regimen. Persons who have traditional cultural values that do not include mental health

TABLE 10-2 • *Group Identity; Service-Delivery Preferences and issues*

Group Identity (Cultural Orientation)

___ Traditional   Culture _____
___ Nontraditional   Original culture _____
___ Bicultural   Original culture _____
___ Marginal   Original culture _____

Hypothesized Service-Delivery Preferences

Locus of control/locus of responsibility
  ___ IC-IR   ___ EC-IR   ___ EC-ER   ___ IC-ER

Preferred service model
  ___ Medical   ___ Compensatory   ___ Enlightenment   ___ Moral

Possible Service-Delivery Issues

___ Language preference (first language) _____
___ Ability of assessor to communicate assessment findings (competence in language
    and/or style)
___ Desire for assessment results
___ Ability to understand results (possible conflict with beliefs)
___ Ability to use resources suggested by results
___ Mental health services unacceptable
___ Somatization is preferred symptom expression
___ Self-concept includes "others" with priority
___ Family may make ultimate decisions
___ Acceptability of service provider
___ Initial versus later problem presentation
___ Culture-specific presenting problem
___ Adequacy of DSM for assessee

services and who also experience external locus of control and responsibility (ER-EC) as credible may also demonstrate an unquestioning faith in the doctor as an authority.

The willingness to make direct and immediate use of assessment findings will vary with the extent to which a client desires control over a personal destiny and perceives his or her efficacy as commensurate with this task. Moreover, the source of decision-making power for compliance with any recommended intervention may lie in the family rather than the client. Whenever the family retains this prerogative, the important family members should participate in any feedback of assessment results.

In addition, there are a variety of other culture-specific considerations contained in Table 10-2 that may affect the assessment process. Of special importance is the issue of DSM relevance for labeling symptoms and planning interventions. If there is an error in diagnosis, there is also an increased likelihood of ineffective treatment as a result of the inapplicable diagnosis.

The possible cultural meanings of each of these potential problems listed in Table 10-2 have been discussed for each group earlier in this book. The list serves as a reminder to be alert to each one of these possible issues prior to developing a plan for assessment that includes not only choices of tests/instruments but the desirability of client-shared decisions for test administration and subsequent use of findings. It is recommended that each assessor prepare a personal list of possible assessment issues relevant for his or her client population, as the list presented in Table 10-2 is not generic. This list is not intended to be definitive, complete, or applicable exclusively to any single cultural group. These problem areas are included here to signal the importance of considering potential cultural issues at the onset of assessment.

Potential Confounds/Problems for Clinical Diagnosis, Personality Description, and Intelligence Evaluation

Psychological assessment has two major purposes: diagnosis in DSM terminology by using either broad- or narrow-band instruments, and personality description using either global or discrete constructs (i.e., traits/behaviors). These discrete traits would also include intelligence and cognition. There are potential confounds in both diagnostic assessment and personality description.

Culture-general and culture-specific symptoms should always be differentiated. Psychopathology should be clearly distinguished from deviance or problems-in-living. Personality description may be confounded by use of a culturally inappropriate personality theory, regardless of whether the theory has been rationally or empirically derived. There are potential confounds with global or specific construct methods for personality description and psychopathology, as well as between personality and deviance.

These confounds can occur because both the DSM and the personality theories were developed from an implicit Eurocentric stance for application to Anglo-Americans and contain only token acknowledgments of cultural contributions to diagnosis or personality development. Trait theories are composed of a variety of constructs and often assume universality of the component constructs. These constructs, however, refer to behaviors, accompanying affects, and meaning in life situations that may differ across cultures.

There are potentials for inadvertent pathologization that may result from using DSM criteria to describe mental illness whenever the client's world view differs markedly from the dominant-culture world view. Personality constructs or traits may be misconstrued as psychopathology when, in fact, these traits have functional value within a particular culture, or may have had such value earlier in life (e.g., with refugees). Personality traits also may be misconstrued as problems from an Anglo-American perspective. Similarly, personality may be caricatured on the basis of inapplicable theory or constructs. For example, the construct "intelligence," as measured by standard tests, may not be relevant for prediction of academic success in different cultural settings and certainly should not have universal currency as an index for intelligent management of an individual life. Table 10-3 is provided for sensitization to these possible confounds and other problems.

Selection of Instruments/Interpretations of Assessment Findings: General Issues

Personality description and assessment of psychopathology or intelligence depend on the tests selected for a particular client and on the interpretation of those tests. As a result, both the selection of particular tests and the interpretation of findings from the tests must be done with unremitting attention to the cultural context. Moreover, selection of tests that contain culturally valid constructs is mandatory for an accurate interpretation of assessment findings. However, selection of tests using criteria for cultural validity is not routinely feasible during the current era of culture-bound psychometrics. As an alternative, the tests selected should expose the assessee to the fewest possible hazards in the form of pathologization, caricature, and/or dehumanization.

There are several potential sources of test misinterpretation that may result from selection/interpretation; these require attention to (a) emics and etics (imposed and/or genuine); (b) cultural validity of constructs; (c) cultural utility of test formats; (d) translations of tests, and (e) sources of potential bias (Table 10-4).

TABLE 10-3 • *Assessment Purposes and Possible Problems*

Purpose	*Problem*
Diagnosis (broad-band)	Culture omitted from DSM
Diagnosis (narrow-band)	Culture-general vs. culture-specific; pathology vs. deviance
Personality (global)	Theory may not be generalizable to other cultures because of European or Anglo-American origins
Personality (construct)	Personality vs. pathology; personality vs. problems-in-living; constructs may lack cultural validity
Intelligence/cognition	Standard tests differ in factor numbers and composition across cultural groups; scores may be influenced by assessor's gender, race etc., especially for children

TABLE 10-4 • *Potential Sources of Test Misinterpretation*

Emic/imposed etic—Use of derived etic as genuine etic. Unjustified creation of new emic or misuse of an existing emic.

Construct validity—Failure to use replicated factor analysis to establish construct equivalence by invariance or use of other approaches to construct validation.

Linguistic validity—Inappropriate rendering of affect/emotionality in item content.

Metric validity—Inadequate formats for presentation of test content (i.e., for illiterates and non-English-speaking persons).

Translations—Ignoring accepted rules for establishing construct equivalence (e.g., back-translation, decentering, committee, and key informants) or a clearly stated rationale for translation safeguards. Ignorance of culture-specific response sets and preferences about self-disclosure.

Assessor bias—Erroneous assumptions: similarity or dissimilarity. Beliefs: deficit hypothesis, mandatory assimilation (melting pot), self-contained individualism. Stereotyping. Stage 3 ethnorelativism.

Emics and Etics (Imposed and Genuine)   Whenever an imposed etic is used as a genuine etic without an established research basis, the test may not provide a fair representation of constructs for assessees within a cultural setting other than their own. This is part of the dilemma inherent in comparison of MMPI norms obtained in two different cultural settings, or in using the MMPI in this country, for example, with traditional Hispanic Americans or Native Americans. This issue is not as clear-cut with the Holtzman Inkblot Technique or with the State-Trait Anxiety Inventory, which not only claim to be genuine etics but have substantial research support for their claim. Although there may also be genuine etics among personality theories (e.g., those of Raymond Cattell and Hans Eysenck), there is also a growing sense that a five-factor theory that explicitly includes culture may ultimately be demonstrated to have universal applicability.

Emics have a history of development and usage primarily in European and American society. The majority of tests being used at the present time throughout the world are of such derivation and are constructed on the basis of culture-specific psychometrics. There are not only fewer available emics from non-Euro-American cultures, but for many previously discussed reasons, there is a lack of interest in their development for applications with the diverse cultures in this country. As a result, the majority of tests in use with culturally different populations in the United States are imposed etics.

However, emic measures do not necessarily have to be designed for a single cultural group. The stimulus materials, administration, and scoring/interpretive procedures may be individually focused to qualify as legitimate and useful emics. This is especially applicable to measures of problems, life events, or behaviors that may be useful when the components or items have been scrutinized for their presence, frequency of occurrence, affect, and meaning within each cultural group. Chapter 8 described some of these measures and suggested the need for genuine emic instruments for some cultural populations in this country. The problem here, as Table 10-4 indicates, involves the construction of new emics or use of existing sets of stimulus materials as emics for particular cultural groups, when there may be insufficient reason to do so.

Although there has been substantial controversy over this issue, new emics for distinct cultural groups in this country appear to be justified in only two instances. First, when the assessee has chosen to retain or redintegrate a traditional culture with a world view that is alien and/or incomprehensible to the dominant Anglo-American culture, the creation of emics is mandatory. For example, a traditional Hopi person constructs reality in a manner that cannot be readily comprehended by an outsider. This world view affects all perceptions and guides behavior in ways that do not make sense using Anglo-American perceptions and beliefs. Similarly, an African American who has redintegrated a traditional African world view and construes all behaviors and activities in Afrocentric terms may be regarded as outrageous and even bizarre by many middle-class Anglo-Americans.

Culture-specific assessment and interventions are required for culture-specific problems, problems arising from a poor fit with the dominant society because of the alien world view, and subsequent aggravation as a result of discrimination. In addition, culture-specific interventions are more likely to be used as a result of assessment that is emic in nature.

Second, for assessees who are refugees or migrants with special problems arising from earlier dislocation, trauma, and/or relocation stress, emic measures will facilitate problem delineation and subsequent interventions. Chapter 7 indicated some of the problems experienced by these groups and some unique assessment information that can be useful in addressing these problems.

Construct Validity   Interpretation of personality assessment findings uses constructs that may be called traits or factors, as well as other descriptive terms. Thus, the demonstration of equivalence of these constructs across cultures assumes critical importance. Although the major methodology for demonstrating construct equivalence—replicated factor analysis—may have serious shortcomings, it does represent a bona fide attempt to demonstrate equivalence by means of factor invariance. The question here for assessors is, "Has the particular test to be used for a traditional-culture individual shown factor invariance?" If there has been factor similarity but not equivalence, the items or content responsible for lack of equivalence should be related to cultural differences in expression of the construct. In addition, it is especially desirable to demonstrate the cultural validity of constructs by methods other than factor analysis.

Linguistic Validity and Metric Validity Linguistic validity refers to the accuracy of reproducing the affective dimension of a construct in test content. This is extremely difficult to accomplish, because there may be cultural differences in the subjective experience of a particular construct.

Metric validity pertains to the adequacy of formats used for presentation of test content. This may be an infrequent problem, because it appears primarily for assessees who are inexperienced in taking objective tests, are illiterate, and/or do not speak English.

Translations Translations of standard tests should be used whenever the assessee's first language is not English. Existing translations of tests for psychopathology, personality, and intelligence are discussed in this book. However, there are two additional problems for assessors. If several translations of the same test are in existence and/or use, which one should be used? Second, how can an assessor evaluate the adequacy of any existing translation?

There are several translations of the same test for Hispanics and Chinese. The translation that represents the client's idiomatic first language most closely should be used. For example, a Mexican-American client may be handicapped by a translation prepared for Puerto Ricans. Although there are no absolute standards for evaluating the adequacy of a translation, there are accepted rules to provide a reasonable indication that careful and systematic procedures have been used. These rules for establishing construct equivalence in translations were presented in Chapter 6.

Similarly, as Table 10-4 suggests, response sets that are culturally determined or occur with high frequency in a particular culture (e.g., acquiescence in some Asians) will influence cultural validity. The willingness to be self-disclosing as a result of cultural norms will affect test performance. By the same token, there may be selective willingness to self-disclose that is dependent on the nature of the personal content to be shared and the role or identity of the person who will receive the disclosure.

Assessor Bias Bias (discussed in Chapter 6) is related to errors in diagnosis. For the most part, this bias is below the threshold of awareness and is therefore unacknowledged and unquestioned. Nonetheless, bias in the form of unquestioned belief in the deficit hypothesis or in a compelling societal need for assimilation can exert an influence that will distort the interpretation process and assessment findings. In addition, bias can also result from incorrect assumptions of similarity or difference, particularly between African Americans and Anglo-Americans (Neighbors, Jackson, Campbell, & Williams, 1989). An incorrect assumption of similarity can result in the decision that similar symptoms are equivalent. An incorrect assumption of difference can result in ignoring certain symptoms because of the belief that all persons must exhibit the same symptoms for a particular diagnosis.

Similarly, a tacit acceptance of self-contained individualism as the proper and/or unique form of self-concept usually will result in failure to recognize that ensembled individualism produces an entirely different self-concept. A self-concept that emerges from acceptance of ensembled individualism provides an emphasis on a collectivity that may include not only the family and/or extended family but the cultural group and even the society of origin as well. In the instance of a pan-Asian or pan-Indian identity, many original societies may be included in the collectivity.

Stereotyping often occurs without intent, malice, or awareness, simply because of the shared stereotypes that each cultural group has about other cultural groups. An awareness of conventional Anglo-American stereotypic expectations for behaviors of other cultural groups is essential for assessors. This awareness should be accompanied by knowledge of how stereotyping can affect judgment in interpretation of tests.

Finally, there is the bias that occurs as a result of ethnocentrism. As Chapter 1 suggested, most assessors will be at ethnocentrism-ethnorelativism Stage 3, or minimization and toleration of differences. Training for Stage 4, acceptance, also was outlined in Chapter 1.

Selection of Group-Specific Instruments for Diagnosis, Personality Description, and Intelligence

Clinical Diagnosis   The validity of DSM categories for each multicultural group has not been established. Assessors will know that cultural beliefs may be difficult to distinguish from schizophrenia and that only organic disorders, schizophrenia, bipolar disorders, major depression, and certain anxiety disorders and phobias are distributed across all cultures. Even for the disorders with worldwide distribution, there will be differences in symptom patterns and intervention priorities. However, there has been little awareness that acceptable procedures are available for establishing the validity of all DSM categories for each cultural group in the United States (Marsella, 1978). This dilemma is further compounded by the presence of bias in the form of false assumptions and stereotypy. As a result, as Table 10-4 suggests, assessors continue to have genuine and pervasive problems in clinical diagnosis that uses the DSM.

There are, however, ethically responsible approaches to these diagnostic problems that include the use of a clear, stepwise procedure and preferences for certain narrow-band instruments as aids to diagnosis. A stepwise procedure for an interpretive process leading to diagnostic categorization would include:

1. A category-specific examination of symptoms/test data.
2. The functionality of symptoms within the life setting.

3. Possible cultural contributions to symptomatology.
4. Culture-specific symptomatology.
5. Collection of data leading to a research basis for multicultural practice.

As a first step, whenever the data have some resemblance to schizophrenic or personality disorders, a possible cultural contribution to misdiagnosis of these disorders can be considered by using moderator measures, such as when there has been a research history examining diagnostic error in a particular cultural group (e.g., schizophrenia in African Americans or Hispanic Americans). For personality disorders, it is important first to examine the data for DSM cultural bias in the categorization, and second to examine the assessee's culture for an alternative explanation.

A second step is to examine the life situation in which the assessee is enmeshed. Do the diagnostically significant behaviors/symptoms have any functional value for coping? Are these behaviors evaluated by family and community as interfering with responsibilities? How have others responded to these behaviors over a period of time? To accomplish this examination, it will usually be necessary to interview family and/or community members.

A third step is to examine any potential cultural contribution to the kinds of symptoms presented. For example, if physical symptoms, psychosomatic symptoms, phobias, or somatic delusions predominate, do these behaviors have a context in problems-in-living that are acceptable and understandable by family and community? The distinction to be made here is between deviance, or problems-in-living, and residual deviance, or diagnosable psychopathology.

A fourth step is to compare the behaviors/symptoms with known culture-specific psychopathologies. This is of particular importance when the behaviors appear bizarre, psychotic, and/or out of context with ordinary and anticipated behaviors. For this purpose, assessors should prepare a list of culture-specific disorders for their multicultural populations of concern.

Finally, it is necessary for assessors to collect baseline data from their multicultural populations as a routine part of practice. As Marsella (1978) suggested, this baseline data should be described by frequency, intensity, and duration. Later, as a consequence of networking with other assessors of the same populations, objective symptom patterns can be established by using multivariate techniques.

Ordinarily, clinical diagnosis of Anglo-Americans is provided by checklists and rating scales as well as tests. However, broad-band devices, including widely used structured interview schedules such as the Diagnostic Interview Schedule (DIS), the Research Diagnostic Criteria (RDC), the Schedule for Affective Disorders and Schizophrenia (SADS), and the Structured Interview for DSM-III Personality Disorders (SIDP) have severe limitations for use with multicultural populations (López & Núñez, 1987). Although there has been some limited research using the DIS and the SADS with Native American and Hispanic-American populations, there is still too little data to justify use of even these instruments with these populations.

Although the limitations for MMPI use with multicultural populations in this country were summarized in Chapter 9, reiteration at this point is necessary. The MMPI-1 and MMPI-2 should not be used with Native Americans without local or tribe-specific norms and a provision for examining the obtained profiles against independent collateral data of community origin. The situation is even more complicated for other groups. For African Americans and Hispanic Americans, the use of moderator variables is imperative unless there is acceptable collateral information that the assessee has identified with the dominant Anglo-American culture and is similar to the standardization population on an acceptable array of sociodemographic variables. Moreover, the use of a subculturally appropriate translated version of the MMPI is mandatory for Hispanic Americans or Chinese Americans and other Asians who do not speak English as a first language. Although the language caveat must be applied for Asian Americans, there is an additional problem: Adequate moderators for independent measurement of group-specific cultural orientation are not available at present. As a result, the MMPI should be used with extreme caution for Asian-origin persons, even if independent data on world view is available.

In addition to the stepwise procedures for examining data, and the limited applicability of broad-band assessment, there are instruments for narrow-band or single-construct descriptions of affective disorders, anxiety disorders, and substance-use disorders in multicultural populations. The descriptions then can become part of the database for inferences with regard to diagnostic classification of persons in these populations.

Depression has been measured in multicultural populations by using many instruments, especially the Center for Epidemiologic Studies Depression Scale (CES-D), the Inventory to Diagnose Depression (IDD), the Vietnamese Depression Scale (VDS), and the Lao Depression Inventory (LDI). The CES-D is the most widely used of these depression measures with all multicultural groups. However, it does not include some somatic features or information concerning total symptom duration, and it may constitute an emotional distress index rather than a single-construct measure of clinical depression. There is a Spanish-language version, although there are large differences among Hispanic subgroups in symptom levels. In spite of these reservations, the CES-D can be used responsibly to describe depression, if not to diagnose it.

The IDD was designed to operationalize the DSM criteria for major depressive disorder and to provide an ongoing summary of symptom severity. As a result, it is potentially more useful for DSM diagnosis of depression than are other competitive measures, including the CES-D. Although to date the IDD has been used primarily with Native Americans, assessors should be alert to future research on other populations.

The symptoms of depression vary in different Asian cultures. For example, Japanese have predominantly existential complaints together with interpersonal symptoms, and Chinese present somatic complaints without the dysphoria and suicidal ideation in the Anglo-American syndrome. Although there are Chinese-language versions of some depression measures, these measures probably do not reflect an adequate array of depression symptoms for Asian groups. For Vietnamese and Laotians, the VDS and LDI have been developed. These two measures differ greatly in the adequacy of construction and translation. The VDS is noteworthy for having followed acceptable procedures to maximize cross-cultural construct validity.

Anxiety has been measured multiculturally by using the State-Trait Anxiety Inventory (STAI) for adults and, for children, the State-Trait Anxiety Inventory for Children (STAIC), and there are Spanish-language versions, the IDARE and IDAREN. The translations were done by using acceptable procedures to maximize idiomatic equivalency. These tests were factorially derived, and more work needs to be done to demonstrate factorial invariance across cultures. Nonetheless, these tests may be used in both English and Spanish versions for Hispanic Americans. However, these tests were not intended to provide DSM diagnosis of Anxiety Disorders of Childhood or Adolescence or Anxiety Disorders in adults. As a result, their multicultural diagnostic usefulness is limited to describing an etic state-trait anxiety domain. Correspondences between specific diagnostic criteria and item clusters or factors can be inferred on the basis of test data.

There is need for an adequate description of alcohol abuse and dependence in multicultural populations as a basis for clinical diagnosis of some substance use disorders. The patterns of use differ between populations, and there has been no systematic identification of group-specific factors that promote, maintain, or diminish these problems. Three instruments have been used with these populations: the Alcohol Dependence Scale (ADS), the Michigan Alcoholism Screening Test (MAST), and the Alcohol Dependency Behavior Inventory (ADBI). Although these instruments are in use for descriptive purposes, at present their value lies in the development of a database for frequency, intensity, and duration of alcohol-related characteristics in each of the multicultural populations. It will be necessary to develop multidimensional instruments, using this database, that include attitudes, values, and beliefs in addition to behaviors. These instruments can then be validated for each of the multicultural populations prior to between-group comparisons and use for clinical diagnosis.

Personality Description   Three major instruments for personality description have substantial evidence of cross-cultural validity. These instruments are the Eysenck Personality Questionnaire (EPQ), the Holtzman Inkblot Technique (HIT), and the Tell-Me-A-Story Test (TEMAS). All of these instruments can provide both personality and psychopathology information. The psychopathology information is supplementary and usable only on an inferential basis for DSM diagnosis. Special caveats for personality description apply to the EPQ and the HIT, which, in spite of being genuine etics, may provide only limited information, because interpretation is based on only a small number of factors. The interpretive potential of the TEMAS is not limited by theoretical origins, because it is a synthesis of constructs selected to be situationally representative, relevant to major concerns in daily living, and comprehensive.

However, except for the TEMAS, there is need for a greater variety of personality measures of a descriptive nature for multicultural groups, because of the continued absence of culture-specific personality theories that have an adequate research history and acceptance by assessors. As emics, these measures will require careful data collection of base-rate data and examination by community members for accuracy and relevance to valued outcomes. Some examples include checklist and questionnaire measures of adaptive and non-adaptive coping skills, acceptable interventions, and stressors (e.g., Hispanic Stress Inventory and items developed for the Rosebud Sioux).

Premised on the relative success of the TEMAS with multicultural populations, a second potential source of descriptive personality data may be found in picture-story tests. These tests, as emics, have the advantages described above but also have a built-in cultural context emerging from the interaction of culture-relevant stimuli and the thematic content provided by the assessee in telling portions of his or her life story. As indicated in Chapter 8, the life story presents roles of class, ethnicity, culture, and race as perspectives for self-description and behavioral decisions. It has proven much more difficult to develop culture-specific picture-story tests because there is no consensual set of theoretical constructs to use for the development of scoring variables. However, the TEMAS may have suggested a direction for development of relevant scoring variables on the basis of accumulated theoretical, empirical, and practical knowledge. The key to this development lies in an immediacy of relevance to the specific cultural context with review by community members.

Intelligence　Description of the use of intelligence tests for multicultural populations will be limited to the standard tests, particularly the Wechsler, the SOMPA, and the K-ABC. With the exception of school settings, the standard tests have the broadest application with these groups and continue to be more controversial than tests explicitly designed for multicultural use. Theories of intelligence remain Eurocentric in their construct composition, and the derivative standard tests have been constructed either to measure school learning or to provide samples of behavior across an array of functions believed to be relevant for intelligent behavior. School learning, however, is not the only criterion of intelligent behavior, and the functions represented on standard tests may be incomplete or not representative for all groups. However, the debate concerning the fairness of these standard tests continues, with documented advocacy on both sides (e.g., Barrett & Depiner, 1991; Padilla & Wyatt, 1983).

It is clear, nonetheless, that group differences have been reduced by more careful matching on selected sociodemographic variables. In addition, whenever representativeness of sampling in multicultural groups has occurred, the argument for relevance to these groups is strengthened. Translations, however, have not necessarily resulted in more comparable versions, nor have they compensated for an absence of cross-cultural construct validity, although they have made test materials and administration somewhat easier to understand. Similarly, group-factor differences provide evidence of deficits in cross-cultural construct validity. These group-factor differences should always be used in culture-specific interpretations and comparisons by group.

Many of the unsettling issues regarding the fairness of standard intelligence tests with multicultural populations have been thoughtfully reconstrued by the SOMPA and the K-ABC. The SOMPA provides a compensatory solution by juxtaposition of Anglo-American and culture-specific norms. Criticism has been levied at the equation of culture and social environment as a working assumption. Nonetheless, the SOMPA provides sensitivity to cultural differences in its assessment of intelligence. The SOMPA, however, is a less sophisticated and more controversial device than the K-ABC. Constructs representing intelligent behavior were developed for the K-ABC from recent research. For example, a processing construct has both sequential and simultaneous modes. A nonverbal administration potential increases the range of application of this test. The sophisticated psychometrics included more careful and comprehensive selection of sociodemographic variables and provision for both construct and criterion-related validity. The SOMPA attempted to provide an alternative model, but the K-ABC retained the original model and refined the constructs, format, administration, and psychometrics of standard intelligence tests.

A Flow Chart to Facilitate Applications

A description of multicultural assessment practice and Tables 10-1 through 10-4 have summarized some of the information that was described in earlier chapters. However, to make practical use of this information during a particular assessment transaction, a flow chart is also provided (Figure 10-1).

Figure 10-1 has six steps to describe a process of decision-making and some of the varieties of services that should be acceptable to many multicultural clients. These steps include a particular style that will characterize the entire assessment process (Step I). These styles will differ somewhat for different cultural groups.

A relatively brief or more prolonged development of relationship will precede test administration. At this point, one or more moderators will be intro-

FIGURE 10-1 • *A Stepwise Flow Chart to Describe Competent Assessment Services for Multicultural Clients*

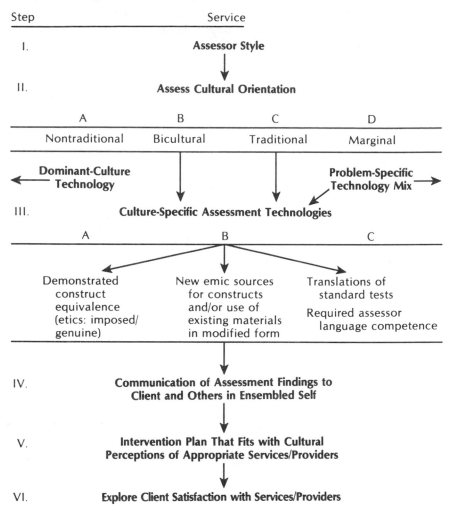

duced for assessment of cultural orientation (Step II). As a result, the assessor will have data that are relevant to selection of assessment materials. As Figure 10-1, Step IIA suggests, assessees who have adopted a dominant-society world view and behaviors would be given assessment materials that have origins in current assessment technology, without any modifications.

Assessees who are marginal in their identity orientation will often be uninterested and/or unwilling participants in the assessment procedures. For such assessees, the appropriate materials may be a mixture of assessment technologies from the dominant society and culture-specific methods. A mixture of methods can provide a problem-specific focus for assessment and usually results in a more time-limited process. The rationale for this approach is that the clients may be unwilling to be assessed or have only minimal tolerance for assessment procedures and/or ensuing interventions. With such clients, assessment procedures and subsequent interventions need to be practical, brief, and perceived as relevant to the presenting problems.

Bicultural assessees should have a choice in the kinds of assessment procedures they will receive. Knowledge of the available options should be provided by a culturally competent assessor, to be certain that the client fully understands the options and the decision-making prerogative.

For assessees who retain their traditional cultural identities, a culture-specific assessment technology should be most appropriate (Step III). Three major kinds of culture-specific technologies are available. The choice from one, or more than one, of these alternatives will depend on the availability of culturally valid tests for the specific assessment purpose.

These culture-specific technologies include tests that have demonstrated cultural validity (i.e., construct equivalence) for a particular group or subgroup (Step IIIA); new culture-specific measures, or modifications of existing materials (Step IIIB); and/or translations of standard tests (Step IIIC).

After test administration has been completed, there should be communication of the assessment findings in a culturally sensitive manner to the client and others who may be included in the client's ensembled self-concept (Step IV). Any intervention plan discussed at this time should include services that are compatible with client perceptions of relevant remediations for the presenting problems. These interventions should be accomplished by providers who are perceived as capable of performing the services (Step V). Finally, there should be routine use of client-satisfaction measures that have been constructed to be culture-specific (Step VI). Applications of these measures would suggest the cultural appropriateness of the interventions and the cultural competence of providers, including the assessor.

Cultural Competence

Worst-case scenarios have been presented in the form of confounds and problems, to suggest some of the possible consequences of assessment whenever assessors are neither culturally sensitive nor culturally competent. Of course, these scenarios will not apply to assessees of multicultural origins who use English as a first language, have acted on the desire to assimilate, and have adopted an Anglo-American world view and behaviors.

Cultural sensitivity is a precursor to cultural competence. Cultural sensitivity simply implies awareness of another culture based on knowledge and firsthand acquaintance. This awareness may be developed in supervised/unsupervised professional and other work settings (i.e., job placement, Peace Corps, practicum, internship, professional practice) and/or by personal experiences (e.g., residence, travel, language education, personal relationships).

Practitioner cultural competence begins with acknowledgment and acceptance of cultural differences. To honor the world views of other cultures, practitioners should appreciate the influence of their own culture on their thinking and behavior. This has been referred to in Chapter 1 as Stage 4, or acceptance, and implies comfort with ethnorelativistic thinking. In addition, practitioners must recognize the culturally prescribed communications, etiquette, and problem-solving approaches that arise from unique cultural histories. This has been referred to as "style" consistently in this book. There must be emphasis on understanding the meaning of behavior within its cultural context. Such understanding includes the client's conception of health/illness and the configuration of acceptable and available support networks.

Cultural competence is based on experience and explicit training. Cultural competence is the ability to provide services that are perceived by clients as relevant to their problems and helpful for intervention outcomes. These services are perceived as legitimate because they mesh with health/illness beliefs and are provided by using a style of service delivery that is perceived as credible and giving. These services include assessment and intervention at the practitioner level, although cultural competence should also be apparent at agency, policy, and consumer levels (Cross, Bazron, Dennis, & Isaacs, 1989).

Professional Ethics and Cultural Competence

The norms, standards, and expectations for appropriate behaviors are contained in statements of ethics. Professional ethics for psychologists (American Psychological Association [APA], 1981) expressed concern with individual self-worth and dignity. General principles covered confidentiality, competence, moral and legal standards, professional relationships, responsibility, public statements, and welfare of consumers.

These APA standards were examined for ethno-cultural biases in those principles that explicitly mention cultural differences (Pedersen & Marsella, 1982). In Principle 1(a) (Responsibility), there is neglect of the multiplicity of cultural values in this society. A cultural definition of exactly what is entailed by "objectivity" and "appropriate services" is always necessary. In Principle 2(d) (Competence), the professional qualifications for multicultural services are not stated. In Principle 3(b) (Moral and Legal Standards), the expectations of service providers take precedence over the standards of multicultural consumers. Pedersen and Marsella concluded that ethical guidelines should protect both consumers and providers, recognize the inevitable conflicts of interest between cultural groups, provide practical examples and/or case studies, and include an option for "responsible disobedience" to protect the ethical values that undergird the guidelines. Moreover, there also must be official sanction for guidelines with flexible oversight.

In response to these concerns, new guidelines for ethical practice were prepared by the APA (American Psychological Association, Board of Ethnic Minority Affairs [APA], 1989). These guidelines addressed several major areas including (a) cultural knowledge as provided by relevant research/practice; (b) self-awareness by providers of their own cultural backgrounds and amelioration of their own biases/prejudices, as well as understanding of clients' cultural backgrounds; (c) respect for diverse values/beliefs as they affect world view, psychosocial functioning, and expressions of distress; (d) use of clients' preferred languages; (e) awareness of the impact of social, environmental, and political conditions on problems and interventions; and (f) an advocacy stance with regard to discrimination and racism as affecting client welfare.

A second response to the concerns voiced by Pedersen and Marsella contained specific standards for assessment (Ibrahim & Arredondo, 1986). There is need for appraisal of the client as a cultural entity prior to any other assessment strategy. This standard has been explicitly recognized in Chapter 7 of this book. The use of moderator indices to assess the client's identity orientation emphasizes understanding of world view in the context of the larger society. A second recommended standard is that "multisource, multilevel, and multimethod approaches to assess the capabilities, potentials, and limitations of the client" be used (Ibrahim & Arredondo, 1986, p. 350). Chapters 8 and 9 of this book have provided detailed information concerning these approaches.

There are some rules that transcend cultures, but there are no metaethics (Barnlund, 1979), and morality is variable and culture-specific. Ethics are culturally contextualized and consequently are relative. The communication between different cultural groups always entails risk, because these groups/cultures have unequal power and differences in psychological boundaries. Moreover, different systems of rules governing communication may be used. As a result, the symbols used in communication may be neither consistent nor understood. The complexity of these issues almost demands the acquisition of the world view of another culture in order to understand the values and behavior of individuals who share that particular construction of reality.

In spite of these difficulties, it will be necessary to develop a system of rules and symbols that can be shared by provider and client. Culture-specific styles or etiquettes of service delivery provide a step in this direction. Such a system would be clear as to who does what to whom under what circumstances and with what sanctions in cross-cultural professional settings (Dana, 1990).

This rule system would require the development of culture-specific ethical codes that not only identify attitudes, beliefs, ideas, and values but also suggest the rules for appropriate professional conduct (Asuncion-Lande, 1979). Each of these codes would contain a list of those interests, motives, and needs that have ethical implications that should be respected by professional providers. As ethical codes address different cultural priorities for satisfaction of potentially competing needs, such codes would be cultural and not professional in nature. Because moral restraints to practice are typically culture-specific, application of these rules to professional psychological services and service delivery entails a second step.

However, these are indeed difficult tasks for professional psychology. It is unfortunate and a commentary on current training that clinical psychology students do not feel adequately prepared to deal with ethical issues, or even apply the existing APA Ethical Code (Bernard & Jara, 1986; Bernard, Murphy, & Little, 1987; Tymchuk, 1985). Nor do these students feel prepared to cope with ethical issues that are not explicitly stated in the APA Ethical Code (Meyer, 1988; Rubin, 1986). Graduate training programs are attempting to remediate these dilemmas (Eberlein, 1987; Fine & Ulrich, 1988). However, it is apparent that other considerations in the selection of potential professional psychology service providers are being overlooked (Dana, 1987), and that current training is apparently inadequate with regard to ethics.

Nonetheless, there are training illustrations that can have byproducts in enhanced awareness of ethical issues (López et al., 1989). There are also examples of potential dilemmas involving individual clients, available in the literature (Cayleff, 1986; Dana, 1990, p. 19); a casebook of multicultural examples would be a welcome addition to courses in ethics. This casebook would provide examples of cross-cultural dilemmas for students and practitioners, material not contained in currently available casebook installments (American Psychological Association, Board of Professional Affairs, Committee on Professional Standards, 1988).

The above-mentioned problems apply to the development and implementation of ethical standards for practice with multicultural populations in this country. However, the major obstacle to the use of ethical standards for services to multicultural groups in the training of predominantly Anglo-American professional psychologists does not lie in the difficulty of developing such standards. A more basic consideration is the level of ethnocentric-ethnorelative development of professional psychology students as a function of their ego development (Loevinger, 1966). Although there is some evidence that training can affect ego developmental levels, whether or not individuals at relatively low levels of ego development can be trained to develop a sense of ethnorelativism remains an open question. Moreover, persons in their mid-twenties do not dramatically change their attitudes during graduate school and may develop a situational cynicism as well (Reinhardt & Gray, 1972; Thurlow, 1987). Nonetheless, the preparation of culturally competent assessment psychologists is a responsibility of the American Psychological Association and accredited graduate training programs. Fortunately, there is both an acceptance of this responsibility and an awareness of the necessity for immediate implementation (Stricker et al., 1990).

References

American Psychological Association. (1981). Ethical principles of psychologists (rev. ed). *American Psychologist, 36,* 633–638.

American Psychological Association, Board of Ethnic Minority Affairs. (1989, March 7). *Draft of guidelines for psychological practice with ethnic and culturally diverse populations.* Washington, DC: Task Force on Delivery of Services to Ethnic Minority Populations.

American Psychological Association, Board of Professional Affairs, Committee on Professional Standards. (1988). Casebook for providers of psychological services. *American Psychologist, 43,* 557–563.

Asuncion-Lande, N. C. (1979). Ethics in intercultural communication: An introduction. In N. C. Asuncion-Lande (Ed.), *Ethical perspectives and critical issues in intercultural communication* (pp. 3–7). Falls Church, VA: Speech Communication Association.

Barnlund, D. C. (1979). The crosscultural arena: An ethical void. In N. C. Asuncion-Lande (Ed.), *Ethical perspectives and critical issues intercultural communication* (pp. 8–13). Falls Church, VA: Speech Communication Association.

Barrett, G. V., & Depiner, R. L. (1991). A reconsideration of testing for competence rather than intelligence. *American Psychologist, 46,* 1012–1024.

Bernard, J. L., & Jara, C. S. (1986). The failure of clinical psychology graduate students to apply understood ethical principles. *Professional Psychology: Research and Training, 17,* 313–315.

Bernard, J. L., Murphy, M., & Little, M. (1987). The failure of clinical psychology graduate students to apply understood ethical principles. *Professional Psychology: Research and Practice, 18,* 489–491.

Cayleff, S. E. (1986). Ethical issues in counseling gender, race, and culturally distinct groups. *Journal of Counseling and Development, 64,* 345–347.

Cross, T. L., Bazron, B. J., Dennis, K. W., & Isaacs, M. R. (1989). *Toward a culturally competent system of care.* Washington, DC: CASSP Technical Assistance Center, Georgetown University Child Development Center.

Dana, R. H. (1982). *A human science model for personality assessment with projective techniques.* Springfield, IL: Thomas.

Dana, R. H. (1985). A service-delivery paradigm for personality assessment. *Journal of Personality Assessment, 49,* 598–604.

Dana, R. H. (1987). Training for professional psychology: Science, practice, and identity. *Professional Psychology: Research and Practice, 18,* 9–16.

Dana, R. H. (1990). Cross-cultural and multi-ethnic assessment. In J. N. Butcher & C. D. Spielberger (Eds.), *Advances in personality assessment* (Vol. 8, pp. 1–26). Hillsdale, NJ: Erlbaum.

Eberlein, L. (1987). Introducing ethics to beginning graduate psychologists: A problem-solving approach. *Professional Psychology: Research and Practice, 18,* 353–359.

Fine, M. A., & Ulrich, L. P. (1988). Integrating psychology and philosophy in teaching a graduate course in ethics. *Professional Psychology: Research and Practice, 19,* 542–546.

Ibrahim, F. A., & Arredondo, P. M. (1986). Ethical standards for cross-cultural counseling, counselor preparation, practice, assessment, and research. *Journal of Counseling and Development, 64,* 349–352.

LaFromboise, T. D., Trimble, J. E., & Mohatt, G. V. (1990). Counseling intervention and American Indian tradition: An integrative approach. *The Counseling Psychologist, 18,* 628–654.

Loevinger, J. (1966). The meaning and measurement of ego development. *American Psychologist, 21,* 195–206.

López, S., Grover, K. P., Holland, D., Johnson, M. J., Kain, C. D., Kanel, K., Mellins, C. A., & Rhyne, M. C. (1989). Development of culturally sensitive psychotherapists. *Professional Psychology: Research and Practice, 20,* 369–376.

López, S., & Núñez, J. A. (1987). Cultural factors considered in selected diagnostic criteria and interview schedules. *Journal of Abnormal Psychology, 96,* 270–272.

Marsella, A. J. (1978). Thoughts on cross-cultural studies on the epidemiology of depression. *Culture, Medicine, and Psychiatry, 2,* 343–357.

Meyer, M. S. (1988). Ethical principles of psychologists and religious diversity. *Professional Psychology: Research and Practice, 19,* 486–488.

Neighbors, H. W., Jackson, J. S., Campbell, L., & Williams, D. (1989). The influence of racial factors on psychiatric diagnosis: A review and suggestions for research. *Community Mental Health Journal, 25,* 300–311.

Padilla, E. R., & Wyatt, G. E. (1983). The effects of intelligence and achievement testing on minority group children. In G. J. Powell (Ed.), *The psychosocial development of minority group children* (pp. 417–437). New York: Brunner/Mazel.

Pedersen, P. B., & Marsella, A. J. (1982). The ethical crisis for cross-cultural counseling and therapy. *Professional Psychology, 13,* 492–500.

Reinhardt, A. M., & Gray, R. M. (1972). A social psychological study of attitude change in physicians. *Journal of Medical Education, 47,* 112–117.

Rubin, S. S. (1986). Cheating, ethics, and graduate training in professional psychology; Crime and punishment or misjudgment and repair. *Professional Psychology: Research and Practice, 17,* 10–14.

Schwartz, G. E. (1984). Psychobiology of health: A new synthesis. In B. L. Hammonds & C. J. Scheirer (Eds.), *Psychology and health: The Master Lecture Series* (Vol. 3, pp. 149–193). Washington, DC: American Psychological Association.

Stricker, G., Davis-Russell, E., Bourg, E., Duran, E., Hammond, W. R., McHolland, W. R., Polite, K., & Vaughn, B. E. (Eds.). (1990). *Toward ethnic diversification in psychology education and training.* Washington, DC: American Psychological Association.

Thurlow, L. C. (1987, June 4). Ethics does not start in business schools. *The New York Times,* D3.

Tymchuk, A. J. (1985). Ethical decision-making and psychology students' attitudes toward training in ethics. *Professional Practice of Psychology, 6*(2), 219–232.

Author Index

Subject Index